Counterculture in Boston 1968-1980s

By Charles Giuliano

Photographs by Charles Giuliano and courtesy of
Jeff Albertson, David Bieber Archive, Steve Nelson,
Peter Simon, and UMass Amherst Archive

Berkshire Fine Arts, LLC
North Adams, Massachusetts

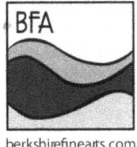

berkshirefinearts.com

Copyright © 2019 by Charles Giuliano
Published by Berkshire Fine Arts, LLC
Book Design by Studio Two, Amanda Hill
All images, except when indicated, by Charles Giuliano, copyright 2019.
All rights reserved. No part of this book may be reproduced or transmitted in any form or by any means, electronic or mechanical, including photocopying, recording, or by any information storage and retrieval system without the written permission of the author. For information or permissions contact Berkshire Fine Arts at 243 Union Street, Unit 208, North Adams, Mass. 01247.
ISBN-13: 978-0-9961715-6-4
Library of Congress Control Number: 2019910647

This book is lovingly dedicated to Astrid Hiemer,
my life partner, mentor, and muse.

Also by Charles Giuliano

Topsy Turvy

Gloucester Poems: Nugents of Rockport

Ultra Cosmic Gonzology

Total Gonzo Poems

Shards of a Life

Love Made Visible: Scenes from a Mostly Happy Marriage, by Jean Gibran (Introduction)

100 Boston Painters, by Chawky Frenn (Essay)

Exhibition Catalogs

Pioneers from Provincetown: The Roots of Figurative Expressionism, by Adam Zucker (Essay: "Sun Gallery and a Return to the Figure in the 1950s")

Lester Johnson: In Memoriam (Essay)

Randall Deihl: An American Realist (Essay)

James Aponovich Recent Paintings (Essay)

Harriet Casdin Silver: The Art of Holography (Essay)

Lester Johnson (Essay)

Contents

Preface vii
Introduction: Counterculture in Boston xi

Bill Lichtenstein's film documents *WBCN: The American Revolution* 1
George Wein brought jazz to Storyville and co-founded Newport Jazz Festival 39
Fred Taylor booked The Jazz Workshop and Paul's Mall 49
Bob Blumenthal, noted jazz critic, started as a DJ at Harvard's WHRB 69
Dexter Gordon: Schnapps in Copenhagen with a bop master 95
David Wilson, *Broadside* publisher, recalls summer we edited *Avatar* 105
Harper Barnes brought journalism to the hippie *Cambridge Phoenix* 141
Arnie Reisman was editor of *Brandeis Justice* and *Boston After Dark/Phoenix* ... 167
Jean Bergantini Grillo was art critic and an editor for *Cambridge Phoenix* 199
John and Leah Sdoucos booked Concerts on the Common for Mayor Kevin White ... 211
Martin Kaplan (Sdoucos insert) relates true story of Stones bust in Rhode Island ... 221
Janis Joplin let it all hang out at Harvard Stadium 239
Jon Landau covered and then managed Bruce Springsteen 249
Steve Nelson booked the British Invasion for the Boston Tea Party 259
Ron Della Chiesa, The Voice of the BSO, started with WBCN 283
Al Perry settled differences between talent and management for WBCN 307
Charles Laquidara concocted mayhem and mishegoss at WBCN 321
John Hochheimer recalls on-air time with David Bowie and Elton John at WBUR .. 351
Roger Lifeset remembers promo guys who broke and managed rock acts in Boston .. 363
David Bieber presides over a million-item archive of rock memorabilia 395

Bibliography 426

Preface

Several of the twenty interviews in this book occurred over the past few years. They were posted to *Berkshire Fine Arts*. My decision this past winter to create this book initiated intensive activity that entailed editing and revising existing texts, as well as creating new ones. The texts were sent back to participants for fact checking. These interactions also suggested others to be included, and so the book expanded in scope. There was some detective work in tracking down sources and encouraging their participation.

As a mandate developed to create an oral history, it soon became apparent that limits needed to be imposed. The book might easily have been two to three times longer than its current form. There was also the issue of redundancy as the commonality of primary events and key players got retold. This entailed some contradictions which provide spice to the sauce.

There was so much potential material to deal with that I made the decision not to include the fine arts. That will be the focus of the next book, *Boston Fine Arts: Museums, Galleries and Artists*.

Many individuals have contributed in bringing this book to publishable form. Closest to home has been the daily support and encouragement of my wife, the writer and editor, Astrid Hiemer. She has seen the ups and downs of multiple projects with many challenges.

For this sixth book since 2014, I am grateful for the technical support of a meticulous editor, Leanne Jewett. With uncanny enthusiasm she has discussed every word in this text. Often she has refined my unorthodox style into some variation of The King's English. That has always been done with respect for the vernacular flavor and jive of colorful dialogues.

Yet again, this book had been impeccably designed by Amanda Hill of Studio Two. She has provided visual continuity to text, balanced by vintage images. Her effort and skill has resulted in books that attain the highest standards of professionalism.

I am grateful to the eighteen individuals who shared their memories of a colorful era in such a lively manner. Their interest, enthusiasm, and generosity were palpable. My sincere thanks to Harper Barnes, David Bieber, Bob Blumenthal, Ron Della Chiesa, Dexter Gordon, Jean Bergantini Grillo, John Hochheimer, Martin Kaplan, Jon Landau, Charles Laquidara, Bill Lichtenstein, Roger Lifeset, Steve Nelson, Al Perry, Arnie Reisman, John and Leah Sdoucos, Fred Taylor, George Wein, and David Wilson.

As the project developed, there was valuable discussion with many individuals. Early on, when I was skeptical about its viability, Arnie Reisman, my editor at the *Brandeis Justice* and later *Boston After Dark/Phoenix* assured me that there was a place for this oral history.

My mentor and friend, the artist Robert Henriquez, has been with me in all aspects of the books from their inception in 2014. Often he has helped me to step back and take the long view. The 2018 Ryan Walsh book *Astral Weeks: A Secret History of 1968* was inspirational and brought national focus to Boston and its seminal role in the counterculture. We shared an exciting evening discussing our books. Similarly, author Richard Vacca discussed the jazz history of Boston.

At times, frustrating effort was entailed in tracking down David Bieber who presides over an archive of some million rock and media items. The author Brian Coleman was an enthusiastic facilitator for that access. It has been productive to bond with others focused on this period and its unique history. The time that Astrid and I spent with Bieber and his associates in Norwood was truly astonishing.

As the project progressed, the issue of archival sources and preservation became ever more relevant. Personal concerns entail the sustainability of my work jammed into file cabinets bursting with documents, slides, and negatives. As I spoke to individuals in this book the subject of their archival plans often came up.

In the course of this research, I was most fortunate to connect with the UMass Amherst archivist Robert Cox. He has particular interest in collecting the social justice activist aspects of the counterculture. When Bill Lichtenstein created the documentary film *WBCN and The American Revolution*, he worked closely with the UMass archive. That critical material has been deposited in Amherst. Other important archives include Northeastern University (*The Boston Phoenix* and Kay Bourne collections) and Boston University (for Ron Della Chiesa). Vacca plans to donate his archive to UMass Boston.

To illustrate this book I have scanned many slides and negatives. To supplement these images I have been generously assisted by Bieber, Coleman, and in particular, the archive overseen by Cox. To date, he has collected the material of eighty photographers. With the permission of their estates, we are grateful to publish images by former *Cambridge Phoenix/Real Paper* staff photographers Jeff Albertson and Peter Simon.

Introduction:
Counterculture in Boston

Now, some fifty years later, the zeitgeist of Boston from 1968 to the 1980s can be seen as one of social and political unrest that inspired unique and diverse creativity. The vibrant counterculture is recalled more through tall tales and acid flashbacks than concise history.

There is truth to the aphorism that if you remember the 1960s, you didn't live them. Too many hipsters are no longer with us. A number of superstars were gone by the critical age of 28. Many of our generation died in Vietnam or on the mean streets of America. The landscape of memory is populated with exquisite corpses.

Having danced over the hot coals of a life in the arts, there is survivor's guilt in telling these chronicles. This project entails dialogues with a range of primary sources. There is ebb and flow to the manner and temperament of each individual that has resulted in a tapestry of colorful threads. The chapters, a series of twenty interviews, range from hipster jive to straight talk.

Consider Chaucer's *Canterbury Tales*. These pilgrims, however, are not traveling to pray over the bones of Thomas Beckett. They have shared tales of art and culture during an exotic era. Against a background of war, civil rights, social and political change, it was a time of drugs, sex, and rock 'n' roll.

This oral history is about Boston during a moment of fusion, confusion, fission, and fizzle. Decades later, there is enough critical distance to debate and appreciate what went down.

There is urgency to record unique events for future generations. The opportunity was seized to document major players in the arts and media and to explore what made the counterculture of Boston so unique and diverse.

Boston ranks tenth in the nation in population, but has some 250,000 college students. That figure increases in a radius of an hour's drive of downtown Boston. Youth culture supported clubs and concerts, art galleries and museums, alternative weekly newspapers, and progressive college and commercial radio stations.

For youth marketing, the critical mass of Boston was essential. During the British Invasion, for example, bands broke out in Boston and toured New England colleges. WBCN routinely launched emerging talent. National acts like J. Geils, James Taylor, Bonnie Raitt, Bruce Springsteen, The Cars, The Modern Lovers, Van Morrison, Boston, and Aerosmith started in local clubs.

Much of this book covers jazz, folk music, and rock. Discussion of the alternative press surveys *Avatar*, *Broadside*, *Boston After Dark*, *Cambridge Phoenix*, *Boston Phoenix*, *The Real Paper*, *Boston Ledger*, *The Old Mole*, *Fusion*, *Vibrations*, *Polyarts*, *What's New*, *Timeline*, and *Nightfall Magazine*.

Initially a failing classical FM station, WBCN emerged as The Rock of Boston. Music was performed in clubs: Storyville, The Boston Tea Party, Jazz Workshop/ Paul's Mall, Lennie's on the Turnpike, Sandy's Jazz Revival, Merry-go-round Room, Lulu White's, and The Paradise.

In assembling the documentary film *WBCN: The American Revolution*, its director, Bill Lichtenstein, set the progressive rock radio station against the social and political agendas of the era. Coverage starts with benign hippie Love-ins on Boston Common in 1967 and ratchets up to anti-war demonstrations by 1968 and beyond. The station rejected Top-40 and developed album-oriented programming.

The prehistory of jazz in Boston starts with George Wein and Storyville in the 1950s. He was a founder of the Newport Jazz Festivals from which he stepped back only recently.

Now in his 80s and booking concerts for the Cabot Theatre in Beverly, entrepreneur Fred Taylor recalls booking Jazz Workshop and Paul's Mall as well as Tanglewood Jazz Festival and Scullers.

From St. Louis, where he grew up as a soul and jazz fan, Bob Blumenthal started as a DJ for WHRB during his freshman year at Harvard in 1965. By his senior year he was covering jazz for *Boston After Dark*. From there he went on to writing for the Boston Globe and Rolling Stone. Currently, he writes liner notes for the box sets of Mosaic Records.

As the former editor of *Broadside*, David Wilson has encyclopedic knowledge of the folk music scene during its formative era. With Sandi Mandeville, we published *Avatar* during the summer of 1968. Wilson discusses the relationship to *Avatar* of Mel Lyman and his Fort Hill-based commune.

Reached by phone in St. Louis, we discussed Harper Barnes' tenure as editor of *The Cambridge Phoenix*. He describes trying to bring professional standards to a feisty but undisciplined hippie weekly.

My former *Justice* editor, Arnie Reisman, hired me and a number of other Brandeis writers and critics when he was editor of *Boston After Dark*. Later renamed *The Boston Phoenix*, the weekly paper launched the careers of many major writers.

Working with Mayor Kevin White, producer John Sdoucos started with Summerthing in 1968. He participated in concerts at Harvard Stadium in 1969, and launched Concerts on the Common in 1970. Creating a network of New England College venues, his production company booked Boston acts like Barry and the Remains, The Hallucinations, and the early careers of James Taylor, Bruce Springsteen, J. Geils, and Aerosmith. Partner Leah Sdoucos adds to the narrative with a focus on the seminal band Barry and the Remains.

Starting with *The Brandeis Justice* and *Rolling Stone*, then *Cambridge Phoenix* and *Real Paper*, Jon Landau is the best known and most successful Boston rock critic of his generation. He is manager and producer for Bruce Springsteen.

Several months after it was launched, Steve Nelson took over as manager of The Boston Tea Party. By the end of a one-year contract the club had a national reputation for bringing major rock acts to the region.

Today DJ Ron Della Chiesa is known as The Voice of the BSO. Before WGBH he started with the eccentric T. Mitchell Hastings, inventor and founder of WBCN.

Al Perry was WBCN station manager and FCC fixer when DJ's pushed the envelope of on-air decorum. He was a negotiator between management and creative talent.

I talked by phone with DJ Charles Laquidara in Maui about his *Big Mattress* years as the top rated WBCN radio host. Howard Stern borrowed a lot from

Laquidara when he tuned in as an undergraduate at BU.

Roger Lifeset was a promo man and scene maker for Warner Bros. Records. His partner was Charlie McKenzie, who with another promo guy, Paul Ahern, managed the major rock band Boston. Lifeset recalled the unique synergy of the small but lively Boston rock world.

Boston attorney Martin Kaplan filled us in on frantic, behind the scenes efforts to get the Rolling Stones out of jail in Rhode Island and on their way to a concert at Boston Garden. Typically Mayor Kevin White took full credit for springing the Stones.

Dr. John Hochheimer joined WBUR as a work/study student at Boston University. Like WBCN at the time, the station was focused on classical music. Under Tom Gamache, a.k.a. Uncle T., the station was experimental after 10 p.m. and on weekends. When Gamache briefly joined WBCN, his slot was taken over by Hochheimer, eventually five nights a week. Progressive programming at WBUR ended not long after John Silber became president of the university in 1971.

In August 1968, David Bieber completed a master's degree program in the BU School of Communications. That September he became music director of WBUR. After the staff lockout in 1971, Bieber focused on advertising, promotion, and marketing. This led to positions at WBCN and *The Boston Phoenix*. Along the way he collected rock memorabilia and today his collection of some million objects is housed in a warehouse in Norwood, Massachusetts.

I spoke with Bill Lichtenstein the day after he wrapped the documentary film *WBCN: The American Revolution*. Since then, the film has been making the rounds of film festivals.

Initially, I contacted Jean Bergantini Grillo to discuss her role as an art critic for *The Cambridge Phoenix* and *Real Paper*. She responded that her primary function was as an editor working with Harper Barnes. She recruited several writers who launched what proved to be major careers.

I am grateful to all those who shared their anecdotes and insights.

Bill Lichtenstein's film documents
WBCN: The American Revolution

In 2006, Bill Lichtenstein was interviewed by the *Boston Herald*. He discussed a film project and asked for readers to contact him if they had tapes of broadcasts, photos, and other documents. That resulted in what he describes as the first open-sourced film.

It is usual to start with material to create a documentary film. In this instance there was no archive related to WBCN. Now there is an extensive one. The idea existed before the material to illustrate it.

The film *WBCN and the American Revolution* makes a case that the counterculture was launched with the 1967 Summer of Love in San Francisco. Lichtenstein argues that the torch was passed to Boston in 1968. He highlights key events from the launch of WBCN in 1968 to the resignation of President Richard Nixon seven years later.

Charles Giuliano You said that the film was wrapped last night. What did that entail?

Bill Lichtenstein You could compare it to Photoshop, but the film was done with an editing program. There are limited desktop capabilities regarding imagery and sound. You then take a film into a studio for color correction to make it look great, and for sound mix. On a desktop system you can fade things in or out and do a certain amount of noise reduction with old broadcasts. In a full recording studio, you can really work with the sound.

We spent about three weeks then outputting it, which was last night. You have to watch it, see that it's okay, then send it out.

CG Start to finish, how long has this film taken?

BL Fifty years. I started collecting stuff when I was there. [Starting in 1970 when he was fourteen.] When we started the project, there were no WBCN archives. A substantial amount of material we started with was what I had collected while at the station. At that point, it was my own collecting of stuff.

In the 1980s, I was working with another producer about doing a documentary on Phil Ochs. The project dragged on for years. We were working with his sister. His brother was Michael Ochs, the famous archivist. He was working with another producer, and the family decided that they would go with that project. It came to an end for us, but the idea of it was on my mind.

In the midst of the Iraq War, post 9/11, George Bush and a lot of National Security issues—what emerged was: why more artists, musicians, and people weren't speaking up. What was going on?

Bruce Springsteen did a benefit for John Kerry and was accused of being too political. In our day if you did a benefit for a Democrat for president you would be accused of selling out.

So there was an idea to tell that story, which Phil Ochs personified. In the 2000s another thing was an explosion of archival material coming online. With Napster all these songs I had forgotten about were suddenly available again.

[Brothers Shawn and John Fanning, along with Sean Parker, launched Napster in 1999 as a peer-to-peer file-sharing network. The software application was easy to use with a free account. The service provided easy access for millions of Internet users to a large amount of free audio files. Approximately 80 million users were registered on its network. It was shut down in 2001.]

Archival material seemingly lost to the ages suddenly reappeared. One was a photo of Danny Schechter [WBCN news director] the day Daniel Ellsberg turned himself in. The photo appeared online of Schechter standing there with a microphone. There was a tape of Bruce Springsteen's first interview, which I heard at the time.

Something happened and the tape disappeared from WBCN. It was in

Maxanne's [Sartori] stash in the production room and it was stolen. The tape we used at the station was ten-inch reels and they run out after 30 minutes. It recorded the interview but at the end a recording of "Blinded by the Light" the tape ran out.

Suddenly it's online, but stops after a minute and a half, which tells me that it was derivative of the actual tape.

Because of those two things I began to think that you could do a film about how media could create social change using archival material that was out there. At the time there was no archive of WBCN or the counterculture of Boston. The material was scattered.

[The David Bieber archive, now some six hundred thousand items, was then in storage and not accessible. That material has been transferred to an industrial space in Norwood where it is being unpacked and catalogued.]

In 2006 the *Herald* did a piece in which they discussed my plan to do a documentary film on WBCN. In the article it stated that if anyone had related material to send it to me. That's what kicked it off.

We collected archival material for a few years, as that's what we needed to drive the story. For most documentaries you tell a story and then use images to put up on the screen. This was the opposite. We had to find what material was there and then how to tell the story.

It was like archaeology. If we found the toe of the dinosaur, then maybe bones from the foot are here. We would find something like a tape of Patti Smith at Paul's Mall. Then we would try to find if there were any photos. We began to cluster sound and pictures around particular events.

What ended up in the film was what we had the best archival material for. From the Tea Party we used The Velvet Underground and Led Zeppelin because we had the material for them.

In 2010 we started doing interviews, and raised money in 2012. We continued to raise money and shoot through 2016. So 2006 to 2010 was pre-production. When we got money, shooting was four years from 2012 to 2016. We started editing in 2017. This past year and a half has just flown.

CG It ended last night.

BL At the end of last year, we had a rough cut and something we could show. It was in pretty good shape a couple of months ago. We showed it to some people and everyone liked it. We've been finishing up since.

CG What's the potential audience?

BL There're two clear target audiences. There are people who remember the era. WBCN is set against the story of how we went from peace, love, and LSD in San Francisco in 1967, hippies on Boston Common in '67, where the message was peace and love will save everything. How did we get from there to Nixon's resignation [August 9, 1974], and everything in between? There was Vietnam, Watergate, Kent State, and the whole story of the 1960s that this is set against. The film touches on the important cultural aspects that impacted WBCN.

CG It is ironic that right now we are talking about Nixon on a day when Michael Cohen, Trump's former private attorney and fixer like John Dean decades ago, is testifying before Congress.

BL The film has gotten a strong positive response from young people. They are struggling with how you use media to create a social, political, and cultural change. They are struck by how much was accomplished during that period.

We focus on the fact, for example, that there were no women on the air at WBCN. There was a protest about it, which resulted in Maxanne [Sartori] coming to town. We have a tape of Jerry Williams of WBZ saying on air in 1970 that women don't belong on the radio. He said that they don't have the voice for it and try to sound authoritative. It's just not appropriate. A woman called in and said, "If I have the radio on I want to listen to a man's voice. If I want to hear a woman rattle on and on, I can call one of my girlfriends."

As a result of the protest, women were given "Bread and Roses" a weekly, one-hour slot. As part of it they read from a 1970s, New York Times obituary which is in the film. It's about a 17-year-old Barnard student who died of a heroin overdose. The obituary quotes her high school principal as saying essentially, she was young, talented, and if she were a boy, you would say she had a bright future ahead of her.

Young people are surprised at how bad it was not that long ago and what it took to change it. WBCN taking the lead and putting women on the air helped to change things. They also love the bands of that era. It's a universal story.

CG Let's talk about the 1960s. A thousand days into Camelot, President Kennedy was assassinated on November 22, 1963. The Beatles appeared on the Ed Sullivan Show on February 9, 1964, pulling America out of months of mourning. Their final tour ended in 1966. In 1967 there was the Summer of Love. WBCN went on the air in 1968. That summer Dave Wilson, Sandi Mandeville, and I published *Avatar*. In Chicago there were riots during the Democratic National Convention. When people talk about the 1960s they really mean starting late and continuing into the 1970s. The counterculture fell off the cliff by the 1980s.

BL In this film, the 1960s began with the Summer of Love. At least the story begins then. Its manifestation in Boston was hippies on Boston Common and their clash with Boston's aristocracy and police.

Right after Kevin White was elected [as Mayor] there were hippies camping on Boston Common. In the wake of Summer of Love they were coming in large numbers by the summer of 1968. There were people on Beacon Hill saying get these kids off Boston Common. They were arresting kids and beating them. It's in the film, and for me, that's where it starts. Ray [Riepen] opened the Tea Party and it went from there.

At the end of the film, Charles Laquidara says, "I think the 1960s ended when radio became not underground but commercial." Nixon resigned, so that's how it's framed. Nixon is the protagonist that this whole thing is set against.

The film presents the role that WBCN played in opposing Nixon by supporting the Moratorium on the Common and the anti-FBI efforts that were going on in that period. Boston was a hotbed of opposition and WBCN was a major part of that.

The story has not been told of the role that Boston had in taking it from peace, love, and LSD to a politicized anti-war mode. WBCN was very clear in helping to create social change.

CG In what sense was Boston different from San Francisco?

BL The heyday of San Francisco was the launch of the counterculture in 1967 with Summer of Love and all those great bands. There was a Free Speech Movement out there, but I think the argument can be made that the epicenter of the counterculture, in 1968, shifted from San Francisco to Boston. Cultural manifestations continued in New York, but they became commercial in fashion, style, and the mainstream of America.

Fringe stuff became part of the mainstream. New York, in commercializing them was not as dangerous, threatening, and radical. San Francisco passed the torch to Boston. The argument of the film is that it developed in Boston. I don't want to say that it was more, less, or better than in San Francisco. But it's surely the story that's not been told. When you see the end of our film you say, wow, I didn't know all that stuff. There was a whole body of things that went on here that was important to the 1960s.

The great, untold story is the reticence of Boston/New England to celebrate its own history.

When Ray Riepen came to Cambridge to attend Harvard Law School [a graduate program], because of him, there was The Boston Tea Party, WBCN, and *The Phoenix*. He had a vision of creating a newspaper like the *Village Voice*.

If you play a "It's a Wonderful Life" game, had he not been born, had he not come to Boston, had he not been accepted at Harvard Law School, what would have been different in the world? Imagine the difference in the 1960s had there never been a Boston Tea Party, never been a WBCN, and never been a Phoenix. Think of the impact that had down the line on all the bands, and the writers.

In my mind Riepen is the most important person in the culture of the 1960s. People have suggested that Riepen would be like Bill Graham if Bill Graham had owned the Fillmore, a major radio station, and the *Village Voice* all at the same time—which he didn't.

Who was on a par with Riepen; Abbie Hoffman, Bill Graham? Riepen's impact on the 1960s was enormous. All of us who have gotten into this field owe it to Ray, and the film makes that case. Yet Ray doesn't have a Wikipedia page. Very few people know who he is, and I don't know why.

My theory is that there is a Calvinist, New England we-don't-blow-our-own-horn kind of thing. But there hasn't been anyone here, like Graham did in San Francisco, to compel that. If you go to the East Village, there are books and walking tours. Guides point out that's where Allen Ginsberg wrote "Howl." That's where they sold the first copy of *Evergreen Review* or where The Velvet Underground performed. Boston has never done that, and I don't know why. There's such an important history here that's never been fully told. That was a part of the mission of the film. We have the actual sights and sounds and stories from people who were there. When you see it, you can decide where the story falls in terms of historical importance. I have not pinned down why, as you say, that this history has not resulted in exhibitions and books. It should all be common knowledge and just isn't.

CG How does Ray Riepen emerge?

BL He's a central character in the film.

CG Curiously at the height of seemingly dominating aspects of the Boston youth market, with a rock club, radio station, and newspaper, he sold these interests and left town.

BL It's not something we can get into, so I can't comment on that. But I can say that the history of business is full of brilliant innovators who started things they didn't stick with. Rolling something out, sustaining it over time, and bringing it to fruition is another skill. Ray's greatest skill was dreaming up world-changing things. As he told me, he was less interested once it was up and running.

We talked a little bit about tensions at WBCN that don't make it into the film. He said, "I got WBCN up and running, but by then I was already onto the *Phoenix*." He wasn't focused on WBCN any more. He started the Tea Party and when that was up he was off to WBCN. As soon as that was running he was off to the *Phoenix*. But, he was owner and operator of each of those. People expected him to be the person in charge.

I know very little of the tension at the *Phoenix* but I know it was there. So that's why eventually he left town. If it had been his intention to run an empire, he could have hired different people to run things, but that would have been a different approach. His primary interest was the entrepreneurial aspect.

He went to LA and tried to replicate WBCN there, but it was more difficult because it didn't have a built-in youth audience. It was a much more diverse city. WBCN worked in Boston because of the nature of Boston. LA was a very different scene and the lack of young people meant it didn't work there.

CG For the time, despite his Midwestern, straight, lawyer persona, curiously Riepen was visionary, and progressive to the point of radical/Avatareque. He was a dream maker. In the zeitgeist there were many doing all kinds of things. There were startups, publications, art galleries, clubs, bands, and entrepreneurs of which few survived.

If you look at the spectrum of what started in and around 1968, there is an interesting pattern. Leadership morphed from visionaries to hip capitalists. When his contract to run the Tea Party expired, Steve Nelson left over a salary dispute. He was replaced by Don Law, who ultimately was a businessman. He had none of the flair and community outreach of Bill Graham. The same might be said of publisher Steve Mindich. T. Mitchell Hastings sold WBCN, and eventually the station was more focused on making money. Other stations sliced off aspects of its style and charisma.

By the mid-1980s what had been the radical counterculture was all about the bottom line.

BL At WBCN it was the announcers who decided what ads ran and not the advertising and sales staff. We weren't interested in ratings, we just wanted to do good radio. Turning down advertising DJ Jim Parry says in the film, "Are you insane?"

Ray says we get a call from some media buyer and they are acting like they are doing us a favor. And we had to tell them, no, the jingle is too ugly for our radio station. There's a story in the film which shows how radical he was.

He hired Bo Burlingham to be news director. He was in the Weathermen until the New York townhouse blew up. [They were making bombs.] That created the Weather Underground. He stayed above ground, and around that time he and his wife, Lisa, decided that they wanted out. He met Ray and Charles and they hired him as news director.

His second day on the job he was indicted with twelve other Weathermen for a plot to bomb federal buildings around the country. Bo went to tell Riepen.

Ray told him, look, I'm running a federally licensed business. I don't think I can have someone indicted for blowing up federal buildings on my payroll. But I own a paper called the *Phoenix* and if you want, you can write for them. You could tell that Ray was proud of the fact that, although he couldn't keep Bo at WBCN, he could get him a job at the *Phoenix*. Ray was very radical and not a hip capitalist in my mind.

In the film, Jim Parry describes him aptly, "Ray was what we needed. He had an understanding of the counterculture, but with the mind of an entrepreneur. He had this vision and it was my way or the highway." He was consistent politically, culturally, and socially with what was going on. It wasn't like he saw a chance to exploit it for money.

CG There is the famous story of Ray calling the station and telling a DJ not to play drum solos. Then Charles Laquidara followed with a show of drum solos. To what extent did Ray interfere with aesthetic decisions?

BL I think not. Ray loved the idea of doing these things. He was not involved in the aesthetic decisions of the station in any way that I knew or saw. I think he was at a party with some people and called in a request.

CG Do you explore the relationships between Riepen and Jessie Benton? They knew each other from Kansas and Jessie wanted help to get divorced in order to marry Mel Lyman.

BL Only in the sense that it led to him taking over a lease that resulted in creating The Boston Tea Party. Jessie called and asked if he could help negotiate a lease on a building. She said she was working with Andy Warhol and Jonas Mekas. They got a Ford Foundation grant to open a Filmmaker's Coop. Ray met with the owner who said, "I have three people looking at the property. If you want it you have to sign the lease right now."

He wrote a check for five thousand dollars, signed the lease, and called Jessie. She said, "Oh, I just heard from the Ford Foundation and there is no money." Other than declare bankruptcy, Ray said, "Why not open a rock club?"

CG Steve Nelson tells the story of being hired to manage the club three months after it was founded. By then Riepen had bought out a partner, David Hahn, who was an MIT graduate and entrepreneur dealing in army surplus.

There was serendipity as the acts that appeared at the club were also heard on WBCN. Back then kids could hear Led Zeppelin for $2.50. Discuss the transition to when hip capitalists saw the potential and top bands moved from clubs to stadiums. Now tickets for concerts sell for hundreds, if not thousands, of dollars.

BL By 1974, acts that appeared at the Tea Party were selling out Boston Garden. That's the third act of the film when WBCN ends up on top of the Prudential Building. An anti-establishment station was struggling to hold onto its values from the top of the Pru.

CG What I am hearing is how the counterculture slid down the slippery slope to the mainstream and commercialism. The cultural landscape of Boston morphed from radical/visionary to commercial.

BL I'm not sure it goes that far. We tell the story in a factual way that's respectful of the people at the station while acknowledging what was going on. You can draw your own conclusion. There is a timeline. Nixon resigned in 1974. When we moved to the Prudential, there were more demands and management started airing national ads. Some felt they couldn't hold onto their core values because of that. Things that were fringe were rapidly becoming part of the mainstream culture. We leave it to the audience to connect the dots rather than make a statement. It was a combination of things.

If the public maintained its radical commitment, it might have been a different story.

As a student in 1973 I did a sociology paper when the *Real Paper* was sold on the theme of "has it sold out?" I called Andy Kopkind and asked what happened? He said, "A bunch of us got together and decided that having a little comfort wasn't counter revolutionary."

CG What was your role at WBCN?

BL I started at fourteen on the "Listener Line." I was finishing a shift and Danny Schechter, then in the first months as news director, asked me if I could do him a favor. He gave me a tape recorder and told me to go up the street a couple of blocks to police headquarters. He said, "There's a protest there over the killing of this guy Fred Hampton. Push the red button and just say to people 'why are you here?' then listen through it and pick out a cut and bring it to me." Very soon I was producing stories for him. They were successful enough that Norm Winer [program director)]offered me a shift. It was on Saturday night, which I did until I was eighteen. Then I went to Brown, but would come back during the summer.

Al Perry later told me what happened. There was a staff meeting and Charles Laquidara was going on and on about high school kids. I said, "If you want to get them to listen, you have to reach out to them." Al said to Norm, "We should give that kid a show." I went on under the pseudonym of "Little Bill."

CG If you visit Boston today, nothing looks the same. Everything that meant so much to us, rock clubs, WBCN, alternative press no longer exists. Even physically, with so much development, the skyline is different. The counterculture proved to be unsustainable, which is a factor in why there has been so little critical attention paid to the era. Out of sight and out of mind.

In the past few years there has been a change. Books like Carter Alan's

Radio Free Boston: The Rise and Fall of WBCN and Ryan Walsh's *Astral Weeks: A Secret History of 1968* and other books have sold well. There is your soon-to-be-released film. The book I am working on now has a bibliography of 32 titles. With aging primary sources, there is some urgency to tell this story. There is a motive to record our history as well as provide a legacy for future generations. Can you discuss why there is a growing interest in looking back at Boston?

BL Much was accomplished during that period including driving two sitting presidents out of office [Johnson and Nixon]. The departure of Johnson is in the film. We helped to end an unpopular war. During that time, there was the first highlighting of the importance of ecology. There was the struggle for equality for African Americans, women, gay and lesbian people. That entailed a dramatic identification of problems and a shift to issues that continue to be significant social problems, including now a criminal president in the White House. These issues have sustained themselves.

For young people today, there is a desire to make the world a better place. With social media they have a set of tools we never had. There is an inevitable look back asking several key questions. Using typewriters and corded phones, how did so much get done in a relatively short period of time? From the arrival of hippies on Boston Common, to Nixon's resignation, was just seven years. If you look at pictures of young people participating in the Love Ins, they have short hair and are dressed in a tweedy, preppy manner. In 1967 the style hadn't yet evolved. In a year or two it exploded, and in seven years all this stuff happened. Another question is what role did media play in these events?

Borrowing a line for Apple, "Today it's never been easier to be heard or more difficult to communicate." With technology of the time WBCN reached some one hundred and fifty thousand. A kid walking down the street today can post to YouTube and reach a half billion people instantly.

Protest in those days wasn't just showing up for a demonstration on Boston Common or calling a Congressman. The whole culture played a role in the change.

I was talking with John Scagliotti about WBCN's role in the change to gay issues, and he said that they had covered them. In 1973, there was the first gay protest in Greenwich Village. In Washington Square Park a number of competing groups were literally about to have fist fights. Bette Midler, who was home listening, literally raced to the park and performed. That changed the whole tone of the rally. John says that, and we have it in the film. WBCN always led with the culture. Covering the first Gay Pride protest we focused on Bette Midler.

People looking for social change: the lesson of that era is that it's not just signing a petition. It was really the whole culture and its music. It's the artists like the guy who created the famous clenched fist that you see on posters. It was created by a Harvard graphic design student. It was used in the Harvard Strike. The confluence of all those elements is an important lesson.

For young people watching the film, it shows how we did it with object lessons for today. As an intern said to me, "Tell me again how you guys got rid of Nixon?" There is a natural tendency to want to look back. What was the influence of Abbie Hoffman, Angela Davis, and Herbert Marcuse?

CG They were all at Brandeis during my undergraduate years. I heard Marcuse, Eugene Debs, James Baldwin, Eleanor Roosevelt, Alan Watts, Max Lerner, Irving Howe, Abe Maslow. They all spoke to us. It was a part of our radical education. Abbie was a senior, along with Martin Peretz, when I was a freshman. I knew Angela from having coffee in the snack bar with my friend Evan Stark. You mentioned that Norm Weiner went to Brandeis.

BL After Kent State we have a clip of Walter Cronkite announcing a national student strike, but the focus was on Boston. He states that 240 schools are on strike. Brandeis was the national center for organization. The first Moratorium started in Boston.

There were people like Noam Chomsky and Howard Zinn. We all know about that inherently. But the story has not adequately been told of their impact on the 1960s. What happened in Boston filtered out nationally. As Danny [Schechter] says in the film, "Boston was a battleground." We didn't have room in the film but Daniel Ellsberg was in Harvard Square at 3 a.m., Xeroxing the Pentagon Papers.

CG What kind of obstacles did you have to overcome in order to make this film? Approaching potential donors one might imagine skepticism.

BL I listened to tapes that we started to find, like the first Bruce Springsteen radio interview with Maxanne Sartori on WBCN. Or the night that Patti Smith, performing at Paul's Mall in a remote broadcast, unleashed obscenities on air.

Or the morning when the FBI busted in the door of the commune Danny Schechter was living in to bust Bill Zimmerman. Danny had a tape recorder running. When they asked if he was a resident of the house, and an individual on their list, he responded that he was a reporter covering the bust. That took chutzpah, as he may have been in pajamas and a bathrobe at the time.

You may have heard this stuff live, but not for all these years.

Layered on that, I went to Florida and met with Jeff Albertson's widow, who is since deceased. I was looking for photos from that era. She said, "Whatever I have you're welcome to. I haven't opened this closet for a year since he passed away." There was a stack of boxes from floor to ceiling. It was all negatives. There were between fifty and seventy-five thousand negatives. There were some contact sheets. He started shooting for the *BU News*, then the *Phoenix* and *Globe*. He had a photographic history of the era.

We called around, but the cost was prohibitive. It was fifty cents or a dollar a scan, times fifty thousand. We struck a deal with [Robert Cox, archivist for the library of] University of Massachusetts, Amherst. They would acquire them, digitize them, and make them available back to us.

Peter Simon said, "I'm interested in doing the same thing. I have all these prints and negatives and they should be in an archive."

So we were finding amazing material, as well as all of these vintage photographs. Let me give you an example.

Ray Riepen was doing well with the Tea Party. He found out that someone was opening a competing club, Crosstown Bus. Long in advance they had booked The Doors. Out of nowhere "Light My Fire" became the number one song in America. They were buying TV commercials, which nobody had ever seen. Their goal was to put the Tea Party out of business.

Andy Warhol had just been on the cover of *Life Magazine*. Ray called him and said, "I've been playing the Velvet Underground here for weeks. You owe me. I'm asking you. Bring a camera, and I don't even care if there's film in it. Be up here next weekend; I need you."

Ray printed handbills. I just saw one online and I swear it was selling for ten thousand dollars. It read: "Be a Part of What's Happening. Be in Andy Warhol's Next Movie." They handed them out all over town. That night [Friday, August 11, 1967] that the Doors were at Crosstown Bus, there was a line of women around the block to get into The Tea Party. Apparently, Crosstown Bus did not even sell out.

Andy was there shooting and shooting. In 2011, when I interviewed Ray, he said that Warhol didn't have film in the camera. A couple of years later, the film was discovered with raw footage of what he shot that night of the Velvet Underground. We licensed the film. Last night, when I was watching it, amazingly, it occurred to me that he was editing it in the camera. It looks like psychedelic movie footage you've seen a million times. There's a flash then a quick cut. But he was doing it in the camera as he was shooting.

In the film, a few moments later, Steve Nelson references "Sergeant Pepper" then Peter Simon talks about "A Day in the Life." There's a short clip of a Beatles film, which they made to go along with the song. It hit me that the style of out of focus, in focus, quick cut, a close shot of someone's face, all of what we equate with 1960s avant-garde filmmaking, began with Andy. This was an example of that from The Tea Party. I would argue that you can't find anything like it before that.

When I saw the material and Warhol footage, I knew that there was a film here. In Boston there was a sense that this will be a film about WBCN. Nationally, there was a feeling of who cares about a radio station in one city. That's what we had to contend with. As a result, we did it completely independently. It was not bought ahead of time by somebody like HBO. So we had to raise all the money independently.

The archives, all of my time and that of others, were not paid for. They were all donated. In the case of archives, people made them available. We got help along the way from many, many people. The final cash outlay for the film will be around $350,000. That seems like not a lot for a serious documentary film.

But the value of Peter Simon and Jeff Albertson's photos alone, if we had to license them, would be well over seven figures. You will appreciate that the film has been done in the WBCN way. You put the word out and hope someone will come along and help. We had a Kickstarter campaign that nearly a thousand people contributed to. People sharing their archives was hugely important.

Most documentary films start because there is material and you are going to make a film about it. Our starting point was let's make a film about a radio station for which there are no tapes. Maybe we can find them.

When I started in 2006, Charles Laquidara told me, "I don't even know how to share a photo on the Internet." In the *Herald* story in 2006 we called this, "The first open-source documentary." If you look on Wikipedia it says that we were the first. It was a novel way of making a movie.

During those seven years you can list the events. There was the Boston Common Moratorium. Abbie spoke and got everyone riled up. They went and trashed Harvard Square. Another landmark was when The Grateful Dead played BU.

CG I covered that gig for the *Boston Herald* Traveler. Later I hung out with them in the greenroom of the Tea Party, then on Lansdowne Street. There was an easy access to bands that no longer exists.

BL There were a lot of people at key events with cameras. Our hope is to create a critical mass of material from that era, particularly in this region, and to create cross references. If someone reads something you wrote, for example, they might ask if there are photographs to look up? At UMass Amherst chances are you can find a photo of that event. Jeff probably has a photo of you in there somewhere. The hope is to contribute to a critical mass of ideas, film, audio, words, and images. Everything I have is going to UMass Amherst. Cliff Garboden's papers went to Northeastern but UMass has his photos. They also have Ray Mungo's papers, Liberation News Service, and a world-class folk archive with Club 47 and Joan Baez. [She attended BU for six weeks.] The hope is not just to have it in boxes, but to put it online.

CG What is the prelaunch buzz for the film?

BL There's a huge interest in Boston. We ask for comments after previews and someone wrote: "Perhaps the first true film about the 1960s."

CG Having worked on this project since 2006, how has it changed you?

BL When I first talked about it with Charles Laquidara, he was skeptical. But he said, "There hasn't been a day that's gone by without someone saying to me that something that I said or did on the air changed my life." That to me was the box that opened to make this film. Not just what the station put out, but the impact it had. We were a part of the resistance. As station manager Al Perry put it, "If we give in to these people, we're finished."

Poster for the documentary film *WBCN and the American Revolution*.

Bill Lichtenstein was the youngest DJ at WBCN. Photo by Don Stanford.

The filmmaker Bill Lichtenstein created the WBCN documentary. Photo courtesy of Bill Lichtenstein.

Lawyer/Entrepreneur Ray Riepen brought album rock programming to WBCN. Photo by David Bieber.

Peter Wolf was an early DJ but left to join J. Geils Band. Photo by Charles Giuliano.

Arnie "Woo Woo" Ginsburg was, for a time, program director. Photo by Charles Giuliano.

Charles Laquidara (right) with Danny Schechter. Photo by Charles Giuliano.

Carter Alan wrote *Radio Free Boston: The Rise and Fall of WBCN*. Photo by Charles Giuliano.

Kenny Greenblatt worked with record companies for WBCN. Photo by Charles Giuliano.

DJ Jim Parry was a neighbor in the Harvard Square Murder Building. Photo by Charles Giuliano.

Danny Schechter was the News Dissector. Photo by Charles Giuliano.

Joe Rogers was DJ for the first WBCN rock broadcast. Photo by Charles Giuliano.

Tommy Hadges was there on March 15, 1968, when Rogers cranked up rock on WBCN.
Photo by Charles Giuliano.

J.J. Jackson, left, WBCN DJ, talked with reporter Dean Johnson. Photo by Charles Giuliano.

Promo man Sal Ingemie, left, with program director Oedipus. Photo by Charles Giuliano.

Marketing director David Bieber, left, with musician D. Klein. Photo by Charles Giuliano.

Charlie "Master Blaster" Daniels was a member of the WBCN extended family.
Photo by Charles Giuliano.

Mark Parenteau was a top WBCN DJ for twenty years. Photo by Charles Giuliano.

Al Perry kept things together at WBCN. Bieber Archive.

Mark Parenteau (left) with Peter Wolf. Photo by Charles Giuliano.

Schechter (left) and Laquidara with news man John Henning (right). Photo by Charles Giuliano.

Peter Wolf on the loose. Photo by Charles Giuliano.

George Wein brought jazz to Storyville and co-founded Newport Jazz Festival

There is a long tradition of Boston as a center for all forms of music. During my teenage years, it clustered around Copley Square, along Huntington Avenue, and into Roxbury. Many clubs featured a core of local musicians fronting headliners on tour. By the 1950s the most famous club of that era, Storyville, regularly booked major artists and their bands.

In 2011 I spoke with George Wein [Born October 3, 1925] about Storyville and his role as a co-founder, and later, sole entrepreneur of the Newport Jazz Festival. He endured setbacks but established the concept of global jazz festivals.

While this book focuses on the counterculture of the 1960s, what follows provides a pre-history of those events.

Charles Giuliano. When I was a teenager, my uncle James Flynn took my sister and me to Storyville to hear Duke Ellington. It was my first exposure to live jazz. As I recall, the club was painted in black, brown, and beige. In addition to Storyville, of course, I would like to talk with you about the Newport Jazz Festival, and what is happening now.

George Wein. I'm pleased with what I have done with the Jazz Festival this year. The Folk Festival is going gangbusters.

CG I understand there was a tough transition going back to Newport.

GW There was an incident at Newport in 1971. That was two years after Woodstock. It was the era when music should be free. We had twenty thousand people in the park and another eight to ten thousand outside trying to break the fences down, which they managed to do. We sent the twenty thousand people home and then we were out of Newport for ten years. That's when I started the Festival in New York, in 1972.

CG I reported on that for the *Boston Herald Traveler*.

GW You reported on the kids breaking the fence down.

CG It ran on the front page of the *Sunday Herald Traveler*. Ernie Santosuosso in the *Sunday Globe* ran a review of the concert, which never happened.

GW I remember you well from those days. You were always a good friend.

CG What I am referring to is actually more recent. Wasn't there a two-year lapse?

GW What happened is that I sold my company four years ago. I was still involved in producing the festivals. I was on a salary with the people. But after a year and eleven months they went bust. I had sold them the name The Newport Jazz Festival. But I had a clause in that contract where it came back to me if they went out of business, or abandoned it, or went bankrupt. They abandoned it, so I just went back there by myself. We had two great years. We had a sponsor that made it possible to get by for two years with both the Folk and the Jazz Festivals.

This year I made the major decision to go nonprofit. Going back after I sold it made me realize that I would like to perpetuate it. These events should continue after I'm gone. The only way to do that is to go nonprofit and then get people involved—people willing to support it. So I'm putting a lot of my life's earnings into it and asking people to join me. If they do, the festivals will go on long after I'm gone.

[In March 2016, bass player Christian McBride became artistic director of the then 63-year-old festival—taking the reins directly from its then 91-year-old co-founder, George Wein.]

I'm going to put a lot of money into it if I get help. I'm working pro bono. I can't take a dime out because I'm putting money in. That's no problem, thank

God. I don't have to make a living out of the festivals. The profit motive is not as strong as when I was supporting a whole business doing jazz events all around the world.

CG So you sold the entire business and not just Newport.

GW I sold the entire business. But I don't want the entire business. I just want Newport, that's all.

CG Newport was a brand.

GW Newport is my legacy. It's a brand that goes with my name.

CG When you went to New York, initially, wasn't it the Kool Jazz Festival?

GW When I went to New York it was the Newport Jazz Festival New York. We have a license on the name Newport and kept it alive. It became the Kool Jazz Festival, but produced by the Newport Jazz Festival. We always kept the logo in there somewhere.

CG Can we go back to Storyville? You were a nice Jewish kid from Newton playing the piano and going to Boston University. How the hell did you open a nightclub?

GW In those days you could do things very cheaply. I didn't have any money. I had five thousand dollars that had been given to me for my education. I didn't use it because of the G.I. Bill. The army paid for my four years of education. I leased a room from a hotel. In those days you could buy tables and chairs for ten dollars; a cash register for sixty dollars; a piano for six hundred dollars. So five thousand dollars went a long way in those days.

CG You started at the Buckminster in Kenmore Square?

GW No. The first one was in Copley Square at the Copley Square Hotel. When I found out the guy was cheating me on the liquor I closed up and went to the Buckminster. I was there for three years and then I went back to the Copley Square Hotel.

CG It is good to clarify this as people have been telling me it started at the Buckminster.

GW No, it started in what became Mahogany Hall. I did two rooms, Storyville and

Mahogany Hall. That was the original Storyville. Downstairs I called Mahogany Hall. I had the big names upstairs and Dixieland downstairs. I opened in the fall of 1950 in Copley Square. I closed after six weeks and opened up in January or February of '51 at the Buckminster. I think in '53 I went back to the Copley Square Hotel. I was there until 1960. That's when I moved to New York. I was doing production and management. I was producing festivals. The management at that time was Albert Grossman who was managing Peter, Paul and Mary then Bob Dylan, and Odetta. He was my partner and I was producing the Jazz Festival and the Folk Festival. I had a partner in Detroit. We did a festival in Detroit.

Then there was the riot in Newport in 1960 and we ran out of money.

[As Marc Myers has reported in the *Wall Street Journal*: "But what began as a chance to swim, find romance and listen to live jazz, quickly turned ugly on the evening of Saturday, July 2. Unable to disperse an intoxicated mob of up to twelve thousand young people seeking access to the sold-out Newport Jazz Festival, New England's wealthiest community summoned the state police and then the National Guard to restore order. When the tear gas cleared, stricter rules for crowd control and alcohol consumption were enforced at outdoor jazz, rock, pop, and soul concerts nationwide. And the Newport Jazz Festival was left with a black eye."]

Then I started working overseas to make a living.

That was the first time the Festival was finished. I went back in 1962 by myself. Then I had another incident in 1971. That's when I went to New York '71 was the Music Should Be Free situation; 1960 was the beer kids. We never had a riot in the Festival. It was always outside. The police in 1960 asked me to keep the music going until two in the morning so they could clear up the streets outside. I had all the musicians extend their playing so they could clean up what was happening. So many people came to town because they kept the bars open until four in the morning.

CG Let's go back to Copley Square. What was a jazz scene at that time and what was your motive to get involved?

GW My roots were at the Savoy where they would keep a band for six weeks—usually a traditional band of some sort. I had Bob Wilbur [reeds], Sidney De Paris [trumpet], Sid Catlett on drums. It was a very nice band. When I went to the Buckminster, I did the same thing. We weren't doing much business. Then we closed for the summer.

Somebody sold me George Shearing for twenty-five hundred a week. It was a fortune. We sold out the entire ten-day engagement of Shearing. You couldn't get in the club. That's when I realized I had to play different attractions and play bigger names. I got involved with everything in jazz from Charlie Parker to Lennie Tristano. Charlie Parker played Storyville twice.

CG As a kid I remember seeing an ad for Billie Holiday. I wanted to see her.

GW We had Billie Holiday, as well as Ella Fitzgerald, Sarah Vaughan, Duke Ellington, Louis Armstrong. Everyone played there. You said you saw Duke there. He played several times.

CG During the summer you ran a club in Gloucester, Massachusetts.

GW Yes, we used to close during the summer and go up to the Hawthorne Inn in Gloucester. There was a fire there at the Hawthorne Inn.

CG My family has a summer home in Annisquam so as a teenager I went to the Hawthorne Inn several times.

GW We had fun. We used a traditional band up there.

CG What was your motivation for going into the jazz business?

GW I never had a motivation. I was going to college. It never entered my mind to have my own nightclub.

CG Where were you playing piano?

GW At the Savoy and at the Ken Club. All the time I was in college [Boston University] I was often playing seven nights and Sunday afternoons. My senior year, I arranged classes so I only had them on Monday, Wednesday, and Friday, so I could sleep Tuesdays and Thursdays. I was part of the jazz world and jazz was my life. I never thought about being a musician or going into the business of jazz.

When I got out of college I went to my grandfather's business and asked him for a job, but they didn't have one for me. It was a paper products business. They were distributors. So I said the hell with it and took a job playing piano in a Chinese restaurant. Somebody came to me and said," Why don't you start your own club?" It was never a motivation, but I was in the world of jazz and music was my crutch. That was my excuse for not getting a job.

CG I remember you playing during intermissions.

GW I didn't play that much when I took over the club, but I would front bands and play outside the club. First I had the Storyville All-Stars and then it became the Newport All-Stars.

Newport happened because of Storyville. I never had the motivation to do a jazz festival per se. When the Lorillards [Louis and Elaine] came into my club [1954] they said, "We would like to do something in Newport for the summer." I came up with the idea of a festival because Tanglewood had a festival—classical festival. So why couldn't we have a jazz festival? The first year it was held at the Newport Casino.

CG A Stanford White building.

GW It's still there and we are still doing things every Friday night during the festival. Then the Lorillards got divorced. They supported it for the first several years—until 1960, when we had that first riot. The Beer Can Riot we call it because the kids were throwing beer cans at the police. There was nothing in 1961. Then in '62 I said, nobody is doing anything, so I'll go back there. I called some friends and raised a little money and went back. That's been my life ever since. I did not know I was a pioneer. We were just doing things. We created the first jazz festival at Newport. Then, when we came to New York, we created the first urban jazz festival.

When we came to New York, we used Carnegie Hall, Avery Fisher Hall, Radio City Music Hall. We had 40 events in ten days.

CG Can we talk about the most famous night at Newport in 1956 with Duke Ellington and Paul Gonsalves.

GW Duke called me the night before. There was a party in Newport and somehow he got the number. It was at the Lorillards' house. He said, "What's happening up there?" I said, "What are you planning on doing?" He said, "Well the medley and then a few things." I said, "You better come in here swinging. The critics are out to get you unless you do something."

The critics in those days were very involved in criticizing everything that happened. It was a new situation to have a brand new festival with every major artist. Everyone had a game. It was really the beginning of major jazz criticism. Up to then there had just been *Downbeat* and *Metronome*. Then came John Wilson in the *New York Times*. It's probably why you were assigned to cover for the *Boston Herald Traveler* later on. We were the establishment. So they didn't want Duke playing the same medley he played everywhere. He needed to do something new, something different.

CG He introduced the *Festival Suite*.

[Personnel: Duke Ellington, piano; Ray Nance, vocals, trumpet; Jimmy Grissom, vocals; Russell Procope, alto saxophone, clarinet; Johnny Hodges, alto saxophone; Paul Gonsalves, tenor saxophone; Jimmy Hamilton, tenor saxophone, clarinet; Harry Carney, baritone saxophone; John Cook, Clark Terry, William "Cat" Anderson, trumpet; John Sanders, Quentin Jackson, Britt Woodman, trombone; Jimmy Woode, bass; Sam Woodyard, drums.]

It was not that well received.

GW No, but then there was the Gonsalves solo on "Diminuendo and Crescendo in Blue" which was the most fantastic thing he had done in years.

CG George Avakian of Columbia recorded the festival and that was a breakthrough to issuing live music and expanding through LPs from three-minute 78s.

GW Columbia said, "We want to record," which was a big thing, so I said, "Okay, you pay the artists." So I would get the artists for nothing, which I thought was a really good deal. They paid Duke that night. But it was a bad deal. We should have gotten royalties on the records. We never got royalties. I forget but I was probably paying Duke five or six thousand dollars for the night. I can't remember the prices in those days.

CG Didn't you have your own Storyville label?

GW I had a little company for awhile, two or three years. But I wasn't in the record business.

CG You recorded Vic Dickenson, Ruby Braff, Wild Bill Davidson.

GW We had about 20 different albums. Jackie Cain and Roy Kral, Ruby, and Pee Wee Russell.

CG Those were 10-inch LPs.

GW We started with 10-inch and ended up with 12-inch. Then we let it go.

CG Do you think you should have stayed in the record business?

GW No, unless I just wanted to spend 24 hours a day making a living grinding out records. You can't do things partway. I tried management. I managed Teddy King and Jackie and Roy, and a few other people like that. Then I realized, you can't do both. I ended up giving my life to what I do best, which is producing festivals.

CG Looking back at your legacy in jazz, you dealt with many of the giants like Miles. Can you tell us what that was like?

GW There's a whole thing about dealing with people like Miles [Davis], [Thelonius] Monk, [Charles] Mingus, Max [Roach] and all the M's. Somehow or other, to make the relationship work, you had to gain their trust. Each one, I gained their trust in a different way.

With Miles once I stopped the payment on his check when he didn't play the gig. He said, "Why did you stop the payment?" I said, "Why didn't you play the gig?" He said, "Fuck you," and I never had a problem with him after that. If I had let him get away with the check, he would have had no respect for me.

So with each one there was something involved with gaining their trust. They understood that my word was always good with them. If I said I was going to pay them, I paid them.

CG At the festivals you often enjoyed creating jam sessions and bringing artists out to play with each other. That didn't always work. I recall an event you did at the Boston Garden with an evening of all-stars. You had Dave Brubeck on stage and then brought out Mingus to play with him. Brubeck would lay down a riff and then Mingus would cut it to shreds. It was like the scene in *Amadeus* with Mozart improvising on Salieri. It was a hilarious Mingus putdown.

GW That was a benefit we did for the Newport Festival after the riot in 1971. Everyone agreed to play, including Aretha Franklin. And we lost money on the event. Nobody believed that so many artists were going to come.

CG Aretha wore an odd outfit like a fluffy snowsuit. She looked like a polar bear.

GW I can't recall all the artists but I remember calling Roberta Flack, Aretha. She said, "If you call me Aretha one more time I'm going to smash you in the face." I was running round like a chicken with the head cut off.

CG Those were the days.

George and Joyce Wein. Photo by Charles Giuliano.

Herb Pomeroy played at The Stables in Copley Square. Photo by Charles Giuliano.

Fred Taylor booked The Jazz Workshop and Paul's Mall

I met Fred Taylor in the early 1970s when I covered jazz, blues, and rock for the former daily *Boston Herald Traveler*. He is a treasure trove of insights and humor. He was known to book comedians more for personal pleasure than sound business strategy.

Taylor ran the Jazz Workshop/Paul's Mall from 1963 to 1978. From 1991 to 2017, he booked Scullers Jazz Club and produced the Tanglewood Jazz Festival from 2001 to 2007. Currently, he is producing a series of concerts for the Cabot Theatre in Beverly.

When Miles Davis formed new groups, the tours often started with a week at the Jazz Workshop. Talent agents and record companies often used his Boylston Street venues, Jazz Workshop/Paul's Mall to launch new acts. One of those was Bruce Springsteen.

We talked about his memoir, *What, and Quit Showbiz*, which is a collaboration with Dick Vacca who wrote *The Boston Jazz Chronicles: 1945–1962*. The book with Taylor picks up that narrative in 1963 with the Jazz Workshop. They taped ten, three-hour sessions. That's 30 times more than what follows.

Charles Giuliano When did you start working at the Jazz Workshop?

Fred Taylor 1963.

CG Were you with George Wein prior to that?

FT No, but my friend John Sdoucos and I were early investors in the Newport Jazz Festival. I knew George from his club, Storyville. He grew up on Grant Avenue in Newton about five blocks from where I lived. We both went to Boston University. He was a musician [piano]. I didn't really know him, but I knew who he was. That was the 1940s about halfway between Newton Center and Newton Corner.

I got to know him when he ran Storyville in Kenmore Square.

CG How did you get into the music business?

FT Everything is by accident. Nothing goes by plan. If I need to go the bathroom, I'll plan that but everything else happens by chance. Originally, I got interested in big band music when I was at Newton High. The RKO Theater in Boston was on the corner of Washington and Boylston Street. They would have a band and a movie. That circuit booked all the big bands. On Saturday, I would see the 11:30 a.m. stage show, see a movie, then catch the second show. That was Louis Jordan. The original sextet was Jordan [saxes, vocals], Courtney Williams [trumpet], Lem Johnson [tenor sax], Clarence Johnson [piano], Charlie Drayton [bass], and Walter Martin [drums]. I also caught Lionel Hampton and Jimmy Dorsey.

Around 1948 I bought my first 78 [rpm record] Dizzy Gillespie's "Salt Peanuts." I loved that. I loved the bop, the rhythm, and the humor of Dizzy.

CG Did you have any musical training?

FT I studied with a very famous woman, Madam Chaloff.

CG Of course, Serge Chaloff's mother.

[Serge Chaloff, (November 24, 1923–July 16, 1957) was a baritone sax player and Boston's most famous musician of that era. At first Chaloff played with Boyd Raeburn's short-lived big band. From 1947–1949 he was one of the "Four Brothers" reed section in Woody Herman's Second Herd. He also played with Georgie Auld, Jimmy Dorsey, and Count Basie, as well as recording as a leader. On baritone sax he was the bridge between Duke's Harry Carney and Gerry Mulligan.]

When I was eleven I studied classical piano with her for two years. Later, I studied popular piano with a guy named Sid Reinherz. For a little while, I took up the trumpet. Not for long, as it was too much. You have to keep your lip up every day. Then I ended up playing the cocktail drum.

During BU one summer I worked at a resort as a busboy. Another busboy was Ed Simon. Of the two bellhops one was a trumpet player and the other played clarinet. On Wednesday, Friday, and Saturday, we did little shows for the hotel audience.

I was the MC. One night I said, "Eddy, while you're playing the clarinet can I play drums?" He said, "Sure." I started playing the cocktail drum with brushes. At the end of the season he said to me, "Gee, I don't want to lug that drum with me." So I said, "I'll buy it from you," which I did for forty bucks. By the way, I still have it.

Herby was in The Don Crayton Orchestra. He was at BU and leaving to study at Syracuse. He asked if I would like to take over the band. I fronted the band playing that drum. My pianist was Creighton Hoyt. He told me about an incredible piano player in his regiment. He was well known on the West Coast and if he ever came East I should catch him.

I saw a Storyville ad, opening Monday, Dave Brubeck. I said, damn, that's the guy Creighton's been talking about. That's what led to taking my tape recorder to the gig. That was 1952 and I didn't get into the music business until 1960, and it was again because of a tape recorder. A friend, John, said, "There's a drummer in Lynn that plays like Basie." I recorded them for four nights. I asked John for some bread and he went into the famous I-ain't-got-no-money shuffle. I said let's make a deal and go in partners to promote this guy. That was my intro to show biz, and I never looked back.

CG When you studied with Madam Chaloff did you meet Serge?

FT No. I had met him once or twice, but he had left with a Boston/New York band fronted by Tommy Reynolds. I only saw him once or twice, but did get to meet him in later years. We actually went out together on a double date. He got knocked off of Woody's [Herman] band. He had a terrible heroin habit.

CG When I was a teenager in the 1950s, I saw him once during the Boston Arts Festival on the Public Gardens.

FT Yes. Herb Pomeroy had a lot to do with that. It was a lovely setup.

CG I believe he was featured with Pomeroy. Did you ever meet the piano player Dick Twardzik?

[April 30, 1931, in Danvers, Massachusetts–October 21, 1955, in Paris. He overdosed while on tour with Chet Baker. He studied with Madam Chaloff and made his professional debut at the age of 14. He played and recorded with Serge, who was eight years his senior.]

FT I didn't know him, but saw him play. As a matter of fact, it was Twardzik who got Serge hooked on smack. Eventually, Serge shook it but started having surgeries and amputations [for cancer of the spine].

When he came off Woody's band, we spent time together. I remember him playing in a wheelchair during a Boston jazz festival. He was living with his mother in the Fenway. I actually booked a date of the Woody Herman All Stars for a Tufts Winter Carnival. I had Serge and Red Rodney [trumpet]. But I wasn't about to play drums in that group.

CG Tell me more about your book *What, and Quit Showbiz?* You spent ten Saturdays, three hours each, with Dick Vacca [author of *The Boston Jazz Chronicles: 1945–1962*]. Thirty hours transcribed is a lot of material for a book.

FT One chapter he's done is called, "Over the Rainbow" and he's put together the whole story of how I came to record Brubeck. He's traced it back to the Strawberry Hills Hotel where I was working that summer. He writes about how I met Herbie, bought his drum, and how he led me to the Don Creighton Orchestra—from there, the link of how I knew about Dave Brubeck. He made a lovely story of how that all went down.

That 78 played a key role in Dave's career. Columbia Records signed him because of the buzz about the record. There were two *New York Times* articles about it. I just did stuff and in my innocent naïve way didn't know that I was ground breaking a lot of things. John Hammond wrote that while EP technology had been developed, musicians were still recording three-minute cuts. Except, he said, a live recording of Dave Brubeck, which had a seven-minute cut of "Over the Rainbow."

I see the ad for George Wein's Storyville and I see the name: Dave Brubeck. Oh, that's the guy Creighton has been telling me about. I went down on a Sunday afternoon.

I had just gotten a tape recorder. I was on my second tape recorder. They had just started coming in. Reel to reel, seven-and-a-half ips. So I introduced myself, and I said, "Dave, my name is Fred Taylor, and I'm a friend of Creighton Hoyt. Dave said ,"Oh, he saved my life in the army. Anything you want to do, go ahead." I said, "I want to record Paul and you." The bass player was absent on the afternoon.

CG Don't tell me you recorded the Storyville Record?

[The Dave Brubeck Quartet Paul Desmond (as) Dave Brubeck (p) Lloyd Davis (d-3) "Storyville," Boston, MA, October 12, 1952, "Over the Rainbow," "You Go to My Head," "Give a Little Whistle," "Lady Be Good." Dave Brubeck - Jazz At Storyville (Fantasy LP 3240, LP 8080.)]

FT Yeah.

CG That was his first record.

FT Not his first. It was a ten-inch LP. Nat Hentoff did the notes. Dave Brubeck and Paul Desmond at Storyville. That had the famous piano solo of "Over the Rainbow."

CG You were the engineer.

FT I was the engineer. It was an accident in that I just went down to get some music for myself. They all wanted to hear it. So we piled into my car and drove to my home in Newton. I still lived with my folks and I had to plug it into a system.

He said, "That's interesting because I haven't been caught playing like that. The bass player was out so we played a little differently." I got a call from him a day later from New York. He said, "You know we may want to put this out." It was Fantasy Records. So I made a deal. I sold him the master for a hundred and fifty dollars. Boy. It paid for my tape recorder and my microphone. Wow, what a deal (*laughs*).

That record was written up in the *New York Times*. John Wilson singled it out as the best new jazz recording of the year. Columbia had just opened an 18-track studio. However, our LP was recorded on amateur equipment, using one mike and achieving natural balance. John Hammond wrote it up a few weeks later. LPs had just come in. People were still recording three-minute cuts but one of the first examples of taking advantage of the LP was this record.

CG George Avakian at Columbia was pioneering the long form on LPs. [For example Duke Ellington Live at Newport, with Paul Desmond in 1956, which came four years later than the Taylor session with Brubeck on Fantasy.]

FT Innocently, I achieved two things.

CG What were they?

FT I managed the best new jazz live recording of the year and one of the first to take advantage of the LP format.
[The 12-inch (30 cm) Long Play (LP) 33 rpm microgroove record album was introduced by the Columbia Record Company at a New York press conference on June 21, 1948.]
Because of all the attention that record got, Brubeck was signed to Columbia Records.
That recording was in '53 I believe [actually October 12, 1952] and Storyville moved from Kenmore to Copley Square about a year later. When Dave returned, he had an album on Columbia. They went to the 12-inch format.
He called me and said, "Hey, do you want to come down and record some more stuff?" I said, "Sure."
His second Columbia album has two of my tracks: "On the Alamo" and "Don't Worry 'Bout Me." If Columbia ever knew they had been recorded on a $79 Tape Master deck they would have thrown it out. But Dave didn't tell them. He just said here's the tape, and it was good enough for them to master it.
In 1978, we had closed Paul's Mall in that year, and I was running something called the Green Mountain Music Festival in Burlington, and one weekend I had Dave Brubeck and Maynard Ferguson. Dave came up to me and said, "There's something I want you to know," Paul had died, and he said, "I was with Paul and he was very lucid almost right up to the end, and he said, "My favorite recording of all time was on the Storyville LP."

CG How many chapters of the book have been done?

FT He's been working on it. He's supposed to have it done in about a month. It's going to be around 400 pages. I told you my title *What, and Give up Showbiz?*
Recently, I heard an interview with Willie Nelson. He was asked why he is still working at 87. He told the story with that punch line. It's about a guy getting on in years who cleans up after the elephants. Since it's such a shitty job, he's

asked if he plans to retire? The answer is: "What, and give up showbiz?"

CG Did you found the Jazz Workshop/Paul's Mall?

FT I'm running around Copley Square and I see this little deli restaurant called Lindy's on Dartmouth Street, right near the corner of Huntington—no, Stuart. I see that there is a stage in the back. So I go in and say, "Is the owner here?" I give him this whole story about recording for Capital with Joe Bucci and we need a place to work for the week. He said, "What do you want?" I said, "Give us three hundred and fifty bucks and that will take care of us for the week."

So he said, "Hmm. I'll tell you what. I'll go fifty-fifty on the register. The first hundred bucks comes out for the bartender." I said, "You do a little advertising. Can I place an ad?"

We ended up making $480, and he was thrilled. He said you have to come back. That man was Harold Buchalter. He owned the Stables and the Show Bar up on Huntington Avenue. There was a ramp that went down into a little basement room. The original Jazz Workshop was started there.

Buchalter relocated because his place was being razed to make room for the highway [Mass Pike extension]. He asked if I would help to promote and book it, so that's how, in 1963, I got started. Some of the musicians included Ray Santisi, Varty Haratoonian, and Herb Pomeroy [Big Band leader], Joe Gordon, and Arif Mardin [musician and producer for Atlantic Records]. That was legendary, and then the state was taking over a whole strip of land for the Mass Pike, so Buckhalter, who was the owner of The Stables and Lindy's and a liquor store, moved all of his licenses over to Boylston Street. He built the new Jazz Workshop and the Inner Circle Steak House on the street floor. A year after the Workshop was built in '63, he extended and built Paul's Mall.

CG In the 1950s, when I was becoming a jazz fan, I recall seeing a Storyville ad in the *Herald* for Billie Holiday? Did you ever see her?

FT Yes, I did. I saw her at Storyville and the following week [July 17, 1959] she died in New York. It was a Thursday night, with not very many people there. They had a beautiful little blue spot on her. She looked angelic and her voice was so beautiful. It was like a moment before death that they talk about sometimes. Little did I know?

CG So you only saw her once.

FT No, I saw her at the Hi-Hat with Roy Haynes on drums and John Malachi was the pianist. I have a tape I recorded with a bit of her singing "Perdido."

CG Where was the Hi-Hat?

FT On the corner of Mass and Columbus. In the 1950s that corner was almost like 52nd Street in New York. There was the Hi-Hat, Wally's Paradise, The Savoy, The Big M, Eddy's, and the after-hours club, oh (*pause*).

CG The Pioneer?

FT Yeah.

CG And Estelle's?

FT Yeah, that's the one I was trying to think about.

CG Then further into Roxbury I used to go to Connolly's Stardust Room [Closed in 1998]. There was a house band with tenor player Al "Bottoms Up" Tyler. They would bring in a headliner. Young Tony Williams [pre-Miles] was a drummer and tenor player. Sam Rivers was a regular.

FT I was there many, many times.

CG When did Jazz Workshop/Paul's Mall close?

FT April, 1978. Costs were escalating and we decided to find another venue with greater capacity. A year ahead we set a closing date because it would take that long to filter down with booking and things. We would find a place and reopen. We came close and thought we would make a deal with the Paramount Theatre, which was just up the street. We had B.B. King in Paul's Mall and the Modern Jazz Quartet in the Jazz Workshop. There were two gigantic acts during the week we closed.

CG You had an interesting relationship with Miles Davis.

FT I first booked him in 1967. It was Monday night, and I came down from the office. They had a Miles doll that you wound up and he turned his back on you. We started at 9:00 p.m. in those days. Miles was sitting at the bar and I went up and said, "Hi Miles, I'm Fred Taylor." I could have said I was Nancy Reagan and it wouldn't have made any difference. I said to him, "How do you like to run your sets?" He said, "I came here to play man." So I said, "We start at nine and close at two with two sets. You're in charge."

They started at nine and played their ass off. At the end of the night he came up to me and said, "What did you think of the band?"

I said, "They sound good, but I'll bet that they sound better by Wednesday."

He said, "You know, you're right." That little meeting bonded us because he hated puff and condescending flattery. He threw it at me, and I came right back at him. That established a relationship, and believe it or not, I was the only one in Boston he would play for. He said so in his book.

CG Right. I read that.

FT I had him do a concert at the Opera House during the Boston Globe Jazz Festival. That was 1967, and at the time, I was suffering from arthritis and was having trouble walking. I needed to have surgery and knew he had gone through it, so I asked him what it was like.

About six months later I had him coming in for a show. I went out to Logan to meet him. We were walking to the baggage area and I said, "Miles, there's something I have to tell you. It's taken a lifetime to be able to say this." Now he's looking at me. I said, "Miles, I'm now hipper than you. I had two hips done baby. Two."

He threw his arms around me in his usual manner and said, "You motherfucker."

CG Who was he playing with?

FT That first time I think it was Herbie [Hancock, piano], Tony Williams [drums]. Ooh, good question [Wayne Shorter, reeds, Ron Carter, bass].

CG Cannonball?

FT No, when Cannonball came in, Joe Zawinul was his pianist. Joe wrote "Mercy Mercy."

CG There were stories about gigs when he wouldn't show up until mid-week. He would be hanging out across the street at the Lenox. Like a lot of cats, they walk through early in the week, then blow it out for a full house on weekends.

FT No. We actually only missed one Monday. He might be a little bit late. No, he did his job. I have no complaints other than that one time he didn't show up on a Monday.

CG How about with Mingus? He would come in with his drummer Danny Richmond. You hired some Berklee kids and it would be a week of rehearsals. By the weekend he had them in shape.

FT One time he had a tenor player, I think his name was Stan Jones, a white cat, and he was bombed. Mingus was halfway through a song and stopped, "This quintet will now become a quartet. Out!"

CG I saw Coltrane once at the Jazz Workshop. How many times did he play there?

FT You saw the only time. That was 1964 with McCoy Tyner [piano] and Elvin Jones [drums]. It was the original group. You saw the show. That was the only week when he played Boston.

CG We avoided the cover charge by standing at the bar. I recall being shocked when the entire set was one song. At one point the band left and Jimmy Garrison [bass] soloed for twenty minutes. They eventually returned and took it out. It is as vivid to me as yesterday. Why only once?

FT I don't know. It's a very good question, and I don't know the answer.

CG When I joined the *Herald Traveler* my first review was Elvin Jones. We met, and I asked if you would introduce me to Mr. Jones. You pointed to the dressing room. Elvin's Asian wife was stripping off his soaked undershirt. He rung it out and a ton of water dripped to the floor.

I said, "Wow, you sweat a lot." That was my brilliant debut as a jazz critic. Elvin was generous and I got some great quotes. After that, everything I knew about jazz was from talking with musicians. They took me to school. During a lot of Workshop gigs, I would meet them for dinner up the street at the Half Shell. Herbie Hancock downed two dozen oysters on my dime. It was a great story. While his band laughed, Roland Kirk [who was blind] cussed out the motherfuckin' white jazz critics who were ruining the music. I wrote it all down.

FT His wife called him The Elvin. She would say, "I'll ask The Elvin."

CG Of the acts that passed through, who were you tight with?

FT Larry Coryell [guitar] was a close friend. Ray Santisi [February 1, 1933–October 28, 2014] was a friend through all the years. I had good relationships with all of the artists. As a matter of fact, I got along great with Mingus. I even got along with Nina Simone.

CG That's a surprise.

FT I had her once at Paul's Mall. Twice I had her in concerts at Symphony Hall.
  I was quite friendly with Harry Chapin.

CG I covered that gig when he had a hit with "Taxi." And I covered Jim Croce, speaking of another guy who died young.

FT Jim was originally the backup guitarist for Harry. Management realized they had another star.

CG I saw Lily Tomlin at Paul's Mall and interviewed her.

FT That was one of her first nightclub dates. She had just come out with that album. [In 1972, Tomlin released This Is A Recording, her first comedy album on Polydor Records.]
  Lily is a very good friend

CG When you booked Chuck Berry at the Mall there was a small turnout and we danced. That was a night to remember.

FT There's a guy I would never work with again. Two weeks before the gig, we got a call, "That's not enough money." We replied, "But we have a contract with William Morris Agency." The response was, "Well. That's not enough money." It's what they asked for and we agreed to. But we had to add another thousand dollars. Then he comes in and pulls, "I don't go on until I have cash in my hand."

CG He was known for that. Sdoucus has stories of gigs with him. Chuck would show up with a guitar, do the gig with a pickup band, then head to the bus station and be off to the next gig. It was all cash and carry until the IRS caught up with him.

FT John and I still work together. We are pretty much in touch. In the winter he's in Florida and has a house on the Cape the rest of the year.

CG I knew John when Don Law was putting the squeeze on him. John was booking the series Concerts on the Common, which is when we got close. We went by helicopter together to Holyoke for the first gig of the Jesus Christ Superstar tour. That was a *Herald* scoop for me.

FT Don Law hung out at our office. We booked some of the acts for him when he was the Social Committee chairman as a student at BU.

CG There are a number of books coming out about Boston in this era. There is definite interest. Do you have a publisher?

FT I had a publishing deal, and was about to sign a contract, when the editor called with bad news. They were closing down the publishing unit. That was University Press of New England, so I was out in the cold again. I just found a literary agent to see if she comes up with a new publisher. The last resort is self-publishing.

CG Is Vacca's book self-published?

FT Yes, and he's done quite well with it.

CG How did you talk for three hours, ten weeks in a row?

FT Very easy. It just flows. I'm looking forward to it and doing book signings and meeting people. I enjoy doing promotion. We hope to get it out in the spring of 2019. We have a proposal that goes out to editors that has two sample chapters. One is on the Brubeck recording and another on Miles.

CG What are some of the other hot topics?

FT Bruce Springsteen. I was the first to present him in Boston.

CG Does that predate the Jon Landau Harvard Square gig?

FT Oh yeah, by far. I was in New York at the William Morris Agency. There was an agent, Phil McKee, who said, "This is a demo I just got from Columbia. They are interested in signing this guy. If they do, would you be interested in booking him?" They played it and I said, "Gee, this is great."

A couple of weeks later, he called and said they signed him. We had him open for David Bromberg. That was his first Boston appearance. I later found out that he hadn't yet signed a contract with William Morris. When he was actually playing at Paul's Mall they got Bruce to sign the contract.

CG Do you remember the date?

FT Not off the top of my head, but I have it written down. I have a logbook that we kept for the Mall and Workshop. For every week, we have the artists, attendance, what we paid them, and liquor sales. When pinning down things for the book, it's been invaluable.

[Columbia signed Springsteen in 1972. The Landau/Harvard Square gig was 1974.]

CG Who do you remember fondly?

FT I was just in the office and picked up an album by Kenny Rankin. What a voice, and he wrote great tunes. I started with Kenny back in '71 or '72, and then he played here. He just died a couple of years ago [2009]. I'm very close with Ahmad Jamal, who introduced me to his protégé, Hiromi. Jimmy McGriff and I were very close. Today there are the musicians out there like Harvey Mason, a great drummer.

In the beginning of the Jazz Workshop, we would bring in a single artist like Sonny Stitt and put our own rhythm section together. So, I would call Muzzy, Ray Santisi [piano], and say, "Listen, I need you and Alan Dawson [drummer], but pick what you think is a really talented young bass player. Let's give them a chance to put their feet to the road."

So I used to bring in one student. Harvey Mason will be here tomorrow. He said, "You know I went to Berklee, but I really learned my music at the Jazz Workshop."

CG What impact has Berklee had on the equation?

FT It has brought in so many talented players. Keith Jarrett was my house pianist. He was going to Berklee. I brought him into the Mall with a trio and he was backing up singers. Miroslav Vitous [bass], who Cannonball brought from Czechoslovakia; I put him in rhythm sections. Berklee has been a spawning ground of musicians.

CG Did Chick [Corea] play in the club?

FT Oh yes, his uncle was the piano tuner. He came from Chelsea. We introduced so many great acts to Boston like Earth, Wind and Fire, The Pointer Sisters, Bette Midler, Bruce Springsteen, Aerosmith.

In the Workshop, George Benson was the guitar player with Jack McDuff. Then he formed his group and we brought him in six times a year. He finally broke out. Joe Zawinul left Cannonball and formed Weather Report. Pat Metheny left Gary Burton to form his group.

There's a musical family tree which just goes on. In fact, I'm going to leave here in about 20 minutes because Grace Kelly [alto sax] is playing live tonight at WGBH on Eric's show. I've been mentoring Grace for about the past four years. She has an album out with Phil Woods.

CG When is your next birthday?

FT Do I have to have one? It was recent, June 8. I was 89, but there's something wrong. I think it's the wrong number. I think I'm going to edit my birth certificate to 1949. It's much better sounding.

CG That makes you younger than me.

FT I'm okay with that.

CG When did you graduate from BU, and what was your major?

FT Economics in 1951. I'm putting shows into the Cabot Theatre in Beverly, a lovely venue. It's been renovated and has 860 seats. I have Jean Luc Ponty [jazz violin] who's making his final tour. Big Bad Voodoo Daddy, then Jake Shimabukuro, an incredible Hawaiian ukulele player, Catherine Russell and John Pizzarelli, Pat Metheny. Those are my dates through December. They have a guy who does classic rock bookings, and I put in these special shows. I do ten to fifteen and they call it Fred Taylor's Jazz Series. In Worcester, at Hanover Theatre, I have Tower of Power. That's my own promotion.

CG Why are you doing this? I assume you don't need the money.

FT Yes and no. I'm subsidizing to keep my assistant and office. I need to find where I can put all the stuff. The office is in Allston. It's the building across the street from The Allston Depot.

CG What will become of the archive?

FT That's what I'm trying to figure out. I have to contact Northeastern. I heard they've done some jazz archiving. BU doesn't want it. David Bieber has something in Norwood I have to check out. Bieber has a ten-thousand-square-foot warehouse. He's one of the biggest rat pack collectors in the world. He developed a New England Music Museum space in there. It also has a performance area. I have to see what makes sense.

CG There is so much ephemera that is at risk of being lost. That's why people are working on books. There is an urgency to preserve culture for future generations. The NEA and Smithsonian should be investing in this heritage. I am shocked that BU isn't interested. George Wein, you, and Don Law are major music entrepreneurs and alumni. Why on earth not celebrate that alumni legacy? Add to that, I'm a graduate of BU's art history program and have a diverse Boston-based archive.

It's a real problem which must be addressed.

FT People are looking back and saying "Those were incredible years."

Hanging with Miles Davis at Jazz Workshop and Lennie's. Photo by Charles Giuliano.

Out of town we heard jazz at Lennie's-on-the-Turnpike. Photo by Jeff Albertson.

Jazz entrepreneur Lennie Sogaloff. Photo by Jeff Albertson.

Fred Taylor is known for his sense of humor. Photo by Charles Giuliano.

Sal Ingemie (left) has a word with Taylor. Photo by Charles Giuliano.

Bob Blumenthal, noted jazz critic, started as a DJ at Harvard's WHRB

Growing up in St. Louis, Bob Blumenthal listened to soul radio stations and attended concerts, including by a local band, Ike and Tina Turner. He borrowed records from the library, which is how he heard Ray Charles, which led to jazz.

For four years as an undergraduate at Harvard University he was a DJ for WHRB. This included live broadcasts at Boston's Jazz Workshop. Starting at Harvard Law School, he could no longer commit to a schedule for the radio station, but a weekly jazz column for *Boston After Dark* was manageable. That led to writing for *Rolling Stone*, *The Boston Globe*, other publications, and liner notes for jazz releases.

Charles Giuliano You are doing liner notes for box sets. Who is the artist for the next one?

Bob Blumenthal Hank Mobley, the tenor saxophonist for Mosaic Records. The label was initiated as mail order only in the early 1980s. They made deals with record companies to produce limited numbers of boxed sets, for example the complete Thelonious Monk Blue Note recordings. They sold five thousand and worked their way along. By drawing upon different labels they established a great library.

[Mosaic Records is an American jazz record company and label established in 1982 by Michael Cuscuna and Charlie Lourie.]

I stopped writing for the *[Boston] Globe* in 2002. I went to work as a consultant to a small jazz label. At that point I said, "I can't do criticism in newspapers and magazines. Those jobs aren't going to be there," and sure enough, they're not.

CG When, where, and how did you acquire a passion for the music?

BB Growing up in St. Louis, there was as much, if not more, black music on AM radio than there was rock 'n' roll. When I was in high school there were two soul stations. One, like WILD in Boston, had a daytime license, meaning that they signed off at sundown. In the winter they went off at four-thirty and in the summer at eight-thirty.

The first jazz radio show I got into was on Sundays, when I was thirteen. It was from three p.m. to whenever signoff was. In the winter, you got an hour and a half, and in the summer, you got four-and-a-half hours. There was a 24-hour black station which broadcast live from two different clubs. Every Monday, Albert King was in some club. Every Thursday, Little Milton was on air. The bands that played with them were young guys who later became well-known jazz musicians. They played instrumental sets before the stars came on.

The big local act at the time was Ike and Tina Turner. I would see them in North St. Louis, which was like going to Roxbury. When I was 13, I got into Ray Charles.

My local library had a lot of records. Washington University was not far from my home; I would go there to do my homework and listen to records.

CG It seems that you were as interested in soul as jazz.

BB Definitely. I discovered jazz through soul music. I heard "What'd I Say" by Ray Charles when I was 13. I bought the album *Ray Charles in Person*, which had a version of the hit record. The live version isn't nearly as good as the studio recording, but everything else on the album was killer, and half of it was instrumental jazz. I thought if Ray Charles plays jazz, maybe there are more Ray Charles records at the library. From there, I discovered all this jazz.

When I came here [Harvard] in September 1965, I liked the Stones much better than the Beatles. They had great taste in R&B songs; they covered like "I Used to Love Her but It's All Over Now." I knew the Valentinos' record when I was

14. [Also known as The Womack Brothers, it was a Cleveland-based family R&B group with brothers Bobby and Cecil Womack.] I loved that record, and when I heard the Stones, I thought they did a pretty good version of it.

Motown was huge during my last few years of high school. The only Motown that was big in Boston was The Supremes. To me they were the lamest of the bands. I much preferred the Miracles and Marvin Gaye.

It's what I listened to on black stations in St. Louis. When I was in high school, you could go and see The Ike and Tina Turner Revue. The equivalent of the Boston Garden was where Ray Charles and James Brown did concerts. White America discovered James Brown on the *T.A.M.I. Show*.

[*T.A.M.I. Show* is a 124-minute 1964 concert film released by American International Pictures. The biggest names in rock 'n' roll, pop, and soul gathered at the Santa Monica Civic Auditorium. Chuck Berry opened with "Maybelline." The Beach Boys, Rolling Stones, Marvin Gaye and others performed. It was the first filmed performance by James Brown.]

I saw James Brown live before the *T.A.M.I. Show*. St. Louis has a much larger black population than Boston. The music was tilted to reflect that. There were only a few good jazz concerts. There was a six-month period when a club tried to have a national jazz policy, when I was 15. I got to hear Coltrane, Sonny Rollins, Art Blakey, Roland Kirk, Dizzy Gillespie. The club then reverted to presenting local acts and that was it. Back then it was easier to hear R&B than jazz. As I said, you could hear Albert King and Lil' Milton live on radio every week.

CG Bob, I have always thought of you in terms of avant-garde jazz. So hearing this means hitting the reset button.

BB David Sanborn, the saxophonist, grew up in a different suburb of St. Louis. We are about the same age. I don't know the guy and met him once. I asked him about radio shows, and he was listening to the same stuff on KATZ 1600. The guys playing trumpet and sax in those blues bands were Lester Bowie, later of the Art Ensemble of Chicago, and Oliver Lake of the World Saxophone Quartet. They were young guys who I heard playing Horace Silver and Art Blakey tunes before the featured vocalists came out.

As I got into jazz, one of the advantages I had was that it all sounded strange. When I was at the library I would play Paul Desmond and say, "He's an alto player;" and Ornette Coleman, "He's an alto player, too." They both sounded strange. In different ways they were both interesting to me.

CG Did you have formal musical education?

BB Just enough to create problems. We lived in an apartment building and didn't have enough money to buy a piano. A neighbor did, and I started lessons. After a couple of years, the neighbor moved, and that was the end of my piano lessons. My school had a program where in fifth grade they would loan you an instrument. By sixth grade you had to have your own instrument. This was before I was into jazz. I got an alto sax from school. The next year came, and we couldn't afford to buy an instrument. My mother had a friend with an old sax in the attic. It wasn't an alto but I took it to school. I was told that it was a C-melody sax and I would have to play violin parts. [The C-melody saxophone is pitched in the key of C, one whole step above the B-flat tenor saxophone.]

I gave it back, and that was the end of my musical education. When I took piano lessons it included theory. I can't tell you what I learned but I had a basic notion of what musical theory meant.

Because I started out listening to everything without any bias, I was able to hear avant-garde things as they were introduced. There's a Coltrane track, "Chasing the Trane," where he plays a fifteen-minute solo at the Village Vanguard. For the first time *Down Beat* ran two reviews. One writer gave it five stars and the other none. The second critic stated that it was an abomination. I said, "What's the problem? The guy's just playing the blues." It was extreme, but straightforward what he was doing. That was my attitude; I moved along with the evolving tide.

When I had a show on WHRB, or started to write, I was the guy who would play or review a Cecil Taylor or Albert Ayler record.

CG What did you major in at Harvard?

BB Government, undergraduate, then three years of Harvard Law School. The first year I started working at WHRB. There were fixed programs that various people would do. My first was *Jazz Round Midnight*. It was Saturday from midnight to three a.m. During sophomore year my show was *Jazz Entrée*. That was Monday to Friday from five-fifteen to six. From six to seven an engineer would play records and I would pre-record intros then I went to have dinner. I did that for a year. For the last two years I had a feature on Monday nights from seven to eight. Each week I would play a whole album and talk about it. That might be Bessie Smith one week and Cecil Taylor the next.

CG What would you say about Cecil Taylor?

BB I would approach it in the context of how people thought of it as jazz. At that time he didn't have many recordings. In 1965 there was one album available and on earlier stuff he might play a Monk or Ellington tune.

CG Did you know him?

BB Yes, I did. I got a call during my show from a guy who said, "You play guys like Cecil Taylor. My friends don't understand me because I love this stuff. Obviously you love it, too. I told Cecil Taylor that I will pay for him to come to Boston and just play for my friends."

Cecil said, "If you can find a Steinway concert grand piano, I'll do it. But I'll play solo because you can't afford to pay to bring anyone with me."

The guy said to me, "You go to Harvard. Do you have access to a Steinway concert grand piano?"

By coincidence, Lowell House, where I lived, had just bought one. He said, "If you can find the piano, your friends can also hear him play. I'm paying to bring him up."

Lowell House said, "You can't just invite your friends. It has to be a university event that anyone can attend."

We put up posters, and Cecil came on a Monday night. He played an hour and a half of solo piano in the Lowell House common room. The place was jammed. I met Cecil before and after the concert. Over time I had other occasions to interview him, but not many.

CG Was he accessible?

BB My general experience is that if you make it clear that you actually listen to the music, and you're interested in the music and not some PR-related stuff, musicians are so happy not to get what they consider inane questions. So they will be very accommodating to you. That's been my experience ninety-eight percent of the time.

I knew his music and where he fit in the scheme of things. He had an attitude, but not toward me.

Did you know Lennie Sogoloff of Lennie's on the Turnpike? If you went out there, he would say you have to meet the musicians. So I met Cannonball Adderley. He wanted me to meet Buddy Rich. I had heard all these horror stories, no, keep away. But he was fine to talk to.

CG I talked with Buddy several times and it was always okay if it was all about him. There was usually a *Tonight Show* or Vegas gig he wanted to plug.

As a Harvard student majoring in government, we assume that kept you in the library. Did you find time to go to clubs? If so, what clubs, and who did you see in the mid- to late- '60s and '70s?

BB First and foremost in those years was the Jazz Workshop. Unlike Lennie's, you could get there by subway. They had a four p.m. Sunday matinee. If you had to study every night, that was an option. During my sophomore year, we came up with the idea of broadcasting the Friday midnight to two a.m. set from the Workshop. In those days, you had to get the phone company to put in a special line and make sure it worked at both ends. For a couple of years, on some, but not all, Fridays, I would be either at the Workshop or in the studio at WHRB. I can tell you who agreed to do it and who didn't. We had Elvin Jones, Freddy Hubbard, Mongo Santamaria. We went to ask Miles Davis. We would go on Tuesday when the bands opened for the week to get permission from the musicians. If they said okay we called the phone company to put the line in.

We asked Miles, and he kind of turned up his nose and walked away. That was his answer. Another time I asked Wes Montgomery. He said, "Look fellahs, I would really like to do it, but I have a family of six kids. If I put my music on the radio, after I die people are going to put out memorial albums and my family won't get a penny. So, sorry, I'm not going to do it." Six weeks later he died. Those are two memorable rejections.

CG Did you ever get to talk with Miles?

BB That was one of only two face-to-face encounters. He was trying to get a friend of his a gig writing in the *New York Times Magazine*. He shot down their writer. They said, "What about Blumenthal? He wrote notes for one of your albums." He said, "Fuck him." So I said I don't have to meet Miles.

CG What album did you write notes for?

BB *Directions*. It was one of the two-record sets that came out when he was in retirement. [Released in 1981, it compiled outtakes from sessions across fifteen years of Davis' career that had been previously unreleased.]

Anything they put out, he had to approve the whole package.

In '73 or '74, when Paul's Mall booked Monday through Sunday, his band was opening on Monday night. I was in New York and there was a club near Lincoln Center called The Watergate. I happened to be there on a Monday night, and there in the audience was Miles Davis. During the break I said, "Aren't you supposed to be opening tonight in Boston?" He just looked at me and laughed like, "Yeah, but my band's there; I'll be there tomorrow." So those were my Miles encounters.

When someone came to town that I liked, I would try to get them on my show. So, on air I interviewed Art Blakey, Horace Silver, Mose Allison, and Charles Lloyd. That was '66 to '67, before I started writing.

So for clubs, the Workshop and Lennie's, when I could get a ride. The Club 47 had already moved to what became Passim's. They occasionally had jazz on Monday nights. When Gary Burton put his band together with Larry Coryell on guitar, they played there. Sam Rivers [tenor player] came back to Boston and played a night there.

I only attended The Boston Tea Party once. The Sun Ra Arkestra opened for the Hallucinations. That had to be the fall of 1968. Sun Ra could play for hours.

CG I heard him at Carnegie Hall during the New York festival. They were playing "Space Is the Place" parading down the aisle with the audience behind. They went outside then back to the stage. For me, Sun Ra sounded like Duke Ellington on acid.

BB The bloom wore off and he got booed off the stage. My friends and I said, "The hell with the Tea Party, they booed Sun Ra." We heard a little of the Hallucinations. We were walking out. On stage the Arkestra was wearing outer space costumes that looked like they came from Woolworth's. As we walked by the dressing room, we saw these guys putting on jackets and ties. We cracked up. That was my Boston Tea Party experience.

CG Were there musicians you formed relationships with?

BB The first guy was Junior Cook, a tenor player with Horace Silver. He had moved to Boston in the late '60s and was touring with Freddie Hubbard at the time. He came to WHRB when I was doing an all-night orgy. Some local musicians came in and we decided to let them play.

CG When did you start writing?

BB I was on the air and got a call. It was January 1969. Larry Stark, the assistant editor of *Boston After Dark*, contacted me. Did you know him?

CG Yes, he was the theater critic when I was the art critic for *Boston After Dark*. Larry has a blog and is still active.

BB He said he used to listen to me. *The Boston Globe* was doing a jazz festival at the Hynes Auditorium in January. They bought a full-page ad in B.A.D. They wanted to review the festival but only had rock writers. Larry said, "If you review it for us, we'll give you free tickets for the concert. All your friends can read about it when we deliver free newspapers to your dining hall." I said, "Yeah, okay, fine."

Tomorrow is actually the 50th anniversary of my first appearance in print. The first article I wrote covered Errol Garner, Nina Simone, Thad Jones/Mel Lewis Orchestra, Dave Brubeck, Roland Kirk, and The Mothers of Invention. This was a period when people were saying that rock is artistic. Roland Kirk sat in with the Mothers that night.

I did a Gary Burton piece, which I didn't get paid for. I got the LP and tickets to the Workshop.

Then I graduated and was going on to law school. I wouldn't have time to do a radio show that locked you into a fixed time each week. But I could write for a newspaper that appeared once a week. With a weekly deadline, I could fit it in. They also started to pay. My first editor was Ken Emerson. [Previously he wrote for *Avatar* and left *Boston After Dark* for the *New York Times*.] We were roughly contemporaries at Harvard. This was the fall of 1969. Pretty quickly Ben Gerson became the music editor. I graduated from law school in 1972 and took the bar exam in June. Denise and I then took our delayed honeymoon and went to Europe for two months.

When we came back B.A.D. was the arts section of something called *The Boston Phoenix*. *The Cambridge Phoenix* has morphed into *The Real Paper*. Jimmy Isaacs came to the Boston Phoenix and everyone else stayed in Cambridge. I came back when it had all happened.

Ben Gerson's girlfriend was Lynn Staley, who ended up marrying Marty Linsky, who was then editor of *The Real Paper*. [She was design director of the

Real Paper before moving to *The Boston Globe*, where she was editor of *the Boston Globe Magazine*, then *Newsweek*.]

When Ben went to New York, my editor was Peter Herbst. When he went to *Rolling Stone*, he asked me to write for them. Kit Rachlis became my editor, and ultimately, Milo Miles. All of these people, to a greater or lesser extent, remained friends. I see Milo more than the others.

CG For a time the Boston Globe Jazz Festival was a major annual event. The regular Globe jazz critic was Ernie Santosuosso. To avoid conflict, they hired guest critics. I believe they asked you.

BB Yes, but that was in the 1980s. John Hammond came from New York one year. They started by bringing people from out of town. Then they decided to engage someone from a local paper to avoid the cost of transportation and hotel. There was a four-year period around '85 or '86 when they asked me to do it.

One way to date it is this: When I started I had a portable typewriter. When they gave me a word limit I had to write the article and count the words. Then edit and count the words. After a couple of years of that, they computerized. People didn't have laptops. *The Globe* had portable computers built for their reporters. They looked like bowling ball cases and weighed a ton. They cost over five thousand dollars each. The last couple of years I did it on these machines for like ten nights in a row. But they wouldn't let me keep the machine because it was too valuable. So Ernie would have to drag the machine to meet me. It was the other side of the Common and I had to drag the thing to the Orpheum or whatever. Ernie had to stand guard over the machine. It was '87 or '88 when that happened. In 1990 I became a *Globe* contributor.

CG What can you tell me about the local jazz musicians like Herb Pomeroy, Dick Johnson, Varty Haroutunian, Ray Santisi, Alan Dawson, Ran Blake, Phil Wilson, John Neves, Hal Galper, Gray Sargent, and Gary Burton?

BB Boston provided an unusual opportunity for musicians like Herb, Ray, Alan, Gary. Berklee College of Music gave them a regular paycheck. It was also flexible enough that when they got the opportunity to go on a short tour they could leave. When Berklee was establishing itself in the '50s and '60s.

There was a studio scene in Boston, if not for commercial releases on national labels, then for local and independent recordings. Musicians could make a living doing local record dates.

There were also touring theatrical shows when Boston was a pre-Broadway tryout town. People like Herb, Ray, Alan, who taught at Berklee, didn't have to be on the road. As a result they didn't have the name recognition nationally and internationally, but they had a livelihood and were able to do their music. At that time music schools like Berklee were the exception. Now every major university has a jazz program.

CG What about the cabaret scene? Did you go to the Merry-go-round Room [Copley Plaza Hotel] or Lulu White's [South End on Appleton Street]?

BB That was all later, after I was out of college and law school. I definitely went to the Merry-go-round Room and heard Mary Lou Williams [piano] there. I had a conversation with her about Filene's Basement between sets. Lulu White's was between '78 and '82. I definitely went there.

If you're talking about when the club scene for jazz was happening, the '80s were as intense as I can recall. Nightstage was open and Green Street was open as Charley's Tap, 1369 Club. Fred Taylor was doing things at the Starlight Roof in Kenmore Square. There was an overload of music. One night I did an eight p.m. set at Charley's Tap, a ten p.m. set at Starlight Roof, and a twelve-thirty a.m. set at 1369 Club. There was Jonathan Swift's in Harvard Square that programmed some jazz. Ryle's in Inman Square. The Workshop closed in '78. I went to Connolly's [Stardust Room in Roxbury] a few times in the '70s. From time to time they would have interesting programs. I heard Abbey Lincoln there. But they weren't on a regular basis as they had been in the '60s.

Do you remember The Garage in Harvard Square? There was a club on the top floor there. I remember hearing the Modern Jazz Quartet and Stan Getz there.

CG In Harvard Square, probably at Jonathan Swift's, I saw Professor Longhair, Roy Buchanan, Dexter Gordon, Allen Toussaint, Anthony Braxton, among others.

BB I saw Braxton at the Workshop. There was a theatre space on Boylston and Dartmouth. [New England Life Hall] It was on Dartmouth or Clarendon going toward Newbury. I heard Braxton there. There were occasional things at Jordan Hall [Huntington Avenue]. There was jazz at Symphony Hall. Was it the Modern Jazz Quartet or Mingus that played there every year with a different guest artist? I was at a Sunday afternoon concert at Symphony Hall, which was supposed to be Oscar Peterson and Sarah Vaughan. Peterson was sick, so Sarah did the whole concert. At the end she just sat at the piano and took requests.

CG I had a similar experience when Peterson didn't show up. We were introduced to Joe Pass [guitar], then unknown, who performed a long solo set.

BB We spoke earlier of the Hallucinations. The greatest rock concert I ever heard in Boston was a double bill at Symphony Hall of Van Morrison and the J. Geils band. We had great seats in the center of the first balcony. Unbelievable.

CG I was at that show and the after party at the Hotel Continental in Cambridge, which was a blast. Van lived in Cambridge in 1968 and was friends with Peter Wolf.

That was the era of drugs, sex, rock 'n' roll, social, and political protest. Compared to that, as a Harvard student, you seemed pretty straight. How did you relate to the zeitgeist of that era?

BB Just because someone went to Harvard doesn't mean they didn't trash Harvard Square. They were disproportionately represented in that exercise. Harvard had a lot of unconventional people. My main focus was the radio station. I was caught up in music and it was different than being a rock fan.

For example, Berklee is having a symposium on Woodstock in April. They asked me to participate and I told them I don't think I'm the right person. Woodstock took place the summer after I graduated from college. I was still up here and about to go to law school. Denise and I had gotten together about a month before Woodstock. We talked about going and ultimately decided not to. I don't think our budding relationship would have survived a weekend in the mud.

I thought about it and was interested enough at that point to pay attention to some of the bands that were coming up, like Cream and Led Zeppelin, but not that I would run out and hear them in concert. I heard the Stones at the Garden when I was in college. So I wasn't divorced from the musical side of all that.

CG I'm trying to understand the relationship of black music, particularly jazz, to the zeitgeist of an era of social and political activism. As one who was embedded in that how did it involve you?

BB My interest in jazz grew along with the Civil Rights movement. By the time I finished high school I had read everything James Baldwin published. My interest in jazz may have encouraged my interest in Baldwin more than my interest in Baldwin encouraged my interest in jazz. To me there was some kind of connection.

Of the songs of the Civil Rights movement I think of Coltrane's "Alabama." [It was written in response to the 16th Street Baptist Church bombing on September 15, 1963, an attack by the Ku Klux Klan in Birmingham, Alabama, that killed four African-American girls.]

To me that was a Civil Rights anthem. The world at large may not know that piece.

Vietnam was an issue, and of course I was anti-war. I had to deal with that, so in that sense, I was countercultural. It was all about how you approach life generally. My first year in law school, when Denise and I got together, she had an apartment. I lived with roommates. We spent every night together in one apartment or the other.

By February we decided to get an apartment together. Our friends who did that got two telephone lines one for him and one for her. We decided to tell our parents that we were living together and they would have to deal with it. For us that was countercultural.

When I was in high school I knew of the relationship of drugs to jazz. Being a suburban Midwesterner I had no contact to the drug culture. I thought if you smoke marijuana next thing you know you'll be shooting heroin and overdose. That's what we were taught.

I remember hearing "male chauvinist" for the first time when I was a senior in college. What did they mean? What were they talking about? So this is about the day-to-day circumstances for a person like myself at that time.

CG Let's talk about the context of the music. For example *The Freedom Suite* (1958) by Sonny Rollins. *Volunteered Slavery* (1968) by Roland Kirk. *Attica Blues* (1972) by Archie Shepp, Art Ensemble of Chicago, or the rage in the sound of Coltrane or Alvin Ayler.

BB For the album release of *The Freedom Suite* in 1958, for the very first time, the liner notes addressed the subject. A year later Mingus recorded "Fables of Faubus." [The song was written as a direct protest against Arkansas governor Orval E. Faubus, who in 1957 sent out the National Guard to prevent the integration of Little Rock Central High School.]

It had a vocal part about Mr. Bones and Mr. Jones as a minstrel-type act between Mingus and Danny Richmond. Columbia Records said, "You can record the music but not the lyrics." A year later, he took it to another record label which recorded it with the lyrics as "Original Faubus Fables." Nat Hentoff was a founder of the label.

Max Roach and lyricist Oscar Brown put out *We Insist!* [subtitled *Max Roach's Freedom Now Suite* on Candid Records in 1960. It contains a suite they began to develop in 1959 with a view to its performance in 1963 on the centennial of the Emancipation Proclamation. The cover references the sit-in movement of the Civil Rights Movement.]

You couldn't be more blunt. There's one track with Abbey Lincoln and Max Roach that had no lyrics. It's her grunting, groaning, and screaming. It was one of the first albums I heard and was a part of the foundation of what I was going through musically. To me it wasn't a point of debate regarding the views expressed. At the same time, I knew it was about something bigger.

If you read interviews with Coltrane, he never got caught up in politics. He just seemed to be focused on the music. That's what conveyed what he needed to express. To an extent he remained above the fray.

Do musicians actually debate some of these issues? I asked Archie Shepp if he ever had a conversation with Coltrane about Malcolm X's approach compared to that of Martin Luther King? Shepp said that the only political conversations he had with Coltrane were about the music business.

Coltrane was radical in another way. Back in the day, nightclub owners told musicians "Play for 40 minutes. Then stop and we sell drinks for 20 minutes, then play for another 40 minutes." Coltrane said "Nah. I want to play for an hour and a half." In Marxist terms, he was interfering with the means of production. Making a protest album would pale in significance to that in a way.

CG Did you have a relationship with Nina Simone?

BB I did not. I had to write about her for *The Globe* when basically she had a nervous breakdown on stage during one of the festival concerts. Did you ever go to the writer's room at Symphony Hall to file? There were overnight deadlines, which I never encountered before *The Globe*. It was very distressing. When I was done, I came out and she was at the stage door laughing and signing autographs. I felt like, "Was this an act?" I should have had more compassion because she was schizophrenic. But it did not encourage me to want to meet her. I saw her in person and wrote about her.

CG Correct me if I'm wrong, but it always struck me that you are more interested in instrumental than vocal jazz.

BB That's true. Now that I listen to more classical music, I'm more interested in classical instrumental music than vocal music. In the realm of popular music, for example, I love the Beach Boys because I don't care what the lyrics say. The harmonies are so incredible and that's what gets to me.

Without drawing a conclusion about hip-hop or rap, the content and lyrics didn't move me to like or dislike the music.

CG Did you have favorite vocalists?

BB Betty Carter. Ella Fitzgerald was an early favorite. She was the one artist I met where I had a Wayne's World moment like when they meet Alice Cooper, "We are not worthy." It was backstage at the Globe Festival. To get to the pressroom you had to go upstairs behind the stage and George Wein said, "Do you want to meet Ella Fitzgerald?" I always loved her. Ray Charles was the guy who got me into it all. There were other singers I liked over time.

CG It's interesting that you say Betty Carter because she was the most instrumental of the jazz singers.

BB She was, and she ran her band and set like an instrumentalist would. That's probably what attracted me to her. I had this argument with Carol Sloane. It's not how she approaches singing. She is a great singer but we had a disagreement over Betty Carter.

Meredith d'Ambrosio doesn't have a national reputation, but she's a fantastic singer.

You ask me, "Have you met people?" If I'm going to write about them, I don't want to get to the point that a friendship would distort my opinion. I just want to deal with the music. On the other hand, when I got to know them, I listened to their music a little differently. I came to really appreciate them, and Joe Williams is an example of that. He was such a fantastic person and a really expressive singer.

CG What about Lambert, Hendricks and Ross?

BB By the time I got to them it was too late. Ross had left and Dave Lambert was killed in a car accident. I did get to meet Jon Hendricks a little and I guess I saw Annie Ross. I listened to their album in the public library as a kid.

I'm trying to think of who I'm missing that's obvious. There are people who influenced me with their style, like Frank Sinatra, Nat King Cole, and Tony Bennett.

When I was visiting the library, now and then I would try to keep up with what the hot new thing was. This was in high school. The two people I listened to who weren't jazz were Bob Dylan and Barbra Streisand. When I got to college, I had heard all the Dylan albums. With Streisand, I lost the thread. I was impressed by both them and loved Dylan's pre-electric recordings. He was part of protest and civil rights, too; "Masters of War," "A Hard Rain's A-Gonna Fall," "The Lonesome Death of Hattie Caroll." They were fantastic songs from that period. They were making a lot of the same points as *The Freedom Suite*.

CG We differ in the sense that for me talking with musician was a means to know the music. In the dressing room I would ask questions and try to listen. They took me to school and the artist has always been the primary source. One approach to criticism is not to talk with the artist, which is an aspect of formalism. In that paradigm the work and critical thinking about it are separate. For me, one informs the other with a respect for boundaries and remaining independent. With time and experience one comes to know what to extract and where to draw the line. So there is a dynamic.

BB In doing liner notes for reissues of box sets, I was doing one for the Art Farmer Benny Golson Jazztet. Art Farmer had died and Benny Golson was alive. I said to the company, "Benny Golson lives in New York and I would like to talk to him." They said, "He's working on an autobiography and doesn't talk to anyone." I said I have a few questions. He invited me to his condo. I had listened to the recordings and was researching the history of the band. Talking with him just made it that much easier. Most of my dealings with jazz people I thought I knew enough to converse with them.

At this point with so many new musicians on the scene, there is such a proliferation of independently produced and small, niche-label productions, I wouldn't feel competent talking to a lot of people. Back then, I could talk to anybody. If I didn't know, I just shut up.

The great example of which was when I was in college. I got a call at 10:30 one night from the radio station. They told me to come and it would be worth my while. They needed somebody to record an interview. There was only one person there who knew how to work the control room and he was on the air. It turned out they were taping an interview with Muddy Waters. I wasn't going to pepper him with questions. I was just going to sit and listen. Peter Guralnick, who was going to Boston University, was there as well. He had met Muddy at Club 47. The Harvard folk director was doing the interview.

I have a question for your book. Do you remember a magazine called *Fusion*? It was published in Boston and had airs of being a competitor to *Rolling Stone*. I wrote for them, and perhaps you can locate someone connected to that magazine.

[*Fusion* was published in Boston 1967 to 1974 and edited by Ted Scourtis until 1970. Writers included Ben Edmonds, Lloyd Grossman, Lenny Kaye, Danny Goldberg, Nick Tosches, Keith Altham, Michael Lydon, Robert Greenfield, Charlie Gillett, Greg Shaw, Geoffrey Cannon, Jon Tiven, Al Aronowitz, Lester Bangs, Gene Sculatti, Ken Barnes, Metal Mike Saunders, Mitchell Cohen and Keith Maillard. The magazine also published pieces by Barry Miles and David Walley.]

CG I'm trying to limit the scope of the book. It's not attempting to be definitive. Hopefully, it will be a resource for further efforts. There is more to this subject than the limits of a single book.

BB Do you know Brian Coleman? He was a publicist for a long time. He was early into hip-hop. He has published a couple of books and thinks that hip-hop albums should have liner notes. Delving into David Bieber's archives, he did a book, *Buy Me Boston: Local Ads & Flyers 1960s to 1980s, Volume One* (Wax Facts Press). It may dovetail with what you're doing. The graphics of ads from various publications provide a sense of the range of venues and acts. It's another way of knowing what was going on.

CG There are a number of specialized books coming out about Boston during the years I am covering. What I'm trying to do is connect the dots. But there is a growing awareness that over a broad spectrum there was a lot going on in Boston. Thanks for sharing your insights about jazz during that era.

Bob Blumenthal. Photo by Charles Giuliano.

Albert King was a blues man Blumenthal listened to as a teenager. Photo by Charles Giuliano.

Blumenthal with Gunther Schuller at Tanglewood. Photo by Charles Giuliano.

Gunther Schuller played tuba on *Birth of the Cool* with Miles Davis. Photo by Charles Giuliano.

Lunch with Ornette Coleman. Photo by Charles Giuliano.

Sarah Vaughan. Photo by Charles Giuliano.

Joseph Jarman of Art Ensemble of Chicago. Photo by Charles Giuliano.

George Shearing performed at Boston jazz clubs. Photo by Charles Giuliano.

Encountering Stan Getz. Photo by Charles Giuliano.

Tête-à-tête with Dizzy Gillespie. Photo by Charles Giuliano

Dexter Gordon: Schnapps in Copenhagen with a bop master

In 1962, tenor titan Dexter Gordon [February 27,1923, Los Angeles–April 25,1990, Philadelphia] was granted a passport and escaped racist harassment in the U.S.A.

After decades of a vicious cycle of addiction and incarceration, he was 39 when he performed at Ronnie Scott's, a renowned London jazz club. Initially, it was just another gig but morphed into a fresh start and new life.

He would return to Los Angeles to visit his ex-wife and two daughters during annual six-week tours. Away from the scene, he got clean and somewhat straight.

The date in London was followed by a tour of England. During that time, he looked for other gigs and contacted Jazzhus Montmartre in Copenhagen. He played there off and on and eventually settled, found a Danish wife, and had more kids.

In 1976, in what proved to be a comeback orchestrated by his manager and third wife, Maxine Gordon, he returned to the States and renewed a career as an ultra cool, progenitor of hard bop, tenor sax. He was a first-generation bop player who influenced the next generation of tenor players, including Stan Getz, Sonny Rollins, and John Coltrane.

With meticulous research, insight, and loving care, his widow has written a compelling biography, *Sophisticated Giant: The Life and Times of Dexter Gordon*

(University of California Press, 2018).

In particular, the biography brought me back to March 1972 when Dexter and I met for lunch, including several shots of potent aquavit on a rainy Sunday in Copenhagen. That was four years before the hoopla that celebrated his return to the mainstream of jazz. He later signed with a major label, Columbia, played global festivals as a headliner, and toured relentlessly. That was capped by an Oscar-nominated role as lead of the 1986 film *Round Midnight* by French director Bertrand Tavernier. In 1960, he was featured, performed, and composed for the Los Angeles production of Jack Gelber's 1959 play *The Connection*. He appeared in a short run of a later Danish production of that play.

For generations Europe had been a refuge for jazz artists, particularly those with bad habits who had endured harassment in the United States. Early on, Paris was home to New Orleans' legend Sidney Bechet. Josephine Baker and Madam Bricktop had European stage and cabaret careers. Seminal tenor sax player Coleman Hawkins resided in Belgium.

They were pioneers in the 1930s and 1940s. By the time that Dexter arrived on the European scene, there were a lot of cats on the lam to jam with. Unfortunately, the sides cut by Bechet and Hawkins were notable for inferior European sidemen. By the 1960s that changed on two levels. There were more Americans abroad, both on tour and longterm, as well as skilled European musicians.

In the mid-1950s, Stan Getz married Monica Silfverskiöld, daughter of Swedish physician and former Olympic medalist Nils Silfverskiöld. Based in Copenhagen, he often played at Jazzhus Montmartre. He returned to the States in 1961, so he and Dexter, kindred spirits, just missed each other.

On many levels Copenhagen proved to be the right fit for Gordon. There was a new generation of European musicians. Not only were they hip to the jive, as numerous recordings with a range of artists document, they were innovative artists on their own terms. The presence of so many American masters was a catalyst for this development.

Dexter's gigs at Jazzhus Montmartre lasted a month or more. The rest of the time he toured a circuit in Scandinavia, Germany, and Paris. From Copenhagen he traveled by ferry and train.

That's where Maxine entered the picture as an experienced road manager. During a train strike, early on, she navigated the band home from being stranded in Lyon.

Mostly, Dexter managed to stay straight. There were notable lapses with consequences. In 1963, he cut *Our Man in Paris*, one of his most memorable of several albums for Blue Note. It featured Bud Powell, piano; Pierre Michelot, bass; and drums, Kenny Clark. Hanging with them, however, resulted in arrest on charges of dealing. He got off on the plea that he was a user, but there was a similar incident that got him banned from Stockholm.

This made his return to Copenhagen difficult. With the help of a physician, who vouched for him, Dexter eventually became a permanent resident. He learned to speak Danish, as I discovered. In the slammer, he taught himself enough French to read *Les Miserables* in the original. Maxine informs us that he was an avid reader.

My week in Copenhagen was a fluke. At the time I was a music critic for the former daily *Boston Herald Traveler*. A colleague from our library had taken a job with the tour company International Weekends. The company organized a weekly package to Copenhagen. If there were seats open for the Friday flight, they were offered to HT journalists for $75.

There was just one catch. You could be out of the office for a week, but had to return with a Sunday piece. Not knowing what to expect, Copenhagen proved to be a challenge. That started with the flight itself in a small commuter plane. It entailed refueling in Gander, Newfoundland, and Reykjavik, Iceland.

From the suburban hotel there was a bus to town. Copenhagen reminded me of Boston and its Back Bay. There was a walking street that combined high-end stores with porn shops. The uniquely liberal Danish approach to the sex industry was a major tourist attraction.

When our group boarded a bus for the live sex show, I opted out. The concierge offered me a ticket to the Royal Danish Ballet. On the previous evening I had seen their *Swan Lake*. I was surprised by a nude production of *On the Beach*.

By word of mouth I found Jazzhus Montmartre. It started in 1959 with Dixieland jazz, and then closed.

On New Year's Eve, 1961, Jazzhus Montmartre was re-opened by Herluf Kamp-Larsen. It evolved into a matrix for jazz in Europe. American artists were booked with a house rhythm section of American pianists Bud Powell and Kenny Drew, with Danish musicians Alex Riel, drums, and Niels-Henning Ørsted Pedersen, bass. NHOP, as he became known, was one of the most renowned musicians of his generation, particularly for tours with pianists Oscar Peterson and George Shearing.

It cost about a dollar cover charge for the small, packed, smoky club. There were benches for cheap beer and pub food. On the walls were plaster masks in an ersatz African motif by Mogens Gylling. They disappeared when the club closed in 1976, but were re-created by the artist during Copenhagen Jazz Festival 2010. The club became a legendary home away from home for a generation of mainstream jazz artists.

Looking for a story I caught up with owner, chef, and waiter Kamp-Larsen. We met for dinner in one of three Chinese restaurants in Copenhagen.

"I started with the club about ten years ago," he said. "At the time, there was no place in Scandinavia to hear live jazz. I bought out the other backers one by one, and now I am the sole owner. I don't make any money on the club, as taxes are very high. Income tax is 41 percent, and there is a new artists' tax on talent we bring in, as well as a 15 percent sales tax. My salary comes from earnings as a waiter.

"I have an apartment in the old section of Copenhagen, where I pay thirty dollars a month for rent, compared to an average of one hundred and fifty dollars. I have a small boat with a cabin, and like to sail on nice days before opening the club for lunch. During two-month holidays in Spain, I can live very cheaply. Recently the jazz musicians union applied to the state to help support the club to bring in major musicians."

Despite low income and high taxes he stated, "I love Copenhagen and would never leave here. I have no desire to visit the U.S. like the jazz musicians who live and work here. Many say it's because they don't want to put up with the hassles of life in the States. I recall when Bud Powell lived here. For a long time he was the house pianist at Montmartre. Right now, Ben Webster from the Duke Ellington band lives here. He loves Copenhagen. Tomorrow is his birthday. Unfortunately, he is out of town playing this week. We just had Herbie Hancock. Also Dexter Gordon lives here and plays frequently. We have a very healthy jazz scene here."

It was disappointing to miss Webster, but I looked up Gordon in the telephone book. He answered in that resonant hipster patois, "What's up, baby?" I introduced myself and asked if we could meet for lunch. He responded, "Solid, baby," and suggested a restaurant.

I had seen him perform during the 1969 Newport Jazz Festival. So I was familiar with his music and stage persona.

With excited anticipation, I was seated when long, tall Dexter at six foot six strode in. There was a palpable shock wave through the restaurant when he made an entrance. Settled into our table, after mutual salutations, he had the shakes, and asked if he might have a taste to get straight. Foolishly, I opted not only to join him but to attempt to keep pace.

Gordon spoke bebop Danish to the formally-attired waiter, who returned with a bottle of frozen aquavit. It poured like syrup into shot glasses, which we knocked back. The alcohol content is about 45 percent by volume. While it relaxed Dexter, by the end of lunch I was completely trashed. Wandering into the street felt like an acid trip, but I managed to catch up to our group for a traditional smorgasbord dinner.

Somehow I scribbled notes that became the *Herald Traveler* piece that follows. After 1976, when he returned to the States, I caught all of his Boston club dates.

With an offering of reefer that first time since Copenhagen in the greenroom I said, "Hey Dexter, remember me? We had lunch in Copenhagen."

Meaning no offense, he floored my by replying, "No, baby." It came to be a riff. Each time I repeated the question and got the same response. With hipster humor it spoke volumes about the life and times of a truly magnificent jazz artist.

What follows appeared in the Boston Herald Traveler, June 4, 1972.

"Ira Gitler wrote an article in which he called me an expatriate jazz man," said Dexter Gordon in a crowded Copenhagen café. "I don't consider myself an expatriate. I still have my American passport. It's a little hard to give up."

In the 1969 Newport Jazz Festival Dexter played in the afternoon with Phil Woods. That was a rare New England appearance for Dexter who hasn't played in Boston since 1965. This summer he will again play at Newport when the historic Billy Eckstein orchestra is reunited.

A tall, imposing man with the frame of a Green Bay Packer, Dexter seems to dominate any room he's in. He has a swarthy tan-tinted complexion with touches of white hair at the temples as sprightly contrast. He is a hearty, mirthful man who delights in his own jokes.

It was a rainy Sunday morning in Copenhagen when I roused him out of bed. Holding his head with one bleary ear next to the phone Dexter complained about his hangover. Later at a café he introduced me to schnapps, a powerful Danish brew which hits you like a ton of bricks. But it is also good for curing hangovers.

Originally Dexter came from Los Angeles. On December 23, 1940, he joined the Lionel Hampton band while on vacation from high school. He later worked for three years with the Hampton band playing tenor sax. When the Hampton band broke up he did a six-month gig with Louis Armstrong. Then he bopped off to the newly formed Billy Eckstein band.

His first taste of Europe came in 1962 when he gigged at Ronnie Scott's club in London. From there he took off for a six-week tour in England. During this time he contracted Copenhagen's famed Club Montmartre. They had a big circuit in Scandinavia where they were still interested in jazz.

"Actually today Stockholm is pretty dull. I just came over for a casual visit, and before I knew it I had been here for two years. At the time I had a hassle from getting my cabaret license. In New York I couldn't get a card because I had a record. The original purpose of the cabaret card was to control the gangster element in nightclubs. It ended up penalizing musicians who had police records and drug problems. Billie Holiday and J.J. Johnson were fighting it but it wasn't until (Mayor) John Lindsey when they done away with it.

"I was cool when I left the States but your record follows you around. Looking back I would say that leaving the States added ten years to my life. I found that there was plenty of work for me in Denmark and the people treated me well.

"While I've been here I worked with people like Ornette Coleman and George Wein's various tours. Still I'm an American citizen but I have a visa. You enter Denmark on an automatic visa of three months. To extend it I have to leave for six months and then come back. I had to do that several times but now I have a permanent residence. I just bought a house and for the first time feel like I have joined the establishment."

By the third schnapps each we were both pretty loose. Dexter's forehead was slightly beaded with sweat.

"What intrigued me about Denmark was that I didn't have to look over my shoulder to see who was behind me. In the States I was getting paranoid. If you're an artist here you get some kind of recognition. Of course here everything is highly taxed. So it's a commitment to stay here. I still do an annual tour of the States, usually for about six weeks. But my time is limited there. This year I will be there in early June and I'll be around through the Newport Jazz Festival."

Recently Dexter signed with Prestige Records a contract for two albums. He also has albums on GPS, a German label, as well as albums on Dutch, Norwegian, and Blue Note Records.

"I'm really excited about the Billy Eckstein reunion which is planned for this summer's jazz festival. Eckstein had been doing vocals with the Earl Hines band. In 1943 he left Hines and took half the band with him. Dizzy Gillespie and Charlie Parker were the heart of the band, which also included me, Gene Ammons and Sonny Stitt, Art Blakey, and Sarah Vaughan. Billy was a trumpeter and trombone player as well as singer, so he was pretty hip instrumentally. The band was really wailing. It was the first bop band. We weren't just playing whole notes. Plus we had some really great writers like Jerry Valentine and Tadd Dameron. This summer John Jackson will play Bird's book. Being in that band with Bird 'n Diz was like college for me. They really influenced my playing. Also at the festival I'll be playing in one of the jam sessions."

By now Dexter finished his steak with béarnaise sauce as well as the schnapps. Letting out a hearty laugh and hoisting his glass he said, "This is the devil." With that final toast, I staggered out to a rainy Sunday in Copenhagen.

Dexter Gordon. Photos by Charles Giuliano.

Dexter Gordon

David Wilson, *Broadside* publisher, recalls summer we edited *Avatar*

As the former editor of *Broadside*, David Wilson has a formidable grasp of the folk/blues music scene of Boston and Cambridge in the 1960s.

He was a founding board member of the alternative weekly *Avatar*. Gradually, the publication was taken over by guru/musician Mel Lyman's Fort Hill commune.

I had been writing for *Avatar*'s New York edition, edited by Brian Keating. Returning to Boston in the summer of 1968, I wrote for *Avatar*. For payment, as a contributor, I was given papers to sell in Harvard Square. With my partner, Arden Harrison, we got to keep the quarters for each copy. We were barely able to pay rent on a Fort Hill apartment and put brown rice on the table.

Issues of *Avatar* became ever more infrequent as Lyman pursued other interests. When it ceased publication, a group formed to continue with *Avatar*. Our issue #25 was confiscated when Lyman decided that it had violated an agreement not to use the name and logo of *Avatar*. That resulted from an act of sabotage by the designer Ed "Beardsley" Jordan.

Wilson and the board met, and by a narrow vote ousted Lyman's minority trustees. He took over as editor, and I joined him as managing editor. There was another act of sabotage by Beardsley/Jordan and I replaced him as design director. After several issues Wilson left *Avatar* returning full time to Broadside, which merged with the *Boston Free Press*.

That fall, I was hired as design director of the weekly *Boston After Dark*. That didn't last long, but I stayed on, launching a career as an art critic. From there I joined the daily *Boston Herald Traveler* as jazz and rock critic.

Charles Giuliano You were publisher/editor of *Broadside*. It was one of the major New England music magazines of its era, with an emphasis on folk music and blues. Can you tell us when it was founded, as well as when it ceased publication?

David Wilson In 1958, Manny Greenhill was running monthly midnight folk concerts at the Hotel Ambassador just off Harvard Square, which I attended with a few friends. It was through those concerts that I began to get a sense of the scope of folk music, and it was so much more interesting to me than was the pop music of that time. In 1959, I went into an Air Force pilot training program, but washed out in mid-1960. While I was away, folk had blossomed in the area, with several coffeehouses featuring regular performances. In late summer of 1961, I took a basement apartment on Newbury Street, which was across the alley from the back door of The Unicorn. I and my roommates became regulars there. In early fall, I volunteered to become program director for the Boston Folksong Society.

In March of 1962, I was feeling frustrated that I missed performances by musicians I would like to have heard, but they were not listed anywhere. If I wanted to have advance notice, others would also. I did some calling around, and visited every coffeehouse I knew about, and organized a schedule of everything I could dig up. With the help of a friend, who worked in his father's office, I typed up mimeo masters and ran off copies of the first issue. We could only get limited numbers from each master, so I ended up doing it three times for each page, and as a result there were three different versions of that first issue. Other friends chipped in their assistance for the next issue and we went to an Itek printing method on the second issue, and photo-offset on the third. We published fairly regularly until 1969, when a combination of market factors pretty much sank us.

CG What was it about folk and blues that particularly interested you? It seems that you became involved initially as a fan. Who were some of the artists that you were listening to in the clubs at the time?

DW The interest I had in folk music grew out of my experiences as a camp counselor and singing camp songs. Eventually, I discovered that a lot of those songs were descended from traditional songs. Combined with an interest in the literary connections of classic English ballads, that gradually got me into folk music. A regret about getting involved professionally with folk music was that I gradually stopped singing and became a listener.

It was an interest in Afro-American work songs and prison songs that eventually led me to blues and gospel. I have always been more interested in the wider variety of traditional songs than the more rigid codification of blues.

I started visiting Club 47 in 1958, where I first heard Joan Baez, Carolyn Hester, and Richard Farina, before I went into the Air Force. They were still programming mostly jazz and classical with only occasional forays into folk. By the time I got back from military service, folk had become their primary focus.

CG We had a club on the Brandeis campus called Cholmondeley's. Because we were so far from Cambridge, a lot of the acts came to us. I recall performances by Mitch Greenhill and Jackie Washington, as well as Lightning Hopkins. My friend Rachel Goldstein was a Joan Baez fan and insisted that I drive her to Cambridge and Club 47. On one of those nights, there was hardly anyone in the place. Joan was sitting chatting with a friend. During her set she asked him to join her for a couple of tunes. Of course that was Bob Dylan. There was a Brandeis group and they opened for her at the Golden Vanity, which was on the Boston University campus. Joanie came to Brandeis on the back of a Vespa to perform in a packed dorm lounge.

DW I remember Chomondeley's well, as we started carrying their schedules in our first year of publication. I attended performances there on a number of occasions.

CG I knew Tim Hardin pretty well. Of course Tom Rush came over from his dorm to play Club 47. Yes, you're right, I do recall hearing jazz there—a group with drummer Al Dawson. During the summer of 1963, when I graduated from Brandeis, I was living on Hartwell Street in Waltham near the campus. Mel Lyman hooked up with Tim Leary and Richard Alpert, who had a commune at 55 Kenwood Avenue in Newton called IFIF. We visited a number of times. That's where I met the artist Bruce Conner. Mel came home with a bag of morning glory seeds. They were like an acid trip. The actor and later BU professor James Spruill was also living with us, as well as John Kostik who founded Omniversal Design.

DW Tim Hardin was ubiquitous. He was always after me to put him on the cover of *Broadside*, and eventually we did. He gave me my first snort of coke, rolling up a dollar bill and saying, "Here, this will clear your sinuses." It did, but the comedown was so god-awful, I was never tempted again. Tom was not only performing in those days, but hosting WHRB's *Balladeers* show at the same time I was doing *Rambl'n Round* on WTBS. He lent me an advance copy of Dylan's new album and that night I played the whole thing on my show. We invited callers to comment, and the response was the most we had ever had up to then. Early callers hated the album, but as the hour went by we got more and more favorable calls, and it ended up a fairly even split. No one felt neutral about it.

IFIF had offices in the West End in the early sixties and my roommate Chuck Schefreen and I visited them. Chuck signed up and we spent some time talking with Lisa Bieberman, who seemed to be the actual manager of the operation. I still remember a few folks wandering around the scene munching from bags of morning glory seeds they kept in their pockets.

CG Jim Kweskin came by our Waltham pad and asked Mel to join his jug band. Mel played five-string bluegrass banjo, so he was eventually replaced by Bill Keith. Mel went to live in Kweskin's attic in Cambridge before they moved to Fort Hill to found their commune.

What are some of the highlights and performances that you recall from the 1960s when *Broadside* became more active in the music community?

DW I need to do a bit of thinking before I answer that one. It is a bit all encompassing. I will say that with the awe I felt for Joan Baez, going to a Bob Gibson concert in 1959, and having him bring her out to do a few numbers, was a thrill. It led me to believe that since he was going to perform at the Newport Folk Festival, he might very well do the same thing there. He did, and I was there and I knew, as many did, that something very big had happened that night.

CG In the summer of 1968, I moved to Fort Hill from New York. There was the Bosstown Sound of MGM Records under Mike Curb. There were hippie concerts on Boston Common as well as a few riots.

Do you remember Jamie Brockett, Ultimate Spinach, Beacon Street Union, Orpheus, Charles River Valley Boys, The Remains, The Lost with Willie "Loco" Alexander, The Barbarians, The Hallucinations, and other groups which played at the original Tea Party?

DW Jamie Brockett, I was not a big fan, and he seemed to make his big splash with a song that was, at the time, a copy of a song in Chris Smither's repertoire about the Titanic.

Ultimate Spinach, Orpheus, and Beacon Street Union were all label-manufactured, local groups which formed the basis for the Bosstown Sound. Priscilla DiDonato, who did cartoons for *Broadside*, was with the Spinach. I worked for a while with the agency, [along with Don Law] Music Productions [John and Leah Sdoucos] that developed Barry and the Remains. They, and the Barbarians, were the first hot '60s Boston rockers. I designed and produced the Remains' first brochure. I introduced Ed Freeman, who did a column for us, to them. He did a more contemporary brochure, and ended up being their roadie when they went on tour with the Beatles. When I was managing the Odyssey Coffeehouse, on Hancock Street, I gave the Hallucinations their first steady gig on the basis of a door split. Peter Wolf was the lead singer for the Hallucinations. Doug Slade played bass and the artist Paul Shapiro played guitar.

I do not think that the Charles River Valley Boys, anymore than the Kweskin Jug Band, can be considered part of the Bosstown Sound. The CRVB released their first U.S. recording in '62 on the Mt. Auburn label, though I believe they had an earlier one in the U.K. They went through a fair number of lineup changes in their time.

CG Did *Broadside* cover The Bosstown Sound?

DW We did cover much of it, especially in so far as the groups sprung out of the folk tradition. It was tricky at that time, trying to stay true to our traditional music readership and the fringes, where folk was fusing with psychedelic, metal, pop, country, gospel, and what-all.

CG Ultimately the Bosstown Sound flopped, and for a time that seemed like the end for a Boston music scene.

DW Later there were great groups, including Boston, J. Geils, The Cars, and Aerosmith to mention just a few.

One difficulty I am having here is that you seem to see the '60s as a much more unified period then I do.

The early sixties were culturally, politically, and aesthetically quite different from the late sixties, and the change, while rapid and dynamic, was organic. Not the least was the freedom that came with the appearance of the contraceptive pill in 1960. That resulted in huge changes in lifestyle and attitude.

I was let go from the Air Force pilot training program during a RIF in June of 1960. It was during the presidential campaign, which eventually came down to Kennedy and Nixon. Later that summer, I got a job working in a Top Value Stamp Warehouse, (remember those?) in Needham. I hadn't any idea what I wanted to do or what course to take.

I took an apartment in Boston, lost my TV stamp job, and got another as a parts inventory clerk at a tractor company in Cambridge. At a meeting of the Folksong Society of Boston I signed up to help out on the program committee. I left that meeting as the Program Director, not knowing zilch about it. But I knew that the Society's platform was of value to performers. I used the position to get to know, and have access to, a lot of the performers around town. Camelot was in blossom. Fresh air and change seemed to be the order of the day and the atmosphere seemed full of hope.

After Kennedy's election, the sit-ins, the wade-ins, and all the other demonstrations became a major cause for me. Folk music was a large component of the struggle. With the connections I had, as program director for the Folk Song Society, it was a big help in gathering the info I needed to start publishing Broadside. Originally, I had intended to call it Funky, but few people I mentioned it to knew what that meant, so I chose *Broadside*. I didn't know that in New York and in L.A., in that same month, two other *Broadside*s had started publishing.

CG What role did Club 47 have?

DW Club 47 was the center of controversy. A scheduled benefit for the SANE, (Committee for a Sane Nuclear Policy) had drawn the iron hand of the Cambridge political structure down on them. They were besieged by inspectors of every conceivable type, suspending their permits, and threatening permanent closure— so much for free speech. The community rallied, legal aid was freely proffered, and eventually the club reopened. In many ways the founders were scarred by the event. The venue became more exclusive, and in some ways a bit paranoid. I was persona non grata there for most of the decade due to an unflattering review for some event or other. Distribution of *Broadside* was suspended on the grounds that the club was nonprofit. Because of our 10-cent cover price, they claimed that they could not sell our issues.

Pot was becoming common and more so among musicians. Narcs infiltrated the scene and busted people. They held their futures hostage unless they would inform on friends. Disillusionment and paranoia was on the rise. I lost a couple of close musician friends because I made house rules barring pot from the premises. With wholesale gatherings going on, and seldom knowing half the people there at any moment, I was unwilling to take chances.

In August of 1962, *Broadside* moved to a big duplex house on Columbia Street in Cambridge. We had one side and the crew running the Café Yana had the other side. They were putting up the out-of-town musicians playing the club. I was constantly meeting more and more of the national performers. It was at that house that I met Dave Van Ronk, Reverend Gary Davis, and Oranim Zabar. It is also where Bob Lurtsema, [Robert J. Lurtsema the renowned late classical music DJ at WGBH-FM] first came into our life.

When the Cuban crisis got me activated, and threatened my still-iffy economics, I became more anti-establishment and politically radical.

CG How did military activation in the 1960s impact you?

DH True to the law, Krohn-Hite, my employer, kept me on the job for the six months required after return from activation and then let me go. It took me awhile to figure out that I was a pawn in a power struggle going on between George Hite and some of his department managers. I left, but George and I remained on friendly terms and our occasional, if rare, meetings were congenial.

CG What was the status of *Broadside* during your military activation and other employment?

DW During activation I came home in the evening and still had a hand in getting out the issues. The day Krohn-Hite let me go was the day that the first anniversary issue of *Broadside* came out. Money was tight. I collected unemployment for about two months.

Carl Bower, who had operated the Golden Vanity, opened the Silver Vanity in Worcester, but it only lasted for a month or two. Worcester was not ready yet.

In May of '63, a pot bust at the Café Yana shut down the club and resulted in the arrest of newcomer John Hammond, Jr. The people involved in running the club sort of evaporated and dispersed. A few weeks later, the club owner asked me if I would be interested in managing the club. I anguished over the offer, but finally accepted. I turned editorship of *Broadside* over to Jill Henderson and Lynn Musgrave, figuring that my continuing as editor would constitute a conflict of interests. Jill and Lynn put their stamp on *Broadside* and gave it a more professional look. I still contributed, mainly getting others like Tom Paxton, Casey Anderson, Peter LaFarge et al. to contribute.

Running the Yana gave me a whole different perspective on the business. We were operating on a shoestring and barely making expenses. We were building a good weekend audience and bringing in top acts: Patrick Sky, Hedy West, Dave Van Ronk, Reverend Gary Davis, Judy Roderick, The Holy Modal Rounders, and Tim Hardin. We even lured John Hammond back. During their appearances, I put most of them up at my apartment.

I booked our biggest act to date, Jean Redpath, and it proved disastrous. JFK was assassinated [November 22, 1963] and the nation went into mourning. We stayed open, but attendance was sparse and we lost our whole nut and whatever bankroll we had built up.

CG How did the club manage after its finances were wiped out?

DW I managed to hold things together into January, but without front money for name performers it was nip and tuck. I was about to separate from the Yana altogether when I was offered a great opportunity. I had the chance to book Mississippi John Hurt for his first Boston appearance. It was for a thousand dollars against half the house. To seal the deal I needed five hundred up front. I brought the offer to the owner of the Yana, but he declined. A day later I went back and offered to rent the club from him for the week for a hundred bucks and he jumped at the opportunity. I started scrabbling for the front money.

Dick Waterman, who had been writing for *Broadside* and hanging out at the Yana a lot, offered to go halves with me and put up the front money. A week before the booking, Hurt appeared on the Johnnie Carson show and the publicity and word of mouth spread rapidly. We did three shows a night for five nights in February of '64 and turned away people at every show. It was the biggest success I ever had before or after.

CG Waterman went on to manage legendary folk and blues artists and was also the first manager of Bonnie Raitt.

DW While running the Yana I had started to manage a few performers including Ray Pong and Jerry Corbitt. The percentage I was making on their bookings and others kept me going. Most of the money I made on John Hurt I lost a few months later when I produced a Bukka White concert. I had started writing again for *Broadside* and I was writing scripts on the spot for WGBH's *Folk Music USA.*

Broadside took strong positions on the boycotting of ABC's *Hootenanny* show for its blacklisting of Pete Seeger. Musicians lined up on both sides of the issue, with many of the mainstream pop folk groups claiming that by going on the show they could change the system from the inside. Some who clearly should have known better could not resist the lure of the big audience. Baez turned them down flat, as did most of the musicians who had any political savvy.

In the first two years we had only published two songs, one by Dayle Stanley and one by Pat Sky. The last issue of Volume Two introduced an ongoing column by Phil Ochs wherein he would introduce a song with a commentary on the background and his reasons for writing it. It was called "All the News Fit to Sing" and it paved the way for similar columns from Tom Paxton and Eric Andersen.

CG It seems that *Broadside* was expanding its presence in the music scene.

DW Well, it all seemed natural and obvious at that time. Singer/Songwriters were coming into their own. You know, at that time they were suspect, considered to be songwriters who could not get real artists to record their material. That seems strange today when most top artists write a lot of their own material.

In April of '64, I again took over editorship of *Broadside*. I got the word that *Folk Music USA* was being cancelled by WGBH. We printed a petition addressed to the program manager of the station. Whether it was due to our efforts, or not, the station got over two thousand protests within a few weeks. The show was renewed. Meanwhile, The Unicorn bought out Café Yana. They tried a variety of programming strategies to no avail, and it closed before the end of the summer. Then the Unicorn announced the opening of another site on Martha's Vineyard, not far from the Mooncusser.

The Beatles arrived in New York and dominated the pop music scene. Radio Caroline, the UK's first pirate radio station, began transmission. The Boston underground was abuzz with plans to launch a similar station off the coast of Massachusetts. The Rolling Stones released their first LP that April. The Who started breaking guitars on stage and the Kinks released their first album. Three thousand Berkeley students blocked a police car with an anti-war activist under arrest. This was the start of the Berkeley Free Speech Movement. Folk musicians were in the vanguard of civil rights and anti-war activities, and though not as well remembered now, the plight of the Appalachian miners. Companies of black and white performers were touring the south, performing in unsegregated venues, mostly churches, campaigning for voter registration and peaceful resistance.

Over the summer, the civil rights movement continued to heat up. In Mississippi, Michael Schwerner, Andrew Goodman, and James Chaney were murdered and their bodies found a month later. Casualties in Vietnam increased, and Johnson fabricated the Gulf of Tonkin incident as an excuse to escalate U.S. involvement.

All the warnings and rants I had been shunned for over the previous two years became a simple matter of fact. The John Birch Society was waxing in strength and supporting the Goldwater presidential campaign. I went off to my summer reserve meeting at Otis Air Force Base and was working in the CO's office. The chatter in the unit among the mission officers was all jingoistic. We were running simulation-bombing runs of Cuba, and we were encouraged to vote for Barry Goldwater so we could go bomb the hell out of Fidel. In the middle of it all, I scooted off for a weekend at the Newport Folk Festival. Talk about something completely different.

Pot busts had become so common that they no longer made the news. LSD, mescaline, psilocybin, MDA, speed, cocaine, and heroin were all on the increase. Each drug had its apostles and demonizers.

There was an ongoing dialogue/diatribe in our pages trying to figure out just what was, and what was not, folk music. Critics, fans, performers, academicians all wrote pieces for us espousing various points of view. Looking back, this deeply divided perspective was fundamental to our eventual foundering.

In October, with each issue containing more and more national advertising, *Broadside* moved out of its editor's apartment (in this case, mine) for the first time, and into an office at 145 Columbia Street. It remained there for the rest of its life. This was mostly due to the efforts of Bill Rabkin, who had come on board as business manager earlier in the year. The staff continued to expand as well with over 20 names on the masthead, all volunteers.

But I made two errors of judgment that year. I had a spat with Dick Waterman over deadlines that ended up with him walking out. It created a breach in a friendship that has never been healed. The second was the result of a three-week jaunt to Berkeley. I returned to find that someone on the staff had committed us to a new series of columns on protest singers. I do not know now what I found so egregious in the first two installments, but I cancelled the column and earned the enmity of its author. His success was, I am sure, sweet revenge, as Jon Landau went on to become one of the most respected music writers of the period.

CG Can you elaborate on the clubs of that era?

DW During the first half of that decade there was a curious split delineated by the river. My intuition is that it originated during the rise and fall of The Golden Vanity [Near Boston University]. That split seemed to have been created more by fans and club management than by the artists. Most of the performers worked wherever they could. Boston and Cambridge never had the "pass the hat clubs" that made up such a large part of the Greenwich Village scene. The Vanity as well as The Gallery, on Hemenway Street, and The Salamander, on Huntington Ave, all became victims of urban renewal at about the same time as the construction of the Prudential Center and the Turnpike Extension. Café Yana dodged the construction by moving from Beacon Street over to Brookline Avenue. In a way, the split may have mirrored the rivalry between BU [Boston University] and Harvard.

Some musicians came to think of themselves as "Charles Street Performers" and resented what they perceived as snubbing from across the river. To this day, probably the most enduring graduates of Charles Street are Chris Smither and Bill Staines. One might, however, make a case for Noel Stookey, who often played on Charles Street and was later Paul in Peter, Paul and Mary.

In Harvard Square, Club 47 and Club Jolly Beaver waxed as Tulla's Coffee Grinder waned. Boston coffeehouses were strung out in a line along the river with a cluster around Beacon Hill. A fancy new club opened on Hancock Street but was short lived. Charles Street had the Turk's Head, where the legendary Rudi Vanelli had performed, the Orleans and The Loft. The Unicorn sat across from the rising Prudential Center on Boylston Street, a block from Pall's Mall and the Jazz Workshop. Café Yana held down the western end of the line. One other coffeehouse that had a reasonable life span was The Rose, in the North End. In the latter half of the decade, as folk rock and psychedelic bands came and went, followed by the rise of the blues bands, we saw larger venues come into being: The Boston Tea Party, The Ark, The Psychedelic Supermarket, and in Allston, The Crosstown Bus.

On the North Shore, Howard Ferguson had opened the King's Rook coffeehouse in Marblehead, and a few years later, added a second and larger venue in Ipswich where they presented local and national performers. Worcester briefly had the Silver Vanity, Springfield had the Pesky Serpent, Martha's Vineyard spawned the Mooncusser, the Unicorn II, and a third club whose name I cannot remember. Hyannis had the Ballad & Banjo and The Carousel.

CG How did you become involved as a board member and editor of *Avatar*? What brought people together to publish an underground newspaper? Discuss dropping out of *Avatar* when it was taken over by the Fort Hill Mel Lyman cult.

DW I am not sure I could ever answer as comprehensive or complex a question as that. I remember four major trends developing in that time frame which contributed to the dynamics you describe: the space program, the civil rights movement, Vietnam War, and experimentation with consciousness-enhancing chemicals.

All of those had influences on the music, including the fueling of the singer/songwriter movement, which started as an aspect of topical folksongs and swept over pop and rock like a tidal wave. Now singing your own material is the rule rather than the exception.

For *Broadside* it created a dilemma. We were unable to find a firm line of demarcation in our content, and in trying to cover the whole scope, we lost a lot of our most committed audience. We failed to attract enough of a more general readership. The requirements of a second class mailing permit at that time also restricted us in our street vendor sales. When big money came in to fund several new alternate press newspapers, they gave their papers free to the vendors. We could not do that, and we lost our vendors to the rather bitter war that was going on between *Boston After Dark*, *Boston Commons*, *The Real Paper*, and the *Boston Phoenix*.

I had agreed to an arrangement with George Papadopoulos, owner of the Unicorn, to edit a rock paper he was putting out called *Weekly Beat* while I continued publishing *Broadside*. As part of the deal, I got to use a lot of his typesetting and photographic equipment. It was at that point that George brought Ed "Beardsley" Jordan in as staff artist. At the same time, we were working together on a music festival jointly with the *Boston Herald Traveler* that we staged at the Commonwealth Armory in Boston. George put *Weekly Beat* on hold for the festival but never reactivated it.

Meanwhile, after the festival, a delegation from several communities came by the office and pitched the idea of an underground paper for Boston. After hashing over a number of ideas, we put out a mimeoed issue or two of something called the *One-Eyed Man* calling for interested parties to join us. We had several meetings at a think tank on Mt. Auburn Street and a committee of seven of us formed a nonprofit corporation. Besides myself, if I can remember correctly, there was Brian Faunce, Sandi Mandeville, Ed Jordan, Lew Crampton, Ed Fox, and Wayne Hansen.

What we did not understand at that point, and did not comprehend for quite some time, was that the last three were followers of Mel Lyman and always voted as Mel told them to. The first two or three issues were published out of the *Broadside* offices on Columbia Street in Cambridge, but then moved to the South End and the former offices of the *Mid-Town Journal*, which was an alternate newspaper of an earlier generation. Fred Shibley, the feisty former publisher, was generous in allowing us access to the space. With that move, I reduced my hands-on participation, but continued to write for the paper.

Shortly after the move, I went to the Broadside office one morning and was met outside by a young man. He told me he had been arrested by the Watertown police while selling *Avatar*s and charged with possession and distribution of subversive literature. I took him into the office, got on the phone to Brian Faunce and told him the story. Then I sent the kid over to the *Avatar* office to answer their questions. Next thing I heard, the kid had Joe Oteri and Harvey Silverglade handling his case and they became the *Avatar*'s legal backstops for all the repression that was about to come down on us.

The story is partly covered in great detail, and pretty much as I recall it, in the article "Incident in Harvard Square" published in *Boston Magazine*.

News dealers in Harvard Square were threatened with municipal inspections, license suspensions, and all the regular bureaucratic reprisals if they continued to sell *Avatar*. We responded by putting more vendors on the street and they got busted left and right, mostly for selling without a license.

One day, better than a hundred vendors, including ministers, college professors, and lawyers, showed up in Harvard Square. Many were arrested and were then represented by Oteri's office. Oteri demanded separate jury trials for each and every one. Faced with the expense, the city backed down and saved face by claiming that so many vendors at any given time constituted a traffic hazard or some such. *Avatar* negotiated a deal as to how many vendors could be in the Harvard Square and the city's concession to the constitutional rights of unlicensed news vendors.

This concession opened the floodgates for all the other papers that wanted to put vendors on the street.

CG When Arden Harrison and I moved to Roxbury, near Fort Hill, we went to work for *Avatar*. Rent was cheap and we made a lot of brown rice. For cash we were given copies of *Avatar* to sell in Harvard Square. As contributors we got to keep the quarters. But sometimes Wayne or some other Hill zealot would come and kick us out because Mel needed a new lens for his movie camera. *Avatar* was becoming ever more erratic as his interests were less involved with the publication. So there started to be a split between the Fort Hill zealots and the off-hill scoffers. That all came to a head with a breakdown in the summer of 1968. A group of us decided to continue with *Avatar*. The meetings were chaotic with everyone having their own idea of what the paper should be like.

In that chaos I emerged as leader/editor. That entailed a meeting on the Hill with Mel. Arden was concerned that I might get abducted or brainwashed into the cult. I knew Mel from when he was hanging around Brandeis with my friend Judy Silver. It was my car when Mel, John Kostick, and another guy, whose name I can't recall, drove south to North Carolina. Mel and I had breakfast with banjo player Obray Ramsey. Mel planted his pot seeds and said that he was headed on to Florida, while John and I, with zero cash and running on vapors, managed to drive back to Waltham.

Since I knew Mel from before he became a "World Savior," I felt confident in meeting with him. I was ushered into his presence in a house where he was maintained by followers. We sat at a table which was probably bugged, and he took pictures of me from time to time. It went well, and he agreed that we could put out a paper but just not use the name *Avatar* as he claimed that it was his paper.

That was fine by me. I decided not to put a logo on the cover. I designed it as an I Ching hexagram, which we threw as a group. There was an architect, Richard Joos, who created a very beautiful and spiritual centerfold that spelled out the text of the hexagram and what it portended for our launch of a new venture. It all felt very holistic and pure.

But Ed Beardsley, the graphic designer for the paper, subverted our effort. On the second page at the top of a spread of news items, he put a small *Avatar* logo, reversed. He had some kind of deceptive explanation. I was too exhausted to grasp his full intent. But it was immediately obvious to the Fort Hill crowd. If you held the paper up to the light, the logo bled through the front page and became an issue of *Avatar*.

That was never my intent. Inadvertently, that became the infamous Issue #25 of *Avatar*. In the middle of the night, the Fort Hill Gang raided the office. They confiscated the entire press run and locked it up in the tower on Fort Hill. I had grabbed a bundle before leaving the office. So I have a couple of copies and a few others (1,000 of the press run of 45,000) were circulated. It is now all visible online. I called the police about the theft but they basically just laughed at me.

It seemed that was it. But shortly later you got in touch with me and said that indeed we would resume publishing *Avatar*, which we did that summer. That's when we first met. Prior to then, I had heard you bad mouthed, so I didn't quite know what to expect.

You stated that you would be the editor and I would be the managing editor. Also, Sandi Mandeville came onboard and did all the typesetting, which back then was a big job. You had to type out copy twice in order to justify the margins. I knew nothing about laying out a paper and production. Ed Beardsley, whom I never liked or trusted, would be the graphic designer. Of course he would betray us again. What a worm.

What were your thoughts and agendas when you took over *Avatar* that summer?

DW In late spring and as a result of the "hijacked" issue, Brian Faunce and Ed Jordan came to Sandi and I and wanted us as board members to join in revitalizing the paper. We had a meeting at the Broadside office and discussed a number of issues among ourselves and with a few other community representatives. Finally, we concluded that only by taking control of the paper away from Fort Hill, and replacing the editorial staff, could we create a publication that would serve a diverse community. The only dissenting voice was Jordan's female partner, Susan, who pleaded for negotiation with Fort Hill. I certainly had no sense that they would be willing to bargain in good faith and suggested that once we had control, we might then consider concessions.

I contacted Marcel Kirsten, a lawyer with whom I had worked while administering the Folk Song Society of Greater Boston, and someone who I was pretty sure was sympathetic to *Avatar*. After examining the articles of incorporation, and upon my request as president of said corporation, he sent out official notice of a board meeting at his downtown offices. Everyone showed up. I proposed that the editorial staff be replaced, a vote was taken and the motion carried four to three. We voted the three Fort Hill reps out of all official positions, replaced them with ourselves, and took over the offices. In a gesture of goodwill, we allowed them to remain on the board. Go figure.

Then I had to convince *Avatar* staffers that we really did have control of the paper and that we could put out one that would serve the wider community. You were pretty resistant as I remember. Together, however, I think the issues we put out that summer were among the most thoughtful, forward thinking, and respectful of the disenfranchised community that we sought to serve, of any that had appeared before. The working relationship I developed with you during that time was, for me, one of the best things that came out of our joint enterprise.

Of course disaster befell us when, in the middle of laying out an issue, Jordan/Beardsley was notified that the film director Michelangelo Antonioni had decided to use Mark Frechette as the lead in the film *Zabriskie Point*. I don't know that any of us had known that Ed was in competition for the role. He freaked at the news and in a fury tore up all the layouts for that issue. We managed to salvage it without him, but whether in fear of reprisal, or bitterness or some other unknown reason, he jumped back onto the Fort Hill bandwagon and we were ousted.

CG Not really. We continued with more issues after that through the summer.

DW We seem to have different memories about that. As far as I know the next and only *Avatar* to be published was the Fort Hill slick *American Avatar*. Do you have any copies of the issues you remember us publishing after the one which Beardsley destroyed and we reconstituted? I can imagine one more, but that's all.

CG I have copies of the issues we published. For the Fourth of July issue, for the cover, I hand separated a color version of The Spirit of '76. There was community unrest and the new mayor, Kevin White, sent us a letter. From City Hall I obtained a headshot and put him on the cover. I surrounded his head with a halo of green stars. The headline was "Whitey Speaks to Hippies." His letter was printed with a decorative border. His assistant, Barney Frank, sent me a colorful note about that. I did another issue with photos by Benno Friedman on the cover and inside. There were a lot of experimental graphics that summer. I also covered the closing of the Institute of Contemporary Art on Newbury Street. That seemed like the end of it after decades of struggle. The headline was "ICA on the Move."

DW I had hoped that in helping to create *Avatar* that it would address the social political arena and Broadside could concentrate on the music. It did not work out that way.

Meanwhile, a splinter group from *The Old Mole*, an SDS paper, had set up offices across the street from Broadside and started publishing a daily report on the trial of Benjamin Spock, which was going on in Boston.

Spock, along with four others, Marcus Raskin, Mitchell Goodman, Michael Ferber, and Reverend William Sloane Coffin, were put on trial for initiating "A Call to Resist Illegitimate Authority," an anti-war document.

When the trial was over, the staff of the *Free Press* proposed that we take over their banner, and we decided to experiment with a joint publication. We had switched from magazine to tabloid format, and we began that integration by printing Broadside from the front cover to the centerfold and *The Free Press* upside down from the back cover to the centerfold. After a few issues, the post office caught on to what we were doing and threatened to cancel our second class mailing permit. At that point, we incorporated the Free Press into the contents, changed our name to *Broadside and the Free Press*, and added a subtitle, "A Journal of Alternate Lifestyles."

Several of the staffers at the *Free Press* continued to write for us, including Keith Maillard, who Canada now claims as one of their premier novelists.

CG I became art director for *Boston After Dark* [later the *Boston Phoenix*], but was in over my head. My assistant, Linda, knew more than I did, and quite rightly, replaced me.

But I stayed on as the art critic with a weekly column, "Art Bag." The editor was a Brandeis colleague, Arnie Riesman. He was really supportive. My pay was $50 a week and I managed to live on that.

Later, in 1969, Tim Crouse, who I had grown up with in Annisquam, left the *Herald Traveler* as its rock critic, to write for *Rolling Stone*. Tim wrote "Boys on the Bus." He recommended me to the *Herald*. I became an established journalist with a daily paper. That lasted until 1971 when the *Herald* lost its TV station and was sold to the *Record American*.

What happened for you after Broadside ceased to publish? In what way did you stay connected to music?

DW Back in 1961, before I started Broadside, I met Harry Oster when he gave a presentation to the Folk Song Society. Harry was originally from Cambridge and a professor at a university in Louisiana. He had done a fair amount of field collecting and produced a number of exceptional records on his Folk-Lyric label. Joe Boyd, a Harvard student and blues devotee, and I, proposed to Harry that we become distributors for his label in New England. When Harry accepted, Joe and I formed Riverboat Records and set out to acquire other little-known folk labels to represent [Like Arhoolie and Yazoo]. When I started publishing Broadside I gave up my half of Riverboat to Joe.

On graduating from Harvard, Joe sold Riverboat to another group of Harvard students, and he went off to the UK. There he enjoyed a glorious career producing Pink Floyd and numerous other legendary musical entities.

Riverboat was eventually sold again, sometime in early to mid-sixties, to Ralph Dopmeyer. Ralph was one of those Cambridge eccentrics of whom there are a multitude of stories. He had a degree in Naval Architecture from MIT, was an expert cabinetmaker, and an enthusiastic sailor. I first met him when he dropped by Broadside to give us a review copy of his first LP on the Riverboat label. It was John Fahey's *Death and Transfiguration of Blind Joe Death*. Over the next year or two Ralph often dropped by the offices to provide us with review copies of new releases, to use our typewriters, or just swap stories.

Ralph knew that I had been involved with founding Riverboat. When he had the opportunity to sail a boat to Europe for refitting, and back again, he asked Sandi Mandeville and I if we would be willing to manage Riverboat while he was away. We worked out an arrangement, and moved his inventory into our offices.

I think it was at the Newport Folk Festival in 1965 that I met John Sdoucos. He was running the press section and the credentials office. He proposed that, after the festival, I come and talk about working out of his Boston office. At that time he and Fred Taylor were partners. Aesthetic differences led to them parting shortly after I got involved.

John set up a booking and management agency called Music Productions managing a local Boston group called Barry and the Remains. He and his wife, Leah, I, and Don Law worked out of the Boylston office just over Pall's Mall. Primarily, we booked major recording talent for college concerts. It was just turning into a big business in those days. John and Leah took me under wing and I often had dinner at their apartment. I remember sitting down one night to find Diana Ross across the table from me.

I helped develop the Music Productions logo, wrote publicity releases, consulted on folk talent for college bookings, and generated Remains publicity materials. We were involved with a summer series of concerts on the Common at the Public Gardens. I did some live remote broadcasts over WTBS-FM one summer. As part of their organization, I got to work with the press section of the Newport Folk and Jazz Festivals for the next couple of years. At the same time as all this, I was managing The Odyssey coffeehouse and publishing Broadside, writing for WGBH-TV, and running Riverboat Records. Don't ask me how. I could not do one tenth of it today.

CG John and I worked closely together when he produced Concerts on the Common. I reviewed those shows for the *Herald* and got to hang out with bands like the Allman Brothers, Jesse Colin Young, and Rod Stewart. I interviewed Richie Havens, who John was managing at the time. Of course, Freddy Taylor was a friend when I covered Jazz Workshop and Paul's Mall. I also was close to Ted Kurland who booked college gigs for jazz artists. Sometimes I was the MC for his shows like Keith Jarrett at Harvard's Sanders Theatre. Ted managed some great artists especially the Boston-based Gary Burton and Pat Metheny. Through Ted I got to hang out with Ornette Coleman, Phillip Glass, and Steve Reich.

DW At the turn of the decade, as the alternative press was in turmoil, the technology that permitted videotaping to become generally available was suddenly attractive. Sandi and I, along with Broadside reviewer Tom Murray and Bill Desmond, Bob Wiener and Larry O'Connell started collaborating. Between '69 and '70 we produced three issues of what was intended to be a publication in video. We titled it *The Broadside Free Video Press* and dubbed it onto 20-minute reels of three-quarter-inch computer tape bought at surplus government auctions and cut to length.

I, too, had met Arnie Riesman [editor of *Boston After Dark*], as he and I were part of the creative team for *What's Happening Mr. Silver*, which was being produced at WGBH. I think he is still doing a quiz show on WGBH-FM, and last I heard was vice president of the American Civil Liberties Union for Massachusetts. At the close of 1969, I consulted with WGBH again on a segment for the PBS New Year's Eve show "Artists Look At the '60s." We did the music segment that looked at the '60s through the music of the Beatles, Bob Dylan, and the emergence of the blues, with a commentary by Taj Mahal.

I thought I might finally have a steady gig when the FM manager hired me to do a weekly show which would feature live music and interviews with musicians. He hired me at 5:30 p.m. on a Friday afternoon and he was fired at 6:00 p.m. The new manager, if he even knew I had been hired, declined to honor the agreement.

Sandi Mandeville married and moved off to California. Our video venture with Broadside metamorphosed into an expanded operation with a dozen projects, all too far ahead of their time. Most of them are now run-of-the-mill and taken for granted. On speculation, we ran a CCTV project in the Sheraton Boston, and a video coffeehouse, The Video Frontier, on Boylston Street. I had married, was living in Brookline and still running Riverboat Records. It was slowly being raided, manipulated, and deconstructed by the bigger corporations. For awhile I had been writing music reviews for you at the *Herald Traveler*, and then we collaborated as publicity agents, as WAG [Wilson and Giuliano], alternating weekly press releases and commentary. When that petered out, you started the fanzine Staple.

I did some writing as well for the *East West Journal* with some new-age musical perspectives.

In 1972 and '73 I had a small Rockefeller Grant to develop some video art. It was great fun, an important learning period for me, but my ideas were still too far ahead of the technology to be practical.

I finally gave up on my first marriage at the end of 1973, and ended up living in the Broadside offices. Those were hard times, though in a strange way, they were also very happy. I was still involved with several diverse projects. I took a job as night desk clerk at the Cambridge YWCA working an 11 p.m. to 7 a.m. shift. I would come home, sleep till noon, get up and work on Riverboat chores, then go back to bed from 6 p.m. to 10 p.m., get up, and go back to the Y.

Off and on during that time, I started working with Kate Frank, recording real time classroom interactions between children with and without physical disabilities. A small grant allowed us to shoot, edit, and produce a series of tapes with portable video recording equipment. Kate used the tapes to build a curriculum with which to teach professionals in the field how to assess strengths and weaknesses of the disabled under their charge.

By the mid-seventies I was pretty jaded with the music industry. Most of the folk, rock, and pop music that came my way seemed not only derivative, but derivative of derivative. Partly that came from listening to a dozen or more new albums every day. The major factor, however, was that the recording industry had transitioned from recording artists to recording sound-a-likes. The profit motive trumped the aesthetic motive. It's not hard to see how that was a natural evolution, even if it obviates the reason for existing in the first place.

Reconnecting with you, coupled with a desire to commemorate the life of our mutual friend, David Omar White, I considered writing again. Before I knew it, I was tempted to parade my ignorance in public again and here we are.

David Wilson, 1960s. Photo by Peter Simon.

David and Me, *Avatar*, summer 1968. Wilson archive.

Ed Jordan (Beardsley) sabotaged *Avatar* 25. Photo by Peter Simon.

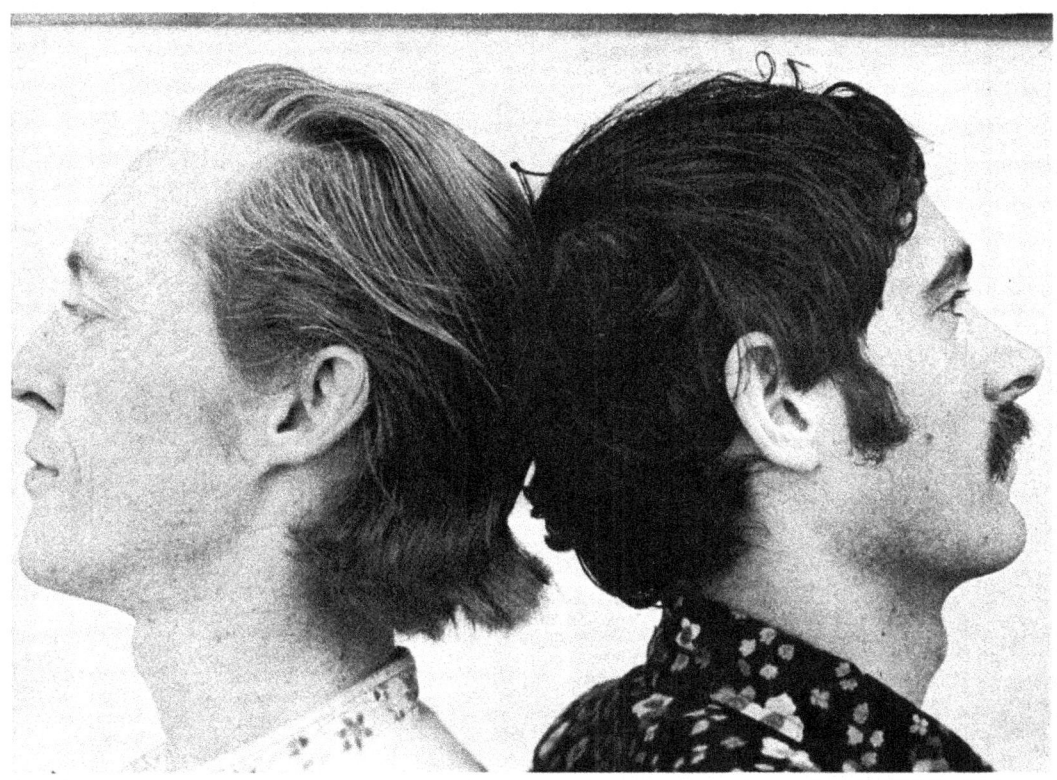

Mel Lyman (left) and Jim Kweskin on the cover of *Broadside*. UMass Amherst archive.

Former *Midtown Journal* publisher Fred Shibley provided *Avatar*'s Rutland Street office. Photo by Peter Simon.

Avatar editors, left to right: Brian Keating, Wayne Hansen. Background: Ed Jordan and Susanne. Photo by Peter Simon.

Arden Harrison was part of Summer 1968, *Avatar* staff. Giuliano archive.

Me with *Rolling Stone* issue on Lyman cult. Photo by Steve Nelson.

Wilson enjoying a laugh on my porch. Photo by Charles Giuliano.

Joan Baez performing in 2013. Photo by Charles Giuliano.

Tom Rush in Harvard Square. Photo by Charles Giuliano.

Tom Rush and Emmylou Harris. Photo by Charles Giuliano.

Ryan Walsh wrote about the Lyman cult in *Astral Weeks*. Photo by Charles Giuliano.

Avatar, volume one, number one. Wilson archive.

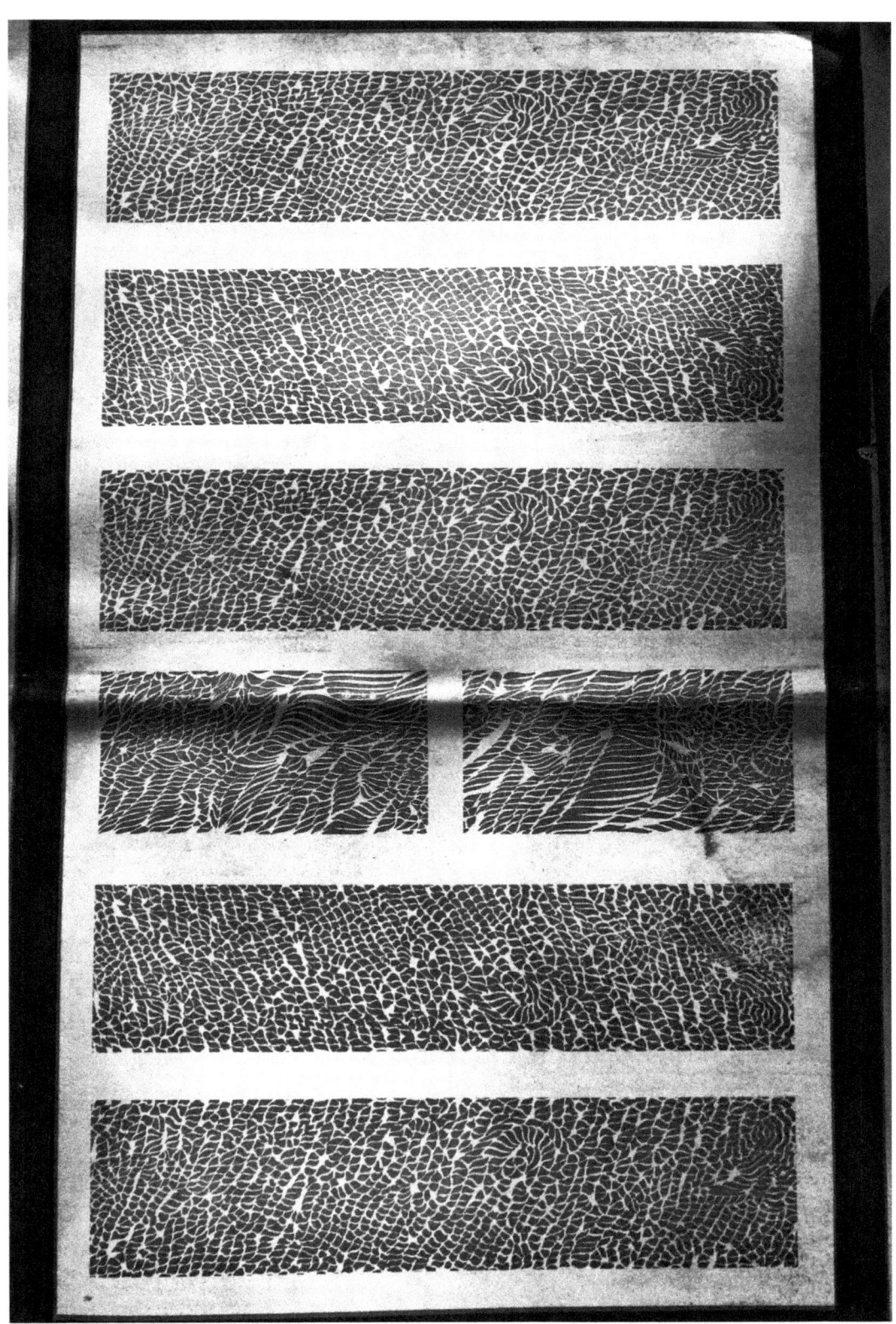

Avatar Issue 25 with I Ching cover designed by Giuliano was trashed by Fort Hill zealots. Giuliano archive.

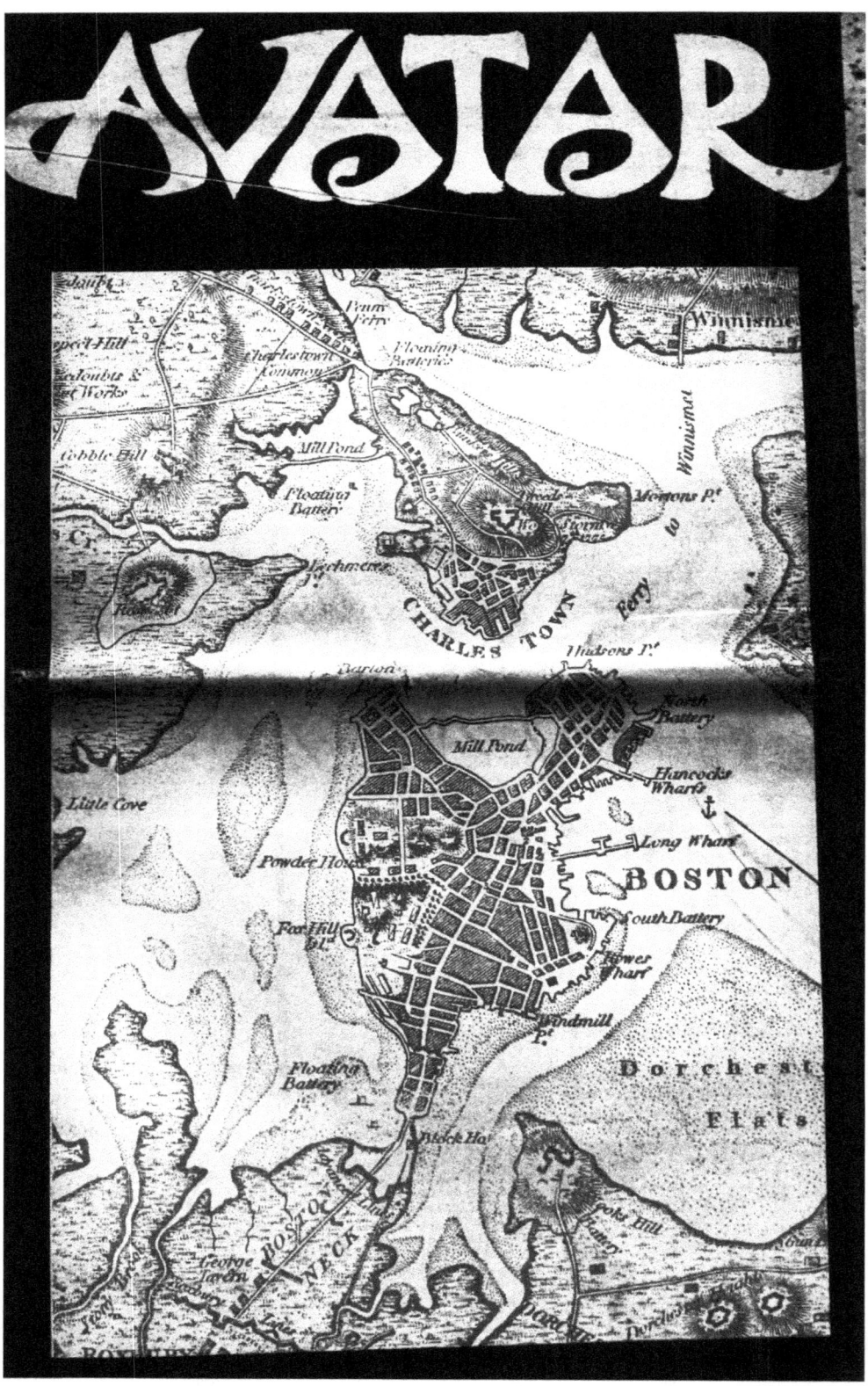

A Summer 1968 Wilson/Giuliano issue that Jordan/Beardsley attempted to destroy. Giuliano archive.

Harper Barnes brought journalism to the hippie *Cambridge Phoenix*

From 1970 to 1973, Harper Barnes was editor of *Cambridge Phoenix*, then a columnist for *The Real Paper*. Back in the day, I had limited contact with Barnes, but we connected for a discussion of events under his watch.

Charles Giuliano Greetings after all these years. Fortunately there is enough distance that you can't take another swing at me. Although I was in little danger as you were having difficulty standing up at the time.

Harper Barnes (*laughing*) I met Bob Woodard some years ago. He married our former executive assistant. The last thing he said to me was, "Nice to see you when you're not drunk." I had a problem.

CG What was her name?

HB Francie Barnard. She was his second wife.

CG Over time things changed. We were not in the same orbit back then. I was largely vilified by your *Cambridge Phoenix* staff. No, I was not the scab who wrote for the paper when it was on strike. When a movie came out, allegedly, the slovenly rock critic was based on me. I never actually saw the film.

HB *Between the Lines* [Fred Barron, screenwriter; Joan Micklin Silver, director; with John Heard, Lindsay Ann Crouse, and Jeff Goldblum, 1977]. Actually, the character was based on George Kimball who died a couple of years ago.

CG He was a piece of work, hanging around bars. When visiting the head, he said, "Keep an eye on my seat." He had a glass eye.

How old are you?

HB I'm 81. Being 70 didn't seem so old, but 80 is different. I'm having trouble with it. It seems awfully old. Overall I'm in good shape. I'm astonished because I certainly drank and smoked enough. I quit drinking about 30 years ago when I met my current wife. It seemed like a good time to make a change. I don't miss it.

I hit my quota 32 years ago when I was living in a motel working at the [*St. Louis*] *Post-Dispatch*. Across the street was the Newspaper Bar and Grill. All I had to do was walk a couple of blocks at the end of the day, then go back and crash at the motel. Roseann rescued me from that. It is one of the many things for which I am eternally grateful in meeting her.

CG At the *Herald* the writers and editors would walk to J.J. Foley's in the South End. Once I had Mississippi Fred McDowell in my care for the day and I took him there. He drank peppermint schnapps and beers.

HB Based on one of Kimball's obits, we were trying to figure who it was he got into a fistfight with over one of his reviews. Somebody literally wanted to punch him out because of one of the nasty reviews he wrote. Usually it was deserved, but at times he took it too far.

CG So you started in St. Louis, went to Cambridge, and then went back to St. Louis. Why on earth would anyone do that?

HB Ray Riepen, a legendary figure around Boston, wanted to buy the *Phoenix*. We were old friends from college. He was at Harvard Law School [for a graduate degree], dropped out, and started the Boston Tea Party. He was building a media empire and flew me in to be the editor.

Ultimately, he found an investor. They bought the paper and made me the editor in April 1970. I wanted to get out of St. Louis, and it lasted for two years. After that I freelanced from Boston for about a year. I came back to St. Louis because there was a Teamsters strike. A group of writers wanted to put together a union-friendly newspaper. They asked me to come back and be the editor. The *Post-Dispatch* was being struck. I got several Pulitzer Prize winners, and we had a tabloid that came out three or four days a week. It was called *St. Louis Today*. We had approval of the unions. That was not a problem, and we gave people a little money. I stayed with a friend of mine in his house. He was my age, and I thought, well, I wouldn't own a house if I stayed in Boston. Life was very pleasant. I got seduced by it. And later, the *Post-Dispatch* offered me a job. I took it and have been here ever since.

CG What was your job?

HB I had several jobs. Toward the end I was critic at large. I had some other positions. I was features director. Then I left to be editor of *St. Louis Magazine* for a few years, and now I am trying to write book reviews. I keep working on a novel set in the St. Louis World Fair in 1904, a murder mystery. I'm not getting very far with it.

CG Have you published anything?

HB Yes. Three books.

[*Never Been a Time: The 1917 Race Riot that Sparked the Civil Rights Movement* (Walker & Company, 2008). A detailed history of the first, and officially, the deadliest of the numerous mass attacks on African Americans that broke out in cities across the United States in the era of World War I. It places the East St. Louis riot in the context of similar racial massacres as far back as the early decades of the 19th century in Philadelphia and other Northern cities. It analyzes the impact of the East St. Louis riot on the early civil rights movement. The book was named the Best Non-Fiction Book of the Year for 2008 by *The Truth About the Fact*, an international journal of narrative non-fiction based at Loyola Marymount University in Los Angeles.

Also, *Standing on a Volcano: The Life and Times of David Rowland Francis* (Missouri Historical Society Press, 2001). It is a biography of the influential Missouri politician who ran the 1904 St. Louis World's Fair and served as Woodrow Wilson's ambassador to Russia during the revolution of 1917. It won the 2002 Missouri History Book Award from the State Historical Society of Missouri "in recognition of superior original scholarship in a book pertaining to the history of Missouri and its people," and the annual book award from the Missouri Conference on History as the "best book written by a Missouri resident in 2001." And *Blue Monday* (Patrice Press, 1991). An historical novel set in the 1930s among the musicians, newspapermen, and corrupt politicians of Pendergast-era Kansas City.]

Last summer was the 100th commemoration of the race riot. It was one of the deadliest race riots in American history. Very little was known about it. Among other things, it was the inspiration for The Silent March. Eight to ten thousand blacks, and a few whites, marched down Fifth Avenue in New York. They tried to end lynching and honored the victims of the St. Louis Race Riot. It was about white people killing black people. During the WWI period there were dozens of race riots across America. They all consisted of blacks being slaughtered by whites. That book sold pretty well.

CG Who founded the *Cambridge Phoenix* and when?

HB Jeffrey Tartar founded it in 1969. After about nine months, Tartar ran out of money. In early 1970 he sold *The Cambridge Phoenix* to Riepen and Richard Missner.

CG Was the idea to compete with the Mindich weekly *Boston After Dark*?

HB That was pretty much an entertainment paper. *The Phoenix* was getting into politics, but it was more of a hippie paper than *Boston After Dark*.

CG Nobody ever described Steve Mindich as a hippie. I worked for Mindich as the art critic before moving on to the *Boston Herald Traveler*.

I was there during the strike when the original partners Mindich and Jim Lewis were fighting for control. Lewis put out *Boston After Dark* with scabs. Mindich and editor Arnie Reisman briefly published *Public Occurrences*. When Mindich bought the *Cambridge Phoenix* and changed the name to *Boston Phoenix*, as we know, the paper became known for its political coverage and many writers went on to have distinguished careers.

HB Mindich bought the name and George Kimball.

The counterculture had reached St. Louis, but hardly was dominant. I remember walking into Harvard Square and being astonished. There were Hare Krishnas, political people, dancing monkeys.

The Boston I knew, basically the Green Line between Back Bay and Cambridge, was dominated by the counterculture.

CG My perception was that you were straight and waspy.

HB Yeah, I was, kinda. I once said that I was the most conservative person at the paper, and I was a screaming liberal. Yeah, the name alone identifies me as pretty waspy. I don't resent that. When we took over the *Phoenix*, it was less than a year old. It was a hippie project and I tried to retain those elements while having serious stuff, like eventually, political writers Joe Klein and Paul Solman.

CG From a distance I sensed that you brought professionalism and journalistic standards to the *Phoenix*.

HB I think that's true. I cut the first graph of every story. I mean that almost literally. They were very young, untrained writers. They tended to put the punch line in the lead. There were paragraphs after paragraphs of philosophizing before they got to the story itself. I trimmed out a lot of that. It was a personal newspaper and I didn't want to take the personality out, but I reshaped some of the stories. That was the main thing I did.

Finding writers was no problem. Cambridge was full of writers. They came from either Boston University or Brandeis. There were a few Harvard people, but not many. I made sure it came out on time, and treated the writers well, I think. The paper itself attracted writers. There was already a core there when I came on—like Chuck Kramer, the film critic. They were pretty darned good. We hired Jon Landau almost immediately. It was Ray Riepen's doing really. Paul Solman and Joe Klein came about a year later.

In 1971 the writers for *Boston After Dark* got disgusted with [Publisher] Steve Mindich. The writers offered to come over entirely or in part to the *Phoenix*. We chose Paul and Joe for various reasons. I thought they fleshed out the paper. We were probably more cultural than political at the time. They came over and made the paper even stronger.

CG Paul Solman I knew from Brandeis. He was a couple of classes behind me. The same was true for Ted Gross, who became the editor of the later *Boston Phoenix*. I believe his brother was a classmate. Of course Landau was also a Brandeis graduate. There was a radical tradition. My editor at *Boston After Dark*, Arnie Reisman, was my editor at the *Brandeis Justice*.

HB From what I could tell, Arnie was a good editor. He had Mindich holding him back. Also from Brandeis, we published an interview with Stanley Bond. He was part of a bank robbery in which a guard was killed somewhere in suburban Boston.

CG It was in Brighton and Officer Schroeder, the father of a large family, was killed. The robbery led to the flight of Susan Saxe and Kathy Powers.

> [On September 25, 1970, *The New York Times* reported:
> The police obtained today warrants charging two women identified as students at Brandeis University and two men with murdering a policeman during a $26,000 holdup yesterday at a branch bank. The warrants were issued soon after Patrolman Walter A. Schroeder died of his wounds.
> Those named in the warrants were: Stanley R. Bond, 25 years old, of Cambridge, also identified as a Brandeis student; William M. Gilday, 41, of Amesbury; Susan E. Saxe, 20, of Albany, N.Y., and Kathy Powers, 20, of Denver, Colo. A fifth man charged with murder, Robert Valeri; 21, of Somerville, Mass., was captured last night.]
> In addition to Abbie Hoffman and Angela Davis, there were other Brandeis students on the FBI's Most Wanted list. I was a freshman when Abbie was a senior. I was close to his wife, Sheila, who was an art major. Martin Peretz [publisher of *The New Republic*] was president of the student council during my freshman year. Arguably, it was the most radical campus in America at the time.
> As I understand it, Gilday was a career criminal taking classes at Brandeis. He radicalized and recruited Saxe and Powers. They were going to rob a bank to raise money for their cause.

HB Stanley Bond wanted to write for the *Phoenix*. This was before the bank job. He wrote an article for us, and I can't remember what it was about, but it was publishable. A month later he pulled the bank robbery. They chased him and caught him in Colorado. He called me because he wanted the story to be first in the *Phoenix*, about why he did the robbery and so forth. He had the usual radical reasons. We consulted an attorney because Stanley was not looked at favorably by the legal profession.

CG Talk to me about Jon Landau. He wrote that famous "I saw the future of rock 'n' roll last night" review of Bruce Springsteen in Cambridge.

[Arguably the most influential rock review of its era stated in part: "Last Thursday, at the Harvard Square theater, I saw rock 'n' roll past flash before my eyes. And I saw something else: I saw rock and roll future and its name is Bruce Springsteen. And on a night when I needed to feel young, he made me feel like I was hearing music for the very first time."]

HB He wrote that for *The Real Paper*. Jon was a columnist, and I was as well. We hired Jon for the *Phoenix* because of Ray Riepen, who had experience in the music business through the Tea Party. He felt that Jon was key to getting record company ads. Landau was respected by the record companies, but the stuff he wrote didn't pull any punches. When he wrote those lines he was not affiliated with Springsteen.

CG There were so many contributors and artists, like cartoonist David Omar White, designer Lynn Staley, who went on the *Globe* then *Newsweek*. Mark Zanger wrote wonderful restaurant reviews. There were rock writers, Steve Davis, James Miller, and James Isaacs; or film critics, David Ansen, Stuart Byron, Stephen Schiff, and Gerald Peary. Arthur Friedman was the eccentric, curmudgeonly theater critic.

But tell me about C. Wendell Smith.

HB Richard Missner owned the paper and kept trying to get rid of Wendell. Ray had gotten Richard involved and then he fired Ray. Wendell wrote these obscure notes that looked like E.E. Cummings poetry about upcoming political meetings. I thought it was perfect. It fit in with the hippie feeling of the paper. I was running Howard Zinn and that contrasted with Wendell's late 1960s hippie/commune notes.

CG As I recall he submitted reams of copy insisting that you run it all. It was printed in six-point and one could hardly read it even if you had the time, interest, and patience.

HB (*laughing*) We did that from time to time. When things were too long, I knocked them down in size. But I think that some did run in six-point. Finally, I fired Wendell because Richard just got on me. I had to fire somebody because I was spending a lot of money. The next thing I knew Wendell chained himself, with a bicycle chain, to Richard's desk. (*both laugh*) He won and Wendell came back to the paper. The times were wonderful.

CG Tell me about Laura Shapiro. She was a feminist writer then evolved into writing on dance. I believe she later wrote for *Newsweek*.

HB She wrote a couple of political cookbooks. Her best-known book was about Fannie Farmer. It had a feminist take. In the beginning, I didn't get feminism. I thought it was an excuse for rich girls to be treated the same as rich boys. I have regretted that feeling ever since. I got into it with her in the beginning. She wrote a long manifesto when Norman Mailer attacked feminism. I would agree with her now, but in those days I didn't get it. I don't know why, but a lot of people vaguely on the left didn't get it. I wouldn't publish the piece and Laura and I barely spoke for a year and a half. She wrote on dance and classical music in the tradition of Jill Johnson of the *Village Voice*. Slowly, I came to understand what it was all about.

CG She had a complex relationship with feminists. Cambridge was a hotbed of activism. At some point, there was an occupation of a Harvard building. Laura gained access as an alleged member of the group and then published, without permission, an insider's report on the protest. It was regarded as a betrayal.

It was out of a Cambridge collective that *Our Bodies, Our Selves* was published. It was recently announced that hard copies would no longer be printed but it is available online. Similarly, The *Whole Earth Catalog* was published as an occasional magazine from 1968 to 1972. I attended the first global Earth Day in 1970 on grounds near Harvard Stadium.

HB You're cursed by a good memory.

CG What was your relationship with Landau?

HB Early on I tried to edit him. He was somewhat imperious, but always very pleasant. Clearly he was headed for bigger and better things. He wrote a story about Muscle Shoals Recording Studio [founded in Sheffield, Alabama, by four studio musicians in 1969]. It's where the Allman Brothers recorded.

[The Rolling Stones stopped by Muscle Shoals Sound Studio in Alabama during downtime from their 1969 American tour. They didn't have a recording permit for America at the time, so the sessions became an extremely hush-hush affair. In just three days, the group recorded "Brown Sugar," "You Gotta Move," and "Wild Horses." They had to sit on the latter song for almost two years because of a legal battle with their former manager, Allen Klein.]

Jon spelled it correctly, Muscle Shoals, which I thought was ridiculous and changed it to Mussel Shoals. He was very kind, but said, "Don't edit my copy again." I gave in immediately because his copy was so incredibly clean.

CG I find it interesting when you talk about cutting first graphs and trimming philosophical speculation. That kind of self-indulgence is happening more and more because of the lack of editors and mentoring. There is nobody to shape and school emerging writers. Journalistic standards are in crisis mode.

HB Absolutely. Our generation, with Hunter [Thompson], you, and me broke the bonds of the old objective journalism. It became permissible to use a personal pronoun occasionally, but it couldn't be fake news. Now there's too much opinion and too little fact coming out in blogs or whatever you call them.

CG What I understood is that the personal pronoun is okay if it is relevant to the story. If something from your personal experience has bearing on the topic, then yes.

HB There was a writer, Stu Werbin, that was true of. I believe he has passed. He wrote a lot for *Rolling Stone*. He wrote for the *Phoenix* but inserted himself in places he didn't belong. He was a fabulous writer. Perhaps he was ahead of the times, but he injected himself too much into the pieces, and I cut it out. He would submit his copy and we would go over it for an hour or so until it met with his approval. It was never a matter of publish it as I want or not at all.

I did have that relationship with Eric Mann, a radical writer. He had gone to prison for breaking into a Harvard office that had selective service numbers. It was 1968 or 1969 when things were pretty violent. He spent a year in prison. He wrote the story of his life, which was fascinating, about how this middle-class guy ended up in prison. I cut the hell out of it. He came in and said, "I didn't realize that I was submitting my memoirs to be copyedited."

I hadn't thought of it as memoirs; I thought of it as a story. It was crucial to understand how personal people wanted to get. With Eric Mann I allowed him to get more personal because I realized he was writing from the heart.

CG Did Steve Davis write for you?

HB Yeah. He was great. He managed to get backstage with Led Zeppelin. As you know he wrote a book about going on the road with them. He was prolific and a wonderful guy.

I think there were more good writers around Cambridge than around New York.

CG That may be true, but for whatever reason Boston/Cambridge has not gotten due recognition and respect for its formative role in alternative culture and journalism.

HB I'm surprised by that.

CG I'm fascinated by your role as a traditional, well-trained journalist editing the new writers. With time, many would evolve from underground to alternative to mainstream publishing. Consider how many went on to write books and screenplays or work in other aspects of media. By bringing some shape to that process, you were a fulcrum character.

HB I was with the *Post-Dispatch* for five years before going to the *Phoenix*. I was pushing in the other direction at the *Post-Dispatch*. I have a story that illustrates the difference between mainstream and alternative press. I did a story about a guy who was organizing grocery workers for the unions. I wrote that "He drove away in a ten-year-old Plymouth Valiant." Maybe it was a Ford Falcon. The editors changed it to "He drove away in a Ford automobile." (*both laughing*) They didn't get it.

Little things like that bugged me in the so-called straight press. On the other hand, thank God for the *Washington Post* and *New York Times*, particularly with what was going on.

CG What was the transition from the *Cambridge Phoenix* to *the Real Paper*?

HB The issue was me being fired. I was the editor for two years. Richard wanted to be more like *The New Republic*. I wanted to hang on to the Wendell Smiths of Cambridge. I thought they gave a funky air that people enjoyed. Finally, he fired me and the staff went on strike. Even the comptroller went on strike.

Through negotiation the *Phoenix* would resume publishing, and I would get a few thousand dollars to go away. The staff would elect an editor who proved to be Paul Solman. It was still the *Phoenix* and lasted about six months. They ran what they wanted and Richard couldn't do anything about it. So he fired Paul and folded the paper. He sold the name to Mindich for several hundred thousand dollars.

The staff immediately started *The Real Paper* and I got arrested. The scab *Phoenix* was being put together in the basement of a building in Central Square. Several of us, me and Jan, my wife at the time, and a couple of other people broke into the room where the copy was being pasted up and we tore the paper up. We got out before the cops came, but they served a warrant on us. The case was eventually dismissed.

When I got fired the *Globe* ran a three-quarters head shot. I got rehired, briefly, then fired again. *The Boston Globe* ran my picture on the front page, flopped the other way. It was the same picture and the headline read "fired again."

Until that point, I was something of a darling of the left wing Harvard/Cambridge, Schlesinger crowd. I had been invited to a party by Arthur Schlesinger's divorced wife. People just snubbed me at the dinner. I think it has something to with tearing up the sheets.

CG How did you get along with George Kimball?

HB He was impossible. I went to the University of Kansas and later taught there. Kimball was there and the leader of the hippies. I knew him vaguely. He showed up in the early days of the *Phoenix*. I didn't think he could write. He submitted a piece about Jo Jo White. He had come from Kansas and played for the Celtics. It was brilliant.

Kimball was a handful. He would get drunk and start fights. He had a glass eye. During a barroom brawl in Greenwich Village a guy broke a whiskey bottle over his head and destroyed his left eye. A lot of people couldn't get along with him. He was terribly sexist and out of control like John Belushi. But I liked him and he gave an angle to the paper.

CG He wouldn't survive in today's social/political climate.

HB Not at all. George wouldn't change.

CG You could fill a book with anecdotes about him. I was tight with PR and record company people. As a favor, I arranged for a big launch party at Castle Hill in Ipswich. It was a great place for a blowout. There was lots of food and booze of which George had his fill. I recall him staggering across the elegant ballroom.

Without stopping, there was a fuselage of projectile vomit. He just walked through it and kept going as though nothing had happened (*both laughing*).

HB George died of throat cancer a few years ago, but if he were around today and acting like that he would surely end up in prison.

CG It's a head scratcher to recall that Kimball and Laura Shapiro worked for the same publication. You say Kimball was all that Mindich got for buying the *Phoenix*.

HB The name had some value. He thought that buying a competitor meant that he would be the only alternative weekly paper in town. *The Real Paper* was launched a couple of weeks after the purchase.

CG Kimball later moved from the *Boston Phoenix* to the *Herald* and turned out to be one of the best Boston sports writers of his generation. His specialty was boxing.

HB I read a book he published with several essays on boxing. I didn't put up with his crap because I knew him back when he was running for Sheriff of Douglas County, Kansas. Of the writers I developed, of which there weren't that many, I am proudest of Kimball. He was the best writer, not to say I developed him, but whom I worked with and got better as he went along.

Hunter Thompson and Kimball gave us a surprise. The [Harvard] Nieman Fellows met at the St. Botolph Club on Commonwealth Avenue. They were on a panel discussion that soon got out of hand. The next day the president of Nieman Fellows posted a sign on his door "From now on all guest speakers will be approved by me."

CG Did you know Bill Cardoso? I was the first to use the word gonzo when telling a story in his apartment. After that I had many conversations with Bill about what gonzo journalism consisted of. He suggested that each story be written in the first person including endnotes with a list of drugs and alcohol consumed while writing a piece. Eventually, that was part of what done him in.

Bill worked on several book projects. One was about legal brothels in Nevada. Another focused on twin brothers, high profile doctors in Palm Springs, who were implicated in murder. Nothing came of these projects.

A collection of his magazine pieces, *The Maltese Sangweech and Other Heroes*, was published in 1984. Some are gonzo but most are straight journalism.

When it had deep pockets, Bill wrote for *San Francisco Magazine*. He convinced them to pay him to cover the Red Sox, then in a pennant race. His pitch was that Boston and Frisco were sister cities. He visited and lived high, hanging at the Eliot Lounge with Kimball and other sports writers. I recall that Kimball got banned from the press box and they covered games from the bleachers.

HB They went to Zaire together to cover the Ali vs. Frazier fight in 1974.

CG That's in *Sangweech* and may have been Bill's best piece. It belongs in a gonzo anthology. When on his game, nobody topped Bill. What an awesome talent.

HB I read a lot of his stuff.

Editing the *Phoenix* was hard work with seven-day, twelve-hour days. A year in, we were very successful. Circulation was increasing. I was getting tired and wanted to get back to writing more. Richard Missner suggested that we hire the former editor of the *Boston Globe Sunday Magazine* to be the managing editor and do all the work.

We had lunch in Harvard Square and it became very clear to me that if we worked together, I would do all the work and Cardoso would be the mastermind. In a way, that was tempting, but I decided not to give up my seat. The last time I talked to Cardoso he had just returned from Ibiza.

Lucian Truscott and I covered the Snake River jump by Evel Knievel [1974]. I believe Cardoso was there.

CG It's in his book.

HB Yeah, I thought we got together there.

CG Lucian Truscott the fourth, wasn't he?

HB Yeah. Lucian was a West Pointer [Class of 1969]. His father was a colonel and his grandfather, was in the movie *Patton*. He took command after Patton slapped the GI in an army hospital. For a while he ran the war in Europe. Lucian followed the family tradition and went to West Point. After his freshman year, on weekends he would go to New York and hang out at the *Village Voice*. While still a cadet he was writing for the Voice.

[He is a member of the Monticello Association, the members of which descend from Thomas Jefferson, who was Truscott's great-great-great-great-grandfather. Starting in 1970, he joined The *Village Voice* as a freelancer and later staff writer. He had previously written for the *Voice* as a cadet, submitting conservative, right-wing letters that the newspaper eventually started to publish. He has published six books.]

He wrote occasionally for the *Phoenix*. Lucian was a hippie in a Lower-East-Side kind of way. He was pretty tough and lived on a barge on the New Jersey shore. He took a boat to cross the Hudson to go to the Voice.

CG Were you the editor of the *Real Paper*?

HB Paul Solman was the editor. It was started by the *Cambridge Phoenix* employees union after Missner sold the paper. It was everybody but Kimball. It started on unemployment insurance. Everyone who was fired had six months of benefits.

CG How did you manage not to be discovered?

HB We weren't getting paid. In the beginning our only income was unemployment insurance. Nobody was getting paid. We got $1,000 from Barney Frank, and that was the nugget Paul used to start the paper. He came over, told us he always liked the *Phoenix*, and wrote a check.

CG How long did the *Real Paper* last?

HB Six or seven years. Maybe not that long. I'm trying to remember. Maybe three years.

[It ran from August 2, 1972 to June 18, 1981.]

Eventually, it couldn't compete with Mindich who was a great ad salesman.

CG Do you recall the art critic Jean Bergantini Grillo? For a time we were rivals when I was art critic for *Boston After Dark*.

HB There was staff there when I took over at the *Cambridge Phoenix*. She was there and I don't have much to say about her. She covered it adequately with a lot of information and listings of local galleries. I feel that's a function of weekly papers to provide that coverage and she did that. She was a good art critic who worked hard.

CG There are so many writers we can discuss from that era. You mention that Harvard was underrepresented in the mix. An exception was Ken Emerson. He started with *The Avatar*. When Dave Wilson and I ran it in the summer of 1968, I contacted him. The prior editor, Wayne Hansen, had him covering local bands, but Ken was more interested in emerging British rock. I remember him writing about Spooky Tooth when they played the Tea Party. He later became a writer and editor for the *Boston Phoenix*. Then he and Janet Maslin, who was a rock writer for the *Boston Phoenix*, joined *the New York Times*. They broke up and Ken stayed on as an editor.

HB Was that after Janet and Laudau?

CG Yes. Ken was a terrific editor. I did a long piece on the Museum of Fine Arts for him, which became a cover story. He took me to school on it and had me rewrite it. I learned a lot from that editing process. The elements were there, but I didn't know how to piece together so much information. He laid out a template to follow, then it all fell into place. It is such a pity that emerging blog writers are not getting that experience.

HB It's amazing. Just consider the movie criticism thing: Maslin, David Ansen, Patrick McGilligan.

CG Deac Rossell of *Boston After Dark* became the first film curator for the MFA. In the 1980s, he was with The Directors Guild. Since 1997, he has taught at Goldsmiths College in London. There are so many careers like that.

Do you recall any of the other underground and alternative papers like *The Old Mole*?

HB I believe that *The Old Mole* was defunct by the time I got to Cambridge. I remember it being pretty radical.

CG How about the *BU News*?

HB I read about that in Ray Mungo's book. There were a lot of BU people. Jeff Albertson was a great photojournalist. We were close friends. They were cranking out journalists. I think Steve Davis was from BU News, as was Stu Werbin. He covered rock for the *Phoenix* and *Rolling Stone*.

CG Landau recruited a lot of local writers for *Rolling Stone*.

HB He did.

CG You were freelancing for the *Real Paper*?

HB I had a column called "Reading." It was every other week on books and magazines. Even when I went back to St. Louis, I kept writing it.

CG That's what George Frazier did for the *Globe*. His column was called "The Literary Life."

HB It got pretty thin toward the end, as I recall. I met George a few times and liked him personally. He glamorized a whole bunch of people that I wouldn't. He lived in a fascinating world. He was drunk every time I saw him. He had a staunch following.

After *All the President's Men* came out, the staff of daily newspapers changed. It became much more career and professional oriented. In the '70s and '80s the women were more interesting than the men. The young women wanted to be like us. I consider myself an old drunk newspaper guy. They wanted to also be old drunk newspaper guys. The men were all trying to win the Pulitzer Prize by getting rid of the President.

CG When were you back in St. Louis?

HB 1972, actually, 1973. I lived in Cambridge for two years, then near Gloucester for a year. Freelancing, mostly for the *Real Paper*.

CG How were you staying alive?

HB I don't know. It seemed easier in those days. When I got fired, Richard Missner gave me three thousand dollars in severance pay. *The Phoenix* employees union negotiated that for me. Somehow I made that last for six months. You stayed with friends and drank beer, which was cheap. Marijuana was cheap. You didn't go to fancy restaurants and crashed in people's basements. I couldn't do it today.

CG Describe your current lifestyle.

HB We live in the middle of the city in a fairly urban neighborhood. There's a French restaurant a block away. We live within walking distance of a lot of bars and restaurants. It's not like living in Boston. It's a Midwestern city.

I've been working on books. The East St. Louis book was the last one. I survive.

My wife [Roseann Weiss] is pretty good at bringing in money. I'm doing all right with a couple of freelance gigs. I introduce movies for a movie club. I do some book reviews. We get by living a middle-class life. My wife is an art consultant. She was head of public art for the regional arts commission. Now she freelances. Her subject is the intersection of art and society.

CG I enjoyed a great conversation with her. She described to me, from time to time, taking issue with some of David Bonetti's art reviews. [Bonetti started with the *Boston Phoenix* then *San Francisco Chronicle* before St. Louis *Post-Dispatch*. He died in Brookline, Massachusetts in 2018.] He could be unkind to local artists.

HB (*laughing*) What I remember was a guy named Bill Cohn, a much-admired, but terrible, local artist. He mentored a lot of girls. He was pretty popular. He died, and there was a show of his work. Bonetti totally trashed it, which was fine. Then he went back a couple of weeks later and trashed it again. Beating on a dead man twice was going too far. You get one swipe at the dead but not two.

CG Do you get any intellectual stimulation in St. Louis?

HB My friends are art dealers and newspaper people. *The Post-Dispatch* was a great newspaper at one point. It was much better than the papers in Boston even in the 1970s, when I was in Boston. It's not a cultural wasteland, but it's not Boston. Per capita, Boston is the most intellectually stimulating city in the country.

CG I agree with that although we now live in the Berkshires and have an entirely different scene. Give me a pullout quote for journalism on your watch.

HB It was very exciting. There were the Pentagon Papers and Watergate, both of which we covered tangentially. We published pieces by Noam Chomsky and Howard Zinn. It was a great time as the Baby Boomers were just getting into journalism. I'm about ten years older. They were doing some great stuff, particularly at the *Washington Post*. Other papers were doing muckraking as well.

CG How did Boston/Cambridge fit into the scheme of things?

HB Boston/Cambridge were in ferment and produced so many great writers who are well known today. It was great to be a part of that. For me the personal highlight of that era was when I got fired and the staff walked out to support me, and we started *The Real Paper*. That was spread out over several months.

There was a story I refused to run and I am proud of that. At the time nobody agreed with me. The former treasurer of the City of Boston, an Italian guy Frank Anzalone, was corrupt and the FBI wiretapped him. They were after money changing hands illicitly. The Federal court wouldn't accept the wiretaps. The FBI offered leaks to the *Boston Globe* but they wouldn't run it. The FBI offered it to *The Phoenix* and *Boston After Dark*. Because it was the FBI, I wouldn't run it. Teddy Gross ran it in *BAD*. I was proud of that decision and it was kind of a liberal thing to do. We didn't like what the FBI was doing to liberal groups. I didn't like the FBI wiretapping a Sicilian.

CG So many are now gone, but we lived to tell the tale. Back in the day, what were your favorite Cambridge watering holes?

HB Jack's and The Plough and Stars. We held editorial meetings in Jack's. The Plough and the Stars was for more serious drinking. Kimball loved the Plough. He had his eye on a seat all the time.

CG In every sense.

Harper Barnes was a journalist from St. Louis. Photo by Jeff Albertson.

Barnes at bat. Photo by Jeff Albetson.

Barnes downs a brew during the softball game. Photo by Jeff Albertson.

Cambridge Phoenix publisher Jeff Tarter. Photo by Peter Simon.

Ray Riepen bought a share in the *Cambridge Phoenix*. Photo by Jeff Albertson.

Sports writer George Kimball (left) out and about with Abbie Hoffman. Photo by Jeff Albertson.

The *Cambridge Phoenix* staff. Photo by Jeff Albertson.

Today Harper Barnes is writing novels in and about St. Louis. Photo courtesy of Barnes.

Arnie Reisman was editor of *Brandeis Justice* and *Boston After Dark/Phoenix*

As an undergraduate, Arnie Reisman was my editor at *The Brandeis Justice*. Later he hired me as design director for *Boston After Dark*. That didn't last long, and I resurfaced as an art critic with a weekly column, "Art Bag." He hired a number of other Brandeis alumni, launching careers in journalism.

Charles Giuliano How did you become the editor of the weekly *Boston After Dark*?

Arnie Reisman I was 26, working as the arts and entertainment editor and critic at the *Quincy* [Massachusetts] *Patriot Ledger*. In the fall of 1968, I got a call from Stephen Mindich, the co-publisher of *Boston After Dark*, a 16-page weekly giveaway about the arts scene—reviews and listings and ads, that was it. Its appeal was to a young audience. The ads reached out to college students, because the publication was basically delivered to area campuses. Actually, *Boston After Dark* began as a supplement inside the Harvard Business School newspaper. Jim Lewis of Chagrin Falls, Ohio, was a student at HBS. When he graduated, he and an MIT colleague, Joe Hanlon, asked if they could spin off the supplement. They got it and opened an office in Boston in early 1966.

By the time I got the call from Mindich, Hanlon was gone. Mindich, a Boston University grad from the Bronx, had come aboard selling ads. He and his ability soon became the backbone of the publication. Now he was Jim Lewis' partner. Steve asked me to lunch.

We had crossed paths several times, since he also served *Boston After Dark* as a theater critic, especially Broadway theater. We met or sat near each other at many a play in Boston. I was moonlighting as a theater critic for *Variety*, the show biz weekly, covering plays on their way to Broadway. Steve also caught me on WGBH's counterculture experimental TV show, *What's Happening, Mr. Silver?* This local public television happening was a weekly attempt at trying to prove that the station was hip and offered something to a younger audience. The host was David Silver, who taught English at Tufts and was himself about three years out of college. What really made him marketable at the time was the fact that he was British. After I gave the only positive published review to the show, the producer, Fred Barzyk, called me and asked me to come to WGBH to help write the program. I not only did that, but ended up on the show as your typical local gadfly.

At lunch Steve asked me to be the editor of *Boston After Dark*. I was 26, about a year older than Steve. He was losing his editor, who was moving away. After some affirming thoughts about running a small paper dedicated to the arts and entertainment, I said yes. Steve offered me more money than I was making at the *Patriot Ledger* and editorial control. My tenure as executive editor lasted three interrupted years, ending in the fall of 1971, during which time I was allowed to take the 16-page arts weekly and turn it into a 156-page news weekly. I quit primarily because I was exhausted, burned out.

CG The publication of *Astral Weeks: A Secret History of 1968* by Ryan Walsh has changed perceptions of the counterculture of Boston. The book has been widely reviewed, mostly positively, with a tepid one in the *New York Times*.

AR I am curious about the kind of coverage it is getting outside Boston. It seems like a book which just as easily might have been tossed aside and forgotten, just as anything like it has been for the pervious thirty or forty years. Perhaps the reason it is being looked at outside Boston is because it's called *Astral Weeks*. That's the title of Van's old album and you don't know it's about Boston until you get into the subtitle. It was a wise choice to call it that. I've been leafing through the book and it would be better if he had an editor tighten up the whole thing by making transitions.

I would like to add my own footnote. There is an anti-Boston bias in the media, particularly among New Yorkers. In sports New York always looks down its nose at Boston. Be it Yankees vs. Red Sox, Celtics vs. Knicks, Bruins vs. Rangers, Patriots vs. Jets. If the Yankees beat the Sox, there is a huge headline in the New York media, and if the Sox win, the story is buried. Boston suffers a passive-aggressive attitude. It never makes an issue of clearing up why it is always viewed as second best.

Some 40 years ago, I pitched the idea for a book which was somewhat in the order of *Astral Weeks*. It was about how, in the cultural scene, Boston was maybe as influential as New York or San Francisco in changing the face of young America. I pitched it to Beacon Press, a Boston publishing house. I've never forgotten the rejection letter which stated, "Who's going to read this outside the city of Boston?" (*laughing*)

CG That's a logical question.

AR I talked about how much of an impact it had on the rest of the country, and that was lost on the guy who was responding to my pitch. I got a reply that what happens in Boston stays in Boston. I dropped the idea, figuring that if I couldn't sell it to a Boston publisher, there was no point pitching it to a New York publisher.

CG There is richness of significant events and colorful anecdotes which deserve to be documented. The primary sources, including you and me, are disappearing.

Last June we were in San Francisco for a theater conference. It was the 50th anniversary of "The Summer of Love." We saw an amazing special exhibition that included the hippie culture of music, media, psychedelics, fashions.

[*The Summer of Love Experience: Art, Fashion, and Rock & Roll*, De Young Museum, San Francisco, April 8 to August 20, 2017]

We also saw Kacee Clanton in *A Night with Janis Joplin*, the touring company of the Broadway musical at American Conservatory Theater.

So San Francisco was revved up and cashing in on tourism related to its counterculture. Clearly, in the late 1960s, they had a lot more going there than what was happening in Boston. They had better bands—Jefferson Airplane, Quicksilver Messenger Service, Grateful Dead, Big Brother and the Holding Company, Country Joe and the Fish—to name a few. Promoting them were psychedelic posters for the Fillmore concerts and graphics for the *San Francisco Oracle*.

AR Compared to that was the fiasco of the MGM Bosstown Sound promotion which totally flopped.

CG That's a part of how Boston unraveled. San Francisco had phenomenal graphic artists. The designer for *Avatar* was Eben Given, an illustrative artist and close friend of Mel Lyman [1938–1978]. He was adequate, but reactionary compared to what was going on in San Francisco.

Lyman and his group were aesthetically conservative. It is not a surprise that the primary assets of the cult derived from Jesse Benton and the estate of regionalist artist and scion of Americana, Thomas Hart Benton. The Kansas lawyer, Ray Riepen, was called on by Jesse to arrange Mel's divorce from Sophie [living with Given] after which they married. Fort Hill was running the Cinematheque based on Mel's passion for Jonas Mekas. For a time, Mel crashed with Mekas, which spawned his ambition to make films.

When the Hill's venture failed, Riepen took over the South End lease and founded the Boston Tea Party. Riepen expanded his empire by acquiring the *Cambridge Phoenix*.

Avatar, Boston's underground paper, under Lyman's overview was conservative compared to what was happening elsewhere. The nation's underground press was serviced by the radical Liberation News Service (LNS).

Under control of Lyman's Fort Hill editors, the *Avatar* was out of sync by lacking a radical, leftist, social, and political orientation. Mel modeled his life and music on Woody Guthrie. He advocated a folk-based, rural Americana during the late 1960s. Fort Hill might well have been located in Kansas.

So consider the contrast between *San Francisco Oracle* and *Avatar*.

AR How true and bizarre.

CG Combining the Bosstown Sound with Lyman's Fort Hill commune, it's significant that *Astral Weeks* documents their marginal impact. That temporarily repressed the brilliant, diverse counterculture and media in Boston/Cambridge that prevailed from 1969 through 1981, when the *Real Paper* folded.

It is interesting that the album format of WBCN, with DJ's not limited to rigid playlists, originated with KSAN in San Francisco. I'm not sure who brought to Boston tapes that inspired formatting at WBCN. The Rock of Boston emerged as one of the nation's most influential stations. Many bands playing the Tea Party broke out when WBCN interviewed, broadcasted performances, and played their songs. That's when Boston evolved from local to national with its immense college demographics. The enormous student population created a youth market disproportionate to Boston's population.

AR You can make a case for Boston/Cambridge evolving as a hothouse for growing talent. It's obviously college based with so many good schools in the area. Many of the best and brightest stayed. I'm thinking of the newspaper business, music, art, definitely theater.

So many great actors began here. After graduate school in New York, I started here as a 22-year-old theater critic. The first thing I was doing was reviewing Theatre Company of Boston, which was functioning out of a dirty old theater in a hotel basement. Two blocks down at the Charles Playhouse was Al Pacino.

[Theatre Company of Boston (TCB) was co-founded by David Wheeler and Naomi Thornton in 1963. Wheeler served as its artistic director until its closure in 1975. Actors including Al Pacino, Robert DeNiro, Dustin Hoffman, Robert Duvall, Jon Voight, Stockard Channing, James Woods, Blythe Danner, Larry Bryggman, John Cazale, Hector Elizondo, Spalding Gray, Paul Guilfoyle, Ralph Waite, Charles Siebert, and Paul Benedict were part of the company.]

All those people came out of here and there was an audience for them. There was an element of sophistication that you don't find in other places.

CG Boston always had a strong theater community. It was a tryout town for shows being developed for Broadway.

AR This past year I had experiences with a show, *War Paint*, headed to Broadway. When they told me it was going to open in Chicago, I spoke with one of the producers. I said, "Fine, you can open it at the Goodman. Everyone knows that theater and it does well. It's been around for a hundred years and I understand that. But back in my 20s and 30s Boston was a real tryout town."

There were three functioning theaters: The Wilbur, The Shubert, and The Colonial. Producers would come in here and work with their shows for a few weeks, which they would also do in New Haven. Then they would open on Broadway.

I asked, "What happened? Because that's not true anymore." The guy laughing on the other end of the phone was the assistant to David Stone, who was one of the producers for *Wicked*. So he was fairly successful.

He said, "I'll give you three good reasons why Boston will never be a tryout town anymore."

I said, "Oh, really, should I be sitting down?"

"Number one," he said, "way too educated."

"What does that mean?" I asked?

"Bostonians will kill a play that New Yorkers will love," he said.

"Are you saying that New Yorkers are not that sophisticated?" I replied.

"No," he said. "That brings me to number two. No tourist in his right mind comes to Boston and goes to see a play. On any given night in New York, one of every three or four seats, on or off Broadway, is sold to a tourist. That takes down the level of sophistication, and the New York commercial market builds on that knowledge.

"That brings me to the third point," he said. "Chicago's Goodman Theatre is a subscription service. They have a database, and people get hit up in the mail or by email. Here's the next season. Here's the next six plays you never heard of. They'll buy tickets just to keep going. They don't know what the hell they're buying tickets for. That's great if you're a producer. It means that you will fill seats with bodies. There is no such thing in Boston."

I said, "There's the Huntington."

The response was, "Nah, not big enough."

CG "ART [American Repertory Theater]?"

AR I mentioned that, but he said, "Rarely do they let you in there. So you have closed the doors on the avant-garde theater world or even the musical theater world. It just doesn't go anywhere if it's in Boston. The taste of Martians!" (*laughs*)

CG What was your role in *War Paint*, which I was lucky enough to see on Broadway?

AR They took it from the documentary we did for PBS.

[March 2009 *The Powder & the Glory*, a 90-minute documentary narrated by Jane Alexander, tells the story of two of the first highly successful women entrepreneurs—Elizabeth Arden and Helena Rubinstein. One hundred years ago these women immigrated to America, and starting with next to nothing, created what is today the $150 billion global health and beauty industry. It was produced, written, and directed by Ann Carol Grossman and Arnie Reisman. It is based upon the book *War Paint: Miss Elizabeth Arden and Madame Helena Rubinstein—*

Their Lives, Their Times, Their Rivalry by Lindy Woodhead. The author had unprecedented access to correspondence and diaries.]

They run it each March. David Stone, the producer of *War Paint* and *Wicked* was also the associate producer of *Grey Gardens*. It was also originally a documentary [A 1975 film by Albert and David Maysles]. It was turned into a musical. Stone saw our film and said, "This is a musical." I said, "What do you want to do?" He said, "I want to buy it from you. We'll have a deal where you'll get a piece of the box office every week."

I said, "Oh. Is there anything I have to do?" He said, "No. Now and then we will send you the creative team to pick your brain." It was the same three guys who did *Grey Gardens*, bookwriter, lyricist, and composer. We had a great time, and the show ran for eight months. It ended because Patti Lupone was in pain and needed a hip replacement. We didn't want to go with an understudy. They're trying to license it to London and LA, which I hope they do.

CG I liked the show, but it wasn't well received by some critics

AR I saw it five times and it grew on me.

CG What's not to like about LuPone and Ebersole?

AR Exactly. They sang their hearts out.

But that was a very sophisticated lesson. The production aide said, "If we listened to Boston, we would have lost our shirts. There's just too much negativity there. I asked, "What happened to New Haven?" He said, "The same. We don't try out anything there either."

CG After my summer as managing editor for *Avatar* in 1968, you hired me as design director of *Boston After Dark*. That didn't last long, but I stayed on writing a weekly column "Art Bag."

AR "Art Bag!" I remember "Art Bag."

CG The *Globe* had Edgar Driscoll, Jr. who covered The MFA, Copley Society, and blue movies. Those x-rated reviews were his best work. Back then papers reviewed *I Am Curious (Yellow)* and films like that.

The art world was digging itself out of annihilation. The ICA on Newbury Street, under Sue Thurman, was booted out of New England Life on Newbury

Street. Its assets [including a fine library] were stored in the abandoned tin-hut home on Soldier's Field Road in Brighton.

In 1968 Drew Hyde, and architect Edwin Child, worked with Adele Seronde in the public art program of Kevin White's Summerthing. With the backing of Assistant Mayor Kathy Kane, Hyde resurrected the ICA. Drew had close ties with White and for a time there was a gallery at the New City Hall. Drew and I curated a show Images at City Hall that had a focus on the new realism.

The only consistent space for emerging artists was Gallery 11 in a basement of Tufts University. In one of my first "Art Bag" columns I asked for artists to get in touch with me. Out of that evolved The Studio Coalition, which staged America's first Open Studios. It was a great success, which led to cover stories in *The Gallery Guide* as well as a major Boston article in *Art News*. Soon Boston artists were included in the Whitney Annual exhibitions. Later, the Boston Visual Artists Union was formed. It was an exciting era and my *BAD* coverage was a part of it.

You responded with some edge to our interview with former *Cambridge Phoenix* editor Harper Barnes. His paper and *Boston After Dark* were similar and different. Both were seeking the same primarily young audience. After all these years, your remarks evoked a rivalry. Can you give us a sense of that era?

AR You're reading in an edge that doesn't exist. There was a playful edge. It was my chance to jump in to what he said. I was shocked to learn that Harper is now 80.

Back then we had a dozen meals maybe even 20. It was early on, around 1970, and I don't recall who made the first call. It was a Ray Riepen vs. Steve Mindich thing. We were hearing that there was potential violence. Hawkers were being harassed. They were beaten up and papers were taken out of vans and tossed in the Charles River. There was a lot of nonsense that went on.

It's a bit foggy now but I recall how pissed Steve was when Ray Riepen announced that he planned to buy the competition rather than put his money into *Boston After Dark*. That was, what, spring of 1970? Both papers hired hawkers making a minimum amount of money. They were standing on corners selling papers for fifteen cents.

CG Twenty-five cents.

AR Apparently, the hawkers went to get papers [*BAD*] and they were pushed aside. Goons arrived and took papers out of the truck and tossed them in the river. I heard that the thugs were hired by Riepen. Over which Mindich was pulling his hair out. He said, "I can't go down that dirty road. This way madness lies." He said, "I have to have a meeting. I don't care where we have it." He told me to stay out of it.

It proved to be a onetime event and nothing happened after that.

CG Harper spoke about vandalizing the flats of the scab *Cambridge Phoenix*. Our design director, Ed "Beardsley" Jordan, tore up flats of an issue of *Avatar* which Dave Wilson and I created. So that kind of criminality was a part of the zeitgeist. It speaks to the passions of the time.

AR Harper and I met secretly and said, let's not be like them, the guys that own us. Let's be friends. Harper was a new guy in town. [From St. Louis] We picked DuBarry's on Newbury Street as a place where it was unlikely that we would run into anyone we knew. We would have lunch and talk for an hour. That was about it. With the exception of features, it was obvious we were going to cover the same things: plays, movies, concerts, news. For news they would have perhaps more of a Cambridge bent than we had. We would meet and share each other's list of what was coming out two days later.

We were sharing information and not really trying to out scoop one another. We developed a friendship. Paul Solman, my news editor, had friends on the *Cambridge Phoenix* as well. [He later took over from Barnes as editor and became editor of the spinoff *The Real Paper*. He is business correspondent for the PBS *News Hour*.]

I was friends with Vin McClellan who did the story of tracking down Stanley Bond who was involved in the Brighton bank heist [with Susan Saxe and Kathy Powers of Brandeis]. Vin got the one and only interview with him as he was going into prison in Colorado.

[Stanley Ray Bond, October 30, 1944–May 24, 1972, was a former convict who enrolled at Brandeis University. He was arrested for a bank robbery conducted to obtain funds for anti-Vietnam War efforts. Previously, he had served as a private first cslass in the United States Army in the Vietnam War. During the bank robbery a Boston Police officer was shot and killed. Bond and accomplices were captured following the robbery. Brandeis students Susan Saxe and Kathy Powers were fugitives. Bond later died in prison awaiting trial when a bomb he built to use for an escape detonated prematurely.)

Vin and I started at the *Patriot Ledger* in Quincy. So there was a lot of camaraderie. Two weekly, alternative newspapers were surviving in the same market. We were both oriented to the college market.

Part of Steven's strategy is that he wanted to have the paper free on college campuses as well as paid on newsstands and to subscribers. The Post Office said you can't do that. He studied the postal code and discovered that it is a new publication if it is at least 20% different.

We established the following. The paper to be sold was called *Boston After Dark*. The free paper for college campuses was *BAD*. We changed the front-page pictures and headlines. We changed stories around and had grab bag features that we would use in one or the other papers then swap the next week. So they became 20% different, and he got under the postal code radar. There were a hundred and fifty thousand free papers and perhaps another fifty to sixty thousand that were sold.

CG That's incredible circulation.

AR It was. *The Cambridge Phoenix* surely had similar numbers.

CG Some two hundred thousand weekly circulation was a monster. That was in the range of the daily papers *Boston Globe* and *Boston Herald*. Today, of course, with the internet their circulation and influence is a fraction of what it was in the 1970s.

[A 2012 *Globe* story reports: "The *Globe's* circulation, including subscriptions to BostonGlobe.com, increased 11.9 percent to 230,351, compared with the same six months in 2011, according to the Audit Bureau of Circulations. The *Globe's* Sunday circulation, including digital subscriptions, grew 3.4 percent to 372,541… *The Boston Herald's* daily circulation fell below 100,000 in that period. The tabloid's circulation declined by 14.9 percent to 96,860, compared to the same period a year ago, according to the bureau. The *Herald's* Sunday circulation was 77,764, down 9.4 percent."]

AR At the time we were all young, in our twenties, having fun, doing what we wanted to do. This is the kind of paper I want to work on rather than an established daily. I don't want to go to the *Globe, Record American, Herald Traveler*. I want to stay here because it's the kind of journalism I want to do.

On the other hand, I didn't think that we had much influence on how Boston ran politically. Most of our readers weren't even voters.

Then one day I got a call from Tom Winship [*Boston Globe* editor]. He wanted to eat me for lunch. Mayor Kevin White was running for re-election against Louise Day Hicks. We were picking apart something on White.

[Anna Louise Day Hicks, October 16, 1916–October 21, 2003, was best known for staunch opposition to desegregation in Boston public schools, and especially to court-ordered busing in the 1960s and 1970s.)

Possibly he was buddy-buddy with too many slumlords. I don't recall the actual issue, but we were hammering away.

I got a call from Winship, who was clearly looking down his nose at me on the phone. In a pissant way he said, "Will you guys stop writing this stuff about Kevin?"

I went, "What are you talking about?" He responded, "Do you want Louise Day Hicks to be mayor? What's the matter with you? Are you that dumb politically?" I said, "I'm surprised you're even calling me." He wanted me to lay off Kevin White. This was from the editor of the *Globe*.

[In *The New York Times* obit for Winship, it states: "Mr. Winship did not shrink from pursuing stories wherever they went. He said his most painful decision was to publish an investigation of the finances of the liberal Republican Edward W. Brooke, the first black United States senator since Reconstruction. The inquiry contributed greatly to Senator Brooke's defeat in 1978." So, using Winship's journalistic logic, why did he deep-six Brooke? Was he friends with challenger Paul Tsongas?]

CG Has this ever been made public?

AR You can post it. Be my guest. I've told the story before. It annoyed the hell out of me. I told Mindich but I don't know if he ever told the Taylor family. Imagine the *Globe* calling another journalist telling him to lay off this thing. What, are you working for Kevin White? The bottom line was: part of this turned my stomach because, oooh I thought, he's right. (*laughing*) If I look at the world that way, if I'm chipping away at White, am I elevating the possibility that Louise Day Hicks gets elected as mayor? She was far worse than Kevin White as a possible mayor of Boston. Looking down from atop Mt. Olympus, I thought: Do we have that kind of influence?

You're shaking in your boots at the establishment newspaper, and take time in the middle of the day to call me and tell me to stop it! After that I went, "Oh my God, we are influential, or those who have influence feel that we are strong enough to make waves in this town." After that I felt we needed to tackle more political stories.

CG As I reported in the Harper Barnes interview years ago, he took a swing at me. The widely held assumption of Barnes and his staff, then on strike, was that I was one of the writers for the scab paper. I never understood why I was on their enemies list. Discussing it recently, a friend from that time said, "Because you were a Mindich man."

What does that mean? I worked for Mindich, but I never felt I was a Mindich man. My loyalty was to you starting when you were my editor at the *Brandeis Justice*. Then you were my editor and mentor at *BAD*. I never planned to be a journalist. It was something I backed into. But you were amazingly tolerant in giving me an opportunity.

AR You were enthusiastic about a field that I felt needed to be covered. You had insights and a real passion for it.

CG My feeling at the time was that under Mindich, other than you, *BAD* was commercial. By contrast, *Cambridge Phoenix* under Barnes was more like a cult. That may have changed later with the *Real Paper* as it passed through editor and staff changes. One thinks, for example, of the *Village Voice* vs. *The East Village Other*.

AR Keep in mind that up until the sale, both papers were making money. Both were in the black. [*Phoenix* owner Richard] Missner's paper was never in trouble, though he thought it was when the staff threatened to form a union. Then he was going to have to pay out too much money. Lord knows, papers didn't pay very well. But they paid enough, because at that time things didn't cost that much.

My relationship with Steve was love/hate but it was much more love than hate. He was a hip capitalist and pleased as punch to be selling full-page ads to Sack Theatres and Jordan Marsh. He was trying to prove that he had entrepreneurial skills, and he also had the savvy to know that there couldn't be 25 to 40 Steve Mindichs. He had to have me, and you, and everyone else who had a different way of communicating. We could reach people he was trying to reach better than he could do, except for his occasional theater review, because that was his passion. He was never going to be the theater editor nor did he want to be.

I was living in Mexico and Mindich called me to come back. I had left in a huff at the end of 1969 when he and Lewis were feuding.

CG Why did he want you back?

AR Now you hit the button. *The Phoenix* was coming to town. The reason I knew that was because I was asked to be the editor. That meant jumping ship and I really didn't want to do that. Jeff Tartar, another Brandeis guy, was starting the paper. Jeff worked for me at the *Justice*. He was my news editor. Personally, I didn't think Jeff could do it. He has worked for *Time Magazine* and taken some shrapnel in Vietnam. He had money. I agreed to a meeting with him and his uncle, who was going to be the finance man. It seemed like it was a toy, and how long were they going to play with it.

Mindich was building something, and this didn't look the same. Mindich started poor and he had something to prove. It was summer of '69 and a lot was going on, including Woodstock. I told Mindich, and said this is what's coming to town. I watched the blood drain out of him. This was going to be competition. He asked what are they going to do? I said, "Well A, they're going to cover Cambridge. They will be an entity for a while. I know Jeff, and he's going to hire people. He was interested in the idea of combining news [politics] and entertainment."

My line to Mindich was, "Let's do a *Village Voice* in Boston." Steve wanted to do it. But Jim Lewis, who started the whole thing and hired Steve to be advertising director before they became partners said, "Over my dead body. I see where the future is and it's not in news. I don't want to go that way."

Jim was entirely into youth marketing and wanted to be even more college related. He wanted to cover what was happening on campus and he wanted to be a college newspaper. I had a meeting with Steve and said, "I really have no interest in doing that. I have much more interest in doing the news thing. Why don't you just fight it out? When it's over, if you still want me, come get me."

Somewhere around October, I quit. Dave Sterritt from the *Christian Science Monitor* replaced me.

CG I worked for him. Eventually, he went back to the *Monitor*.

AR I left to work on a novel and I didn't know what the heck I was doing. My, then wife, Nicole Symons, and I drove all over the country like Kerouac in *On the Road*. We ended up in San Miguel de Allende where we lived for three months. We were there for the beginning of 1970.

CG As I understand, Nikki is deceased.

AR She died 30 years ago. We broke up in 1978.

CG I remember her fondly. She had rose-colored glasses.

AR Exactly, real ones. We remained friends. We were staying in San Miguel with her uncle, who left Madison Avenue to become an artist.

This was the pre-computer era. A kid on a donkey with a sombrero knocked on our door. He said (*in a comical accent*), "Is there an Arnie Reisman here?" I answered, "That's me." He said, "There's a phone call for you." (*laughing*) "Where the hell is it?"

"Back in the post office," he replied, which was like a mile down a hill. So I said, "Oh, can I get on your donkey?"

"No," he said, "it's not going to hold you."

There was an operator I had to call back. She said, "There's someone called Steven Mindich in Boston."

So Steve gets on the phone and says, "I won. Jim has packed it in and gone back to Chagrin Falls, Ohio. I get the paper. What do you want? Come on back."

Paula [Lyons a TV consumer journalist], my wife of 36 years says, "You never asked him for a piece of the paper!"

I said, "I want editorial control and $25,000 year."

He said, "You got it." So I went back.

CG That was pretty good money in those days.

AR This says a lot about Steve. It was the spring of 1971. In the office, we got wind that Stop and Shop was pulling a fraud on consumers. This was the height of Cesar Chavez and produce strikes in California. We were told that there's a phony union label on all the lettuce heads at Stop and Shop. They're slapped on in Cambridge.

Paul Solman had an idea. "This may backfire but I want to send Jane Goldberg." She was our listings editor. He said that she had an innocent manner and that people trust and unload on her. "Send her," he said, "See what happens. If it doesn't work, it doesn't work."

After hours and hours she comes back. She said, "You're right and the produce manager admitted it. (*laughing*) He showed me where they slap the labels on."

She wrote a huge story. I got the art department to create a graphic, which was a head of lettuce with an ax going through it and blood pouring out.

I went to Mindich and said, "Here's your front page." At the time, Stop and Shop was running like $25,000 worth of ads.

Steve said, "You've got to be kidding me. We're not doing this, are you? You really can't do this."

I told him, "This is news and we can't sit on it."

"How did she get this story?" he asked. "Did she tell him she was a reporter?" (*laughing*)

We called in Jane to talk with Steve. She said, "I think I told him." We're saying don't tell him that and Paul is saying you must have told him.

She said, "I was taking notes."

So, we said, He must have seen her taking notes. Oh good. A notebook and a pencil. Good."

This is going on, and all of a sudden Steve said to me, "You can't do it. Build another front page. You can't do it." This was just before dinnertime.

He went off and wrestled with it and around midnight he came to me and said, "Okay, run it. I've been doing a lot of thinking and decided where I have to come down. Otherwise, I'm a total hypocrite. I'm coming down on what's morally correct here. You guys discovered a story that they're using fraudulent labels, and I can't sit on that. If I lose the damned account, then that's just the way it is."

We ran it. The next day all hell broke loose at Stop and Shop. The produce manager was fired. It was a big story at the time. The *Globe* was calling, asking how we got the story. We told them to do their own work and hung up on them. It wasn't Winship this time.

The PR person, Bernard Solomon, known affectionately as "Bunny" called Steve the next day. He said, "Well, you got us. We're sorry it happened. We shouldn't do this and are going to make amends."

He was big about the whole thing and saw it as a public relations fiasco. They had inadvertently walked into it and they never pulled their ads. Steve was ecstatic and ran into my office and kissed me.

Whatever you might say about him, he came around, and I'll never forget him for this.

CG When I worked for *BAD* I recall that Jim and Steve both had separate offices, as well as personal assistants. One, I recall, was Gladys, and I don't remember the name of the other woman.

AR Jim's was Gladys, and Steve's executive secretary was Billie.

CG There was a sense of intense competition, and they were part of the Jim and Steve show, or should we say melodrama.

I recall an incident when they launched the new City Hall with a gala celebration. Somehow Jim got too enthusiastic and spent the night in the men's room. Gladys had to show up and rescue him with a change of clothes.

AR That sounds vaguely familiar, but I don't remember.

CG It was a part of the color of the newsroom and the intense rivalry. I believe it was about when they parted and went to court. Lewis continued to put out a scab paper.

Early on Steve was accessible and a family man. I recall driving around with him in an old car with his son Brad in the back seat.

With success he became more flamboyant and philanthropic. He had money, but never conveyed class and style.

AR His second wife, Dale Roberts, was quite well off financially. The marriage didn't last long.

CG I knew Dale. She was a very nice lady who I knew socially in the art world. Through her, Steve was involved with the ICA, collected art, and was a backer of an art gallery.

AR Then he married the controversial judge.

[Maria Lopez was, for a time, a TV judge criticized for unusual sentencing which resulted in controversy.)

CG A lot of your writers, including myself, were Brandeis grads. Who else?

AR Paul Solman, Teddy Gross, Ben Gerson, who became music editor after Tim

Crouse went to *Rolling Stone*. Gerson and Gross were class of 1969. I was class of 1964. I'm a year behind you. Teddy had a brother, Larry Gross, who taught at Penn. Solman was class of 1966.

CG And Jon Landau.

AR He was class of 1968. It was just people I knew who were writers and wanted to do this thing. It just happened. I walked in and inherited an established staff. There was Deac Rossell in film. Larry Stark covered theater. When we became a newspaper, he became my theater editor. I felt that Larry was doing what you were doing in terms of how he covered every little theater from Boston to the North Shore. What you were doing for art Larry was doing for theater. It was great.

There were a lot of people who walked in and out of the office like [Janet] Maslin. I forget where she went to school.

[Janet R. Maslin, born August 12, 1949, is best known as a film and literary critic for *The New York Times*. She served as a *Times'* film critic from 1977 to 1999 and a book critic from 2000 to 2015. She graduated from the University of Rochester in 1970, with a B.A. degree in mathematics.]

CG I remember a Cat Stevens interview she did for BAD. Didn't she start as a rock critic?

AR She didn't cover film for me. She went to the *Times* to do film. She was doing music for Tim Crouse, who brought her on. When Tim left, he was replaced by Ben Gerson, who I did not know at the time [Several years later he left journalism for law school].

CG I don't think that the prominence of Brandeis in Boston media at that time was a coincidence. While I wasn't a political activist, I would say that, because of Brandeis, I became an arts radical. With an emphasis on dissent, we were encouraged to question authority.

AR Well said. When we were there, the whole thing was question, question, question. Challenge authority. Challenge the status quo. Yeah, I got that feeling.

CG How did that inform your outlook and writers you chose to work with?

AR Well, it informed my outlook to not be a part of the mainstream news media.

CG To what extent do you identify with the Brandeis radical tradition? You didn't make it to the FBI most-wanted list.

AR No, but there was an FBI file which I got through freedom of information. I pursued it, and you had to send a notarized letter. I went to a notary at my friendly bank and she said, "What if they don't have a file. Won't you be embarrassed?" She said, "Okay, what did you do?"

"I edited an underground newspaper," I replied. She said, "Oh yeah. You have a file."

I got the file and it was thick. I'm saying, what the heck is this? (*laughing*) It was a complete Xeroxed issue of *Boston After Dark*. Every article was circled. There was a note that was signed JEH, so I guess it was J. Edgar Hoover. It said, "Is there any reason to dig deeper into this crypto-pinko newspaper?"

CG Why did it all fail? The counterculture we believed in is now gone. The *Phoenix* is gone and WBCN folded. What happened?

AR That's a big teardrop on my face. There are several reasons why it failed. Perhaps there is now enough time, distance, and interest to go back and look at that radical generation.

I had a nice conversation with Mindich five years ago, St. Patrick's Day, when the *Boston After Dark/Phoenix* network ended. I wrote an obit that got printed here on the Vineyard in the *Gazette*. I spoke with Steve and he was not sad but he was mad. He felt the paper died because of his son [Brad]. He said, "I handed off a nice baby to another baby who walked away and went skiing. But times change, and all good things must come to pass."

There was a time to beat the bushes for national advertising, which was spread thin. That was the Holy Grail to survival in the media business. By then, there was social media; so how could a newspaper survive? Brad probably thought, this will never fly, and nobody cares anymore.

I spoke with Peter Kadzis, who was one of the last editors there. He told me that college campuses wanted to read about where to go that night. It had come full circle and kids couldn't care less about the news. You could see it was losing its influence a long time ago.

I recall when Nixon resigned, and a few months later, the Vietnam War ended. Paul Solman said to me, "This is bad. Because we were right, and now what do we do? There's nothing to yell about. Jimmy Carter is slithering into the White House. He'll be above it all with a tin ear. A good-hearted man ended up as the best statesman that ever came out of the White House."

Everything went to sleep, and while we were sleeping, the Republican Party grew six more heads. You have an entire generation which didn't even grow up under Reagan, and that's the youth market.

Young people have to be mad and not want fake news. Now with progressive technology and the Internet there are so many horses out of the barn. Maybe we will live long enough to see another alternative media. It just won't be Steve Bannon's *Breitbart*.

One other thing about my FBI files. I wrote them in 1970 requesting to get weekly updates on their Most-Wanted lists. There were so many radicals on it from Saxe and Powers to Bernadette Dorn. We wanted to write stories about them, so that woke the sleeping bear.

At that time, I had on staff Bo Burlingham, who went on to edit *Inc. Magazine*. [Currently he writes for *Forbes*.] He was under the watchful eye of the FBI every day that he came to the office. They parked outside and he would go bring them coffee.

He asked, "Why are you following me?" They answered because of Days of Rage. He was a Weatherman. A federal judge in Flint, Michigan threw everything out. So the guys waiting for their coffee disappeared.

So here's my guy from Princeton, smoking a pipe, who's wanted for Days of Rage because he punched out a cop in Chicago [DNC convention 1968].

Sid Blumenthal also worked for us as a news reporter. Yes, this is the same Blumenthal who rose to levels of controversy inside the Clinton Administration. But you could have fooled me. Each time during the '90s and later, when I saw photos of Sid, I was amazed. The Sid I knew was unrecognizable. Each time he came into my office, he was hiding behind long hair that draped in front of his eyes. Who knew what he looked like?

CG To what extent were you a part of the New Journalism? I hated all your joke and gag headlines.

AR (*laughing*) Well. Too bad. It all began when I started at the *Patriot Ledger* when I was 23. I was handed a wire item that Roy Roger's horse had died and they wanted to run something. I put the story together with a headline "Trigger

Mortis." The next morning the publisher came to me and said, "You're good."

CG Harper Barnes talked about how the staff got fed up with Mindich and wanted to defect to the *Cambridge Phoenix*.

AR Yeah, but that's not true. Paul was already friends with Harper. I was feeling my oats about getting more and more work at Channel 2. And I told Paul that I was ready to leave. I was liking the idea of early television. Newspaper work destroyed my first marriage, and I was looking for something that would be easier to deal with. Paul said, "If you do that I'm not staying here." I said, "You don't want to be the editor?" He said, "No, I don't want to deal with this. I'd rather go over there."

That's what happened, so we gave it to Teddie [Gross], and he took over. As far as I heard, Teddie made a lot of enemies. After him, Richard Gaines was the editor forever.

[He started with UPI before the *Phoenix*. He later moved and wrote for the *Gloucester Daily Times*. He died there June 11, 2013 at 69, three months after the *Boston Phoenix* folded.]

 I didn't sense any kind of mutiny until the end there, when I decided to go. The joke is that I was the buffer, so the writers didn't have to deal with the advertising side. Barry Morris was a bigger pain in the ass than Steve. He ate up editorial space with last-minute ads.

When Lewis left, I got his office. Steve said, "It has two doors. One goes to editorial and one goes to advertising. So when someone knocked, depending of which door, I knew what it was about. There were a lot of people coming and going, and it was fine. I lost a couple of music writers to Jann Wenner [*Rolling Stone*] at the time. Tim Crouse left, and for a little while, Bob Blumenthal wrote on jazz for them. He wrote for the *Globe* for a long time.

CG Bob was the dean of Boston's jazz writers.

AR He was another guy looking for something to do while in grad school.

Another guy who came to me fresh out of Harvard grad school in 1970 was David Sipress who has had a career as a cartoonist for the *New Yorker*. That was the talent pool.

CG What was unique about journalism in Boston compared to other markets? We talk about the New Journalism. Did you sense that? As you have mentioned there

AR I thought of Boston as a very small town for good and bad reasons. You could find out about things pretty quickly. You could stay on top of things and have a say. The bad side was that everyone knew everybody's business.

We started to live through the beginnings of, your phrase, Gonzo or what was called New Journalism under Tom Wolfe. Basically, I thought it was taking your notes and having them published. When I was in grad school in journalism at Columbia I was shown Tom Wolfe and he was just starting out. That would be about 1965. What it showed me was another way of having a style. You didn't have to write like the entire good grey lady newspapers did. You could inject yourself if there was a just cause for doing that. Or at least some descriptive writing that stated I'm not some staid old newspaper guy.

Early on in meetings we would discuss whether we should have an editorial page. That stopped, as there was no need for one. What was the point? Every article kind of had a slant to it. Good or bad it became what they called at the time advocacy journalism. You took sides in how you wrote things.

I remember writing a piece with Bob Katz when he came back from the Harvard Square riots. That was May of 1970 [actually, April 1970].

CG I was there when the cops charged down Mass Ave. It was like the running of the bulls in Pamplona. On Boylston, I managed to duck into a side street and made my way back to the other end of the square. Standing on a corner, I watched school busses full of cops driving by. Three clean-cut looking guys came up to me and started talking about the "pigs." One of them pulled out what appeared to be a Molotov cocktail and offered it to me. I turned it down and have since thought that it was likely that they were undercover agents. All they needed was my prints on the bottle and I would have been a goner. Checking the papers, no Molotov cocktails were used in the riot.

AR Everyone was blaming SDS and the radical groups. Katz was researching a think piece after the riots. He went to the *Globe* and *Herald* and asked to look at their photos. He got copies and brought them in. He said, "Do you notice what I'm noticing?"

I said, "Everyone looks young."

"Young," he replied, "they're thirteen. These are goon townies. It's not SDS. These were kids with an excuse to act crazy and throw bricks at banks and Design Research."

The more we called police, the more he was right. I said, write the piece about how the rest of the media got it all wrong. I felt good about that. I got a call from a *Globe* guy I knew, Bob Levey, who has been married to Ellen Goodman all these years. He was the "Living" page editor. He said, "Pass along anyone writing features who doesn't fit into your paper, I'll hire them. You have good writers." I ended up writing for him in '74 and '75.

CG Compare the *Cambridge Phoenix/Real Paper* to *Boston After Dark*. Was there a difference?

AR I didn't see any. We were doing the same kinds of things and covering the same news stories. We reviewed the same concerts and albums, the same movies and plays. There were the same counterculture things from Ram Dass to drugs coming through. It was a chance to write in a fresher style than the *Globe* and *Herald* were allowing people to do.

I really didn't see that much of a difference.

CG Who were the writing talents of that era?

AR Paul Solman was definitely a talent. He had a good argumentative view of life. He was trying to see both sides of every story. I thought he was really good. One guy I forgot in my original list was Peter Guralnick. He was on one track and was going to cover rhythm and blues until the day he died, and he's not dead yet. He did really deep pieces whether it was about Elvis or Howling Wolf. They were really good and I didn't see that anywhere else.

CG Of course he wrote acclaimed books on Robert Johnson, Elvis Presley, Sam Cooke, Sam Phillips, and others.

AR We had a guy, now approaching 90, Charlie Beye, who nobody remembers. He was my food writer, as well as a classics professor at BU. He was very funny and dapper, always with a bow tie. He was very witty and enjoyed the chance not to be writing about Greek classics. He wrote for me for about two years, then said, "I have to stop on doctor's orders. I'm getting an ulcer from eating out all the time."

CG You mention that Jon Landau wrote for you but Harper Barnes says that he was his first hire for the *Cambridge Phoenix*.

AR He wrote two articles for me before that and then didn't write anything after that for four or five months and then just left. To go back to your point it was another Brandeis connection. He actually came through Paul. One day he came into the office and said, "I'm another Brandeis guy and would like to write something." He wrote two music pieces about which I can't remember. It was before Harper came to town. That would have been in the summer of 1970.

CG Did you get to know him?

AR No, not really, not at all.

CG Did you know the Georges, Kimball and Frazier?

AR Yes. They were quite a handful in different ways. Everybody tells the glass eye stuff about Kimball. Deep down inside, he was belligerent. He was mad at the world and I don't know if it had anything to do with losing his eye. I got really antsy around people who were drinking a lot, but I found him to be a good writer.

CG You drink, right?

AR Yeah, but I don't get drunk. I wasn't like them back then. I had to get up early in the morning to deal with the paper.

As far as Frazier goes, I met him three times. He was one of a kind and a very interesting guy. He was a columnist that you just don't find anymore.

CG Looking back at that era in media, arts, and entertainment there are so many monuments the likes of which we may never see again. Thanks for sharing your memories.

Reisman's Response to the Barnes Interview

Nobody left my staff to go work for the *Phoenix* while I was editor. When I announced, in the fall of 1971, I was leaving, my news editor Paul Solman went over to the *Phoenix* and Teddy Gross soon thereafter assumed the editorship of *BAD*. Writers and editors working for me for my three years at that helm included Paul, Teddy, Bo Burlingham, Jon Lipsky, Marty Linsky, Richard Gaines [later a

BAD editor], Mark Phillips [*CBS News* for many years and still there], Charles Giuliano, Charles Beye, Sid Blumenthal, Bob Blumenthal, Ben Blumenberg, Janet Maslin, Tim Crouse, Ben Gerson, Art Kaplan, Peter Guralnik, Jon Landau, Ken Emerson, Deac Rossell, Larry Stark, Judy Quigg Stark, and cartoonist David Sipress [usually found today in *The New Yorker*]. Oh yes, and one of my talented art directors was Lynn Staley, who married Marty Linsky and then went to become the design director for *Newsweek*.

It was not Frank but Ted Anzalone. He was not the city treasurer, but Mayor Kevin White's aide, and married to Joanne Prevost, who ran the Real Property agency in Boston. Teddy Gross ran follow-ups on Anzalone, as he was about to head to trial for money laundering [convicted in 1984 on at least one count], but that story broke in *BAD* when I was there, not because we did the bidding of the FBI, but because Fat Vinny Teresa, a lower-level Mafia member, was testifying at the time and named a City Hall connection. When the local Boston establishment press did not expose that name, we went digging and discovered that Vinny actually said Ted Anzalone's name, so we just quoted the hearing record. No big deal in terms of journalism ethics, but a big slap against city government.

Let me add one more glitch: Before Ray Riepen bought the *Phoenix* from Jeff Tarter; he first tried to join forces with Steve Mindich and become the power behind *BAD*. Ray wanted a media empire. He wanted a newspaper, and back in 1970 he didn't care which one. I was privy to a financial discussion between Ray and Steve. The upshot was Steve was giving this serious thought, but it appears Ray wanted a bigger piece for his money, and I think Steve showed signs of balking or trouble up the road. In short order, while the deal was still percolating, BLAM-O!—Riepen buys the *Phoenix*. I thought Steve was going to have a royal fatal fit—justifiably. But he got right back up, dusted himself off, and found new money to keep hope alive. So, when 1972 came around and the *Phoenix* staff was talking "union," Mindich salivated. He circled over Richard Missner's head—exactly where I would have been. Then another BLAM-O!—Missner sells the *Phoenix* to Mindich, giving him the paper's name, circulation data, advertising rolls, and the all-seeing glass eye of George Kimball.

Editor Arnie Reisman. Photo courtesy of Reisman.

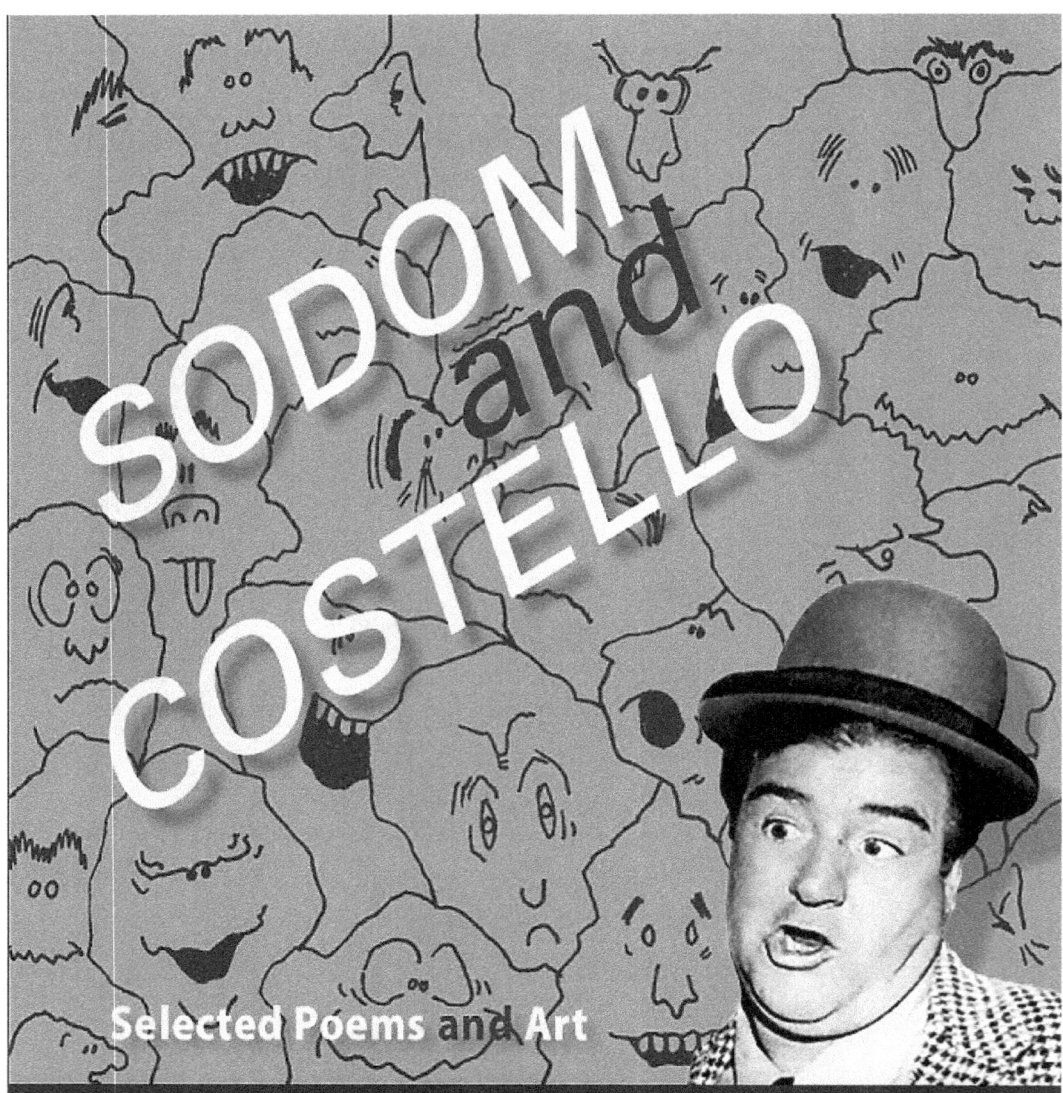

Sodom and Costello, a humorous book of verse by Reisman.

Publisher Stephen Mindich in his car. Photo by Charles Giuliano.

Mindich dressed for success. Photo by Charles Giuliano.

After *BAD* I was hired by the *Boston Herald Traveler*. Here with colleague Ian Forman. Giuliano archive.

Hanging out with Yoko Ono at The Ritz. Giuliano archive.

Applause from John Belushi. Photo by Charles Giuliano.

Covering the Godfather of Soul. Photo by Charles Giuliano.

Jean Bergantini Grillo was art critic and an editor for *Cambridge Phoenix*

In 1969 Jean Bergantini Grillo was hired by publisher Jeffrey Tarter who was launching a weekly paper, *The Cambridge Phoenix*.

I asked her to ID people in a staff photograph by Jeff Albertson. She has kept a lot of vintage material including notes from editor Harper Barnes.

She responded, "I'm holding the original *The Cambridge Phoenix* press kit in my hands. Cover photo by Peter Simon [man at newsstand selling newspapers]. Inside are pages with a list of staff: Jeff Tarter, publisher; Robert Ventola, advertising director [he's the dark-haired man in back behind Jeff that I called Al], Managing Editor Tom Bethell [my personal hero who is not in this photo]; Senior Editor Mark Lieberman [not in photo]; Senior Editor Jean Bergantini Grillo; City Editor April Smith; Stephen Davis, contributing editor; Marsha Clayton Daniel [she's with the blonde streak in her dark hair], contributing editor for cinema; Arthur Friedman, contributing editor for theatre [not in photo]; Laura Shapiro [not in photo] contributing editor for music; Production Manager Steve Diamond [who I think is in the picture]; Staff Photographer Peter Simon; Columnist Joe Pilati; Columnist John Bellairs [whom I don't remember at all]. I have the original statement of purpose, the original ad rate card, and lots of other stuff. I've been saving all this neat stuff for the right time. I'm working on a play about my *Phoenix* days, so have been holding on to these "mementoes." But eventually, I'm donating the lot."

From 1969 to 1972, she was competition as another popular and widely read art critic. We caught up recently to discuss that era. She stated that she thought of herself more as an editor and art reporter than art critic.

Charles Giuliano In the staff photo of the *Cambridge Phoenix* by Jeff Albertson, you said that you were 24 at the time.

Jean Bergantini Grillo I had taught for a year at Waltham High School. A play that I am writing has to do with that year of teaching. Working with kids after school, we were reading *Autobiography of Malcolm X*, and it got me fired.

It was the beginning of my writing career. I was editor of my college newspaper. We were very radical. I was a part of Young People's Socialist League. I got into teaching when my husband was getting an MFA at Boston University. We needed an income. Then I got fired and was desperate to get a job.

There was an ad looking for writers. I sent clips from my college paper. That's how I got hired at *The Cambridge Phoenix*. I was the only person on that paper that didn't know somebody at BU, other than my artist husband.

Jeffrey Tarter [publisher, a Vietnam veteran who had written for *Stars and Stripes*] was older than me, but most of the staff were younger. I was married. It was called *The Cambridge Phoenix* because it started in Cambridge. I always said we should drop Cambridge and just call it *The Phoenix*. It launched in 1969.

I had a lot to do with the establishment of the paper, and my fine arts coverage was an aspect of what I was doing. I hired Laura Shapiro and Chuck Kraemer. I worked with Harper Barnes in editing. When I walked in the door they were bringing in the desks.

I have the first letter that went out with our statement of purpose. "This is our rate card and what we charge for advertising." I was there at the birth of the paper.

CG Describe Jeffrey Tarter.

JBG He was a very buttoned-down kind of guy. He had been in Vietnam. I remember a section he wanted to call "Free Fire Zone'" which was a term from the war. He had a relative that owned Avery Labels and that was where some of our financing was coming from. He was kind of square but had the sense that the *Globe* and *Herald* were not publishing what young people were interested in. Harper was really the one that provided a journalistic point of view. He was the best hire that Jeff made.

I was the senior editor, and art was just one of my duties. Harper was the editor, and I worked under him.

CG I sense that he came in later.

JBG I have the first issue but not here [Rhode Island]; it's back in New York. I would have to look at the masthead. I think that Jeff was the first editor. We had columnists of which I was one.

[There was no editor. Tom Bethell was listed as managing editor.]

CG When did C. Wendell Smith become a part of the mix?

JBG I would have to check that. I'm in touch with him. He is still doing poetry. He's a doctor, you know. He went to med school after *The Phoenix/Real Paper*. I send him my plays and he sends me his poetry.

CG What was the mood and feeling of what you were doing at that time?

JBG In the beginning it was strictly the business of launching a newspaper. It wasn't a radical paper. Later, when it evolved as *The Real Paper*, was when it was radicalized. Initially, we were going to be a newspaper with ad rates. There was a business plan and we were going out to advertisers. Everyone on staff had functions.

[*The Real Paper* was organized by the former *Cambridge Phoenix* staff when the paper was sold to Stephen Mindich. It ran from August 2, 1972 through 1981.]

Somebody had all the movie theaters but didn't want someone to advertise for some reason or other. I thought you have to have advertising. If we pick and choose who advertises we're not going to last long. There was a constant discussion of how radicalized we were going to be. We had to think about, were we just going to be a mouthpiece, or were we going to be a paper?

There was always that push and pull. Abbie Hoffman and some underground people came to speak to us. They were talking about getting explosives and blowing up buildings. I remember thinking, that's kind of dangerous. People can get hurt. I'm not so sure. Some of these people are not that heroic.

I was just trying to make enough money to live. I came from a different background than some of these kids. I went to a state college.

[University of Rhode Island. She was one of six daughters. Her father ran a bakery and the girls all had jobs.]

After a year, *The Phoenix* ran out of money and we were going to try to be a cooperative. I started to bring in food for the staff. One of the staff members [photographer Peter Simon] who said, "I'm not going to work unless I get paid," came in with a brand new car. I was broke and he had family money.

CG Talking with Arnie Reisman and Harper Barnes, there are different takes on Tarter. The perception was that he wanted to create a version of *The Village Voice*.

JBG He had a business model. He didn't want to be an underground paper. He wanted to be an above-ground paper. Those of us who signed on wanted to be above ground, but we were a part of the counterculture.

CG He was founding a paper that would compete with *Boston After Dark* for the extensive [250,000] college/youth market. At that time, *BAD* was entirely focused on entertainment. Because of the diversity of *The Cambridge Phoenix*, the Stephen Mindich paper came around to that at a later time to keep up and compete.

JBG Everyone wanted to cover music. My husband, Stephen, was an artist and that was radical. Parents want their kids to be doctors and lawyers, but nobody tells them to go paint. For us, coming from parents who lived through the Depression, art was a radical thing to do. A lot of the artists I interviewed had a very radical sensibility. I didn't have an art background. I was an English major. I thought of myself as an art reporter. When I interviewed Walker Evans I asked if he kept in touch with the people he photographed? What did he think of them as symbols of destitution? It impressed me that he had feelings for them and wasn't just shooting and running.

CG He and James Agee published *Let Us Now Praise Famous Men*. Belinda Rathbone, daughter of Perry Rathbone, wrote an Evans biography. She discussed how Evans returned and stayed in touch with those families. On holidays he brought them presents.

JBG She probably got that from my interview. Evans talked about that. She may have read my article in *The Phoenix*. As [I was] an English major, Walker Evans wasn't someone I knew about. Literally, I was reading the book before doing the interview. I was as young reporter.

CG You said that everyone wanted to write about rock, so how did it come about that you covered art?

JBG I said one of the more revolutionary things you can do is paint. They pooh-poohed that. Nobody wanted to take my art pictures. [Staff photographers were Simon and Jeff Albertson.] Lois Greenfield, who went on to a great career as a photographer said, "I'll go." None of the guys wanted to take my pictures. They all wanted to do the rock and roll stuff. Lois, who went to Brandeis, went on to a great career. She became the dance photographer for the *Village Voice*.

CG Did you hire Laura Shapiro as a dance writer?

JBG I saw her stuff in the BU paper and said that we had to hire her and Chuck Kraemer. There were people I saw in the BU paper.

CG Jeff Albertson was also from BU.

JGB He was already on staff. I hired Laura and Chuck. [Kraemer was later an on air arts reporter for WCVB and WGBH.]

CG Steve Davis [rock critic] was also from BU.

JBG He was buddies with Peter Simon.

CG So they were all from BU. Talking with Arnie Reisman, my editor at the Brandeis Justice, he worked with a lot of Brandeis graduates. It seems that the alternative media was either BU or Brandeis.

JBG I was from Rhode Island College. I was doing listings, which was critical. People were buying the paper to find out about things. I have all kinds of notes with Harper about how we should do the listings. Years later, I met people who said, "You don't know how important it was to us to be listed in *The Phoenix*."

We started with 320 subscriptions. Later, we had a circulation of 50,000. We went from paid subscriptions to free. Hawkers were something that changed us overnight. That changed distribution. I have a letter from a Brandeis student. It said, "We don't want *Boston After Dark* on our campus. We want *The Phoenix*." *Boston After Dark* had distribution that we didn't have. That's when we went with hawkers and it put us on the map.

CG What kind of money were you making?

JBG It only lasted for a year, then they ran out of money. I was making $8,000 as a teacher. When I was fired we were totally broke. Then, $8000 was the entry salary that Tartar was paying for a senior editor. When the paper ran out of money, we agreed to work as a commune. We'll try to get advertising and make what we make. It was Peter Simon who said, "I have to get paid." He announced that he would not take photographs unless he got paid, then drove in with a brand new car.

CG At that point Ray Riepen and a partner [Richard Missner] bought out Tartar.

JBG We started to get salaries again.

CG Did you know Riepen?

JBG No, no, no. That was the end of Jeff.

CG Day to day the paper was being run by Harper?

JBG Yes. Harper was my editor, then Paul Solman was my editor (as *The Real Paper*).

CG Harper was a trained journalist who had worked at the *St. Louis Post Dispatch*. As he describes it, he was running a hippie paper and wanted to keep that while applying journalistic standards.

JBG I have wonderful correspondence with Harper in which we discussed that. He wrote to me, "Yes, Jean, I agree, we should stop using far fucking out."

CG As I understand it, when Riepen and Missner took over, they wanted to make the paper more commercial. Part of that was firing Harper. The staff rallied and walked out. There was a scab Phoenix but eventually the staff returned with a union. Part of that was negotiating severance pay for Harper. He lived on it for several months. Then Riepen and Missner sold the *Phoenix* to Mindich. There was a pattern of Steve buying competitors and either merging or folding them. That's when the staff formed *The Real Paper* as a cooperative and elected Solman as editor.

JBG I was with *The Real Paper* for a short time. I had been offered a job at the *Boston Globe* as an art critic. At that time Stephen [Grillo] was showing at an art gallery in New York, so our future was to go there. I always saw myself as an editor much more than having a column. I edited everybody's stuff.

When everyone went to Woodstock, I couldn't go. I was editing the stuff that came back. Somebody had to be there. People were coming in saying, "I'll never wash the dirt off my body." I said, "Hand me your copy please."

I saw a lot of people were just destroying themselves with drugs. There were brilliant minds that just fried their brains. Some of us had to work and edit that copy. On top of that I interviewed Walker Evans, Andy Warhol, and Lynda Benglis. I was talking to people with brilliant artistic minds.

There was no support for what I was doing. There was disdain, because they were just interested in rock and roll. But I loved rock and roll. We were at the Tea Party, dancing and doing all that stuff.

My favorite exhibition was something that Marty Mull did [with Todd McKie] called "Flush with the Walls" in the basement men's room of the MFA. We covered it. Nobody else did. The MFA at that time did not have a department of contemporary art. That was shocking.

CG Ken Moffett was the first curator when a department was formed in 1971.

JBG I'm so sorry he is gone. Ken was a great champion of my husband's art. He came to our house and looked at the work. He was a curator willing to get off his butt and look at artists. A lot of curators don't do that.

I interviewed anybody who was doing anything. I did a range of things. I interviewed Boris Mirski who was showing the Boston Expressionists. I saw myself as a reporter. I asked people what was behind what they were showing.

I called a black artist who was having a show. He kept saying, "Yah gottah know Trane." I didn't know what he meant, and I asked my husband who said he means Coltrane. I was educating myself as a reporter to understand what was behind what people were doing. I didn't go in as a critic. I went in as a reporter. I explained the work as a reporter so that the audience who went to see the work would have a better understanding.

CG It was a time of transition and change. The artists were activists. They organized the Studio Coalition, which was the nation's first open studios event.

There were talks that I launched at Parker 470 Gallery. The gallery was mobbed when Tony Thompson moderated a discussion with Perry Rathbone. It was polite until Joan Trachtman, wife of the protest artist Arnold Trachtman, bluntly asked him when the museum was going to appoint a contemporary curator. Not long after Rathbone called me at *The Herald* to tell me that he had hired Moffett. Out of those meetings came the Boston Visual Artists Meeting.

JBG My husband was a part of those meetings and was the first director of the BVAU.

It was a time when America was terrified by young people. *Newsweek* came and interviewed us. They said, "Tell us what's really going on in the world?" Like we had answers. There was a youth quake and I was extremely skeptical. Imagine, adults coming in and asking us for answers. Weren't they supposed to be telling us what was going on?

I saw a lot of drugged-up people thinking that they had the answers and I said, "Sorry." I just saw a lot of fucked-up people. I felt we needed to educate ourselves by listening to each other. The government was fucked up, and things weren't right, but I wasn't ready to go bomb things. I didn't see that as a solution.

CG When did you move to New York?

JBG In 1972.

CG I understand that you became involved in elected politics.

JBG There is a position in New York for a male and female district leader. It's an elected office. You represent your geographic voting area. I was the Democratic leader for the 66th Assembly District. I held that position for ten years. You report to the county Democratic Party. They have a meeting once a month and you fill them in on what's happening. You report on what's happening in your area.

As I got into my playwriting, it was more and more interfering. I retired from that in 2015. 9/11 was the catalyst for playwriting. We live just four blocks away and I saw them come down. I have a niece who got out of one of the towers. After that, I was a food server at St. Paul's. We were feeding the recovery workers. It was a defining moment in my life. I was freelancing at the time. There was a magazine I created. For nine years *Cable Avail* covered the cable television industry. An advertisement segment is called an availability. With a partner we launched the magazine in 1991. With the dot-com collapse we had to shut it down. 9/11 really finished off all that. People wouldn't travel. I worked at St. Paul's for eight months.

Working there I saw so many people change their lives. Actors became ministers and ministers became actors. I had always been writing nonfiction and I decided to do something with creative writing. I sent some stuff to people I had met in the TV industry. Someone I respected said, "These are not scripts Jean. These are plays. Your dialogue is spot on."

I sent work to HP Studios and won a scholarship to their playwrights' workshop in 2005 and have been with them ever since.

CG I understand that you are writing a play about *The Phoenix*.

JBG It's a two-part play and it begins with the seminal moment when I got fired. That catapulted me because I had always wanted to be a writer. I was told to teach. That was the avenue to the middle class. Four of my sisters teach. So that is what I did. I was always meant to be a writer and did criticism when I was in college.

Part Two is about *The Phoenix*. It had difficulties about women. Laura, Lois, and myself had to keep our elbows up. It was a male-dominated place. It was not easy. Harper, I must say, really made it survivable. He came in and said, "It's okay. It's revolutionary to write a grammatical sentence. It's all right to be coherent." They put one of my art reviews [Gongora/Merkin] on the front page. I have a note from Tom Bethell about how much he loved the piece.

Somebody came back from Florida with lurid photos of old people on the beach. There were details of wrinkles and sagging flesh. They thought it was funny and wanted to do a spread. I said, "These are our grandparents and it's going to be us someday. It's not funny."

There was always a push-pull about what are we here for? Did you know that I'm in the Nixon Tapes?

Tricia Nixon came to the MFA to give them a couple of Ming Dynasty vases.

CG I was there.

JBG It was the same day that the photo of a young girl running with her clothes burned off by napalm. I was so incensed that I handed Tricia Nixon a note. I wrote, "Nixon gets toasted while women and children get roasted." Not subtle, but I was furious. How could the MFA allow this to happen? I broke every rule of journalism to use that opportunity to hand her the letter. There was no other avenue to express my outrage.

She handed the letter to a Secret Service agent and I thought, it's the end of that. Little did I know that Tricky Dick read the letter and he was outraged. It was captured on tape in the Oval Office. *People Magazine* called me for comment. I had no idea. That's my claim to fame.

I have always been a radical at heart though I didn't look it. People said, "Oh, she just covers art." But I had a very radical soul. I put it in my writing and work.

CG Did you know George Kimball?

JBG Oh George, OMG. It's like Westerns when they always have a character outside the saloon and everybody tolerates him. He wrote well on sports, but he was a major alcoholic. He came in many times and just fell down, passed-out drunk. I don't care what you do in your off hours, but function and get the copy in. I would come into the office and he would be just blotto. And he had been there from the night before. I can't write his copy for him. That was the whole macho vibe at that office. I had to hold a lot of that together and edit the copy. Which I did, but sometimes it was, "Hello, I can't read this."

For some of them it was a lark and they were rich hippies. For me, it was a job and I needed the money. I took Tartar to court for back pay and won. My buddies were Laura and Lois. Paul Solman and I were close.

CG You describe yourself as holding down the office, reporting, and married. To what extent did you participate in the counterculture?

JBG Totally. My husband and I marched in Washington. We were gassed. I wanted to shake up the art world. When we covered "Flush with the Walls" we criticized the MFA for not including contemporary art. We interviewed Moffett and asked why that hadn't happened sooner. We criticized the MFA for having stolen artwork. I went to RISD and interviewed Warhol. I was trying to show that art could be revolutionary. I wanted art to be covered.

My husband had his first show in New York in 1968. We were constantly moving back and forth. We were much more aligned with what was happening in New York. He was in the Prince Street Gallery and Green Street Gallery. We were on West Broadway painting a gallery space. I said to my husband, "Nobody is going to come down here." The Bowery Gallery started on the Bowery. It was artists taking control of their art. We are going to show our own work because the dealers don't know what's going on. Dealers were taking so much money there was a movement to start a union.

In New York, I worked for the *Village Voice*. OMG. Compared to *The Voice The Phoenix* was heaven. I saw more shit there. I hightailed it out of there and went to work for the *Soho News*. My best experience was with *The Daily News*. I was with them for about four years doing TV criticism. I had such a good time. It was so much fun. But *The Voice*, OMG, it was absolute chaos. But that's another story.

Critic and editor Jean Bergantini Grillo (wearing a skirt). Photo by Jeff Albertson.

Grillo is seated with other *Cambridge Phoenix* staff members. Photo by Jeff Albertson.

John and Leah Sdoucos booked Concerts on the Common for Mayor Kevin White

Music producer John Sdoucos divides seasons between Florida and Cape Cod. He books concerts and festivals coast-to-coast.

"I just got off the phone with the Mayor of Denver. We are planning something with them," he said, "but I'm all yours."

We explored a career that started when he was a junior at Boston University. It was a short walk to Storyville where club owner and entrepreneur, George Wein, hired him to do promotion. That expanded in 1954 when Elaine Lorrilard fell by the club. She asked Wein to do something for the poor little rich people of Newport, Rhode Island.

In 1968 he started booking talent for Summerthing, then Concerts on the Common in 1970. His company, Music Productions, did it all from booking and managing, to launching music festivals. He created a network of colleges in New England extending to Virginia and Pennsylvania. From clubs to colleges, he sustained musicians like Barry and the Remains, The Hallucinations, Barbarians, Bruce Springsteen, James Taylor, and Aerosmith. Later he launched New England tours for British Invasion bands like Jeff Beck, Yardbirds, Cream, Led Zeppelin, and The Who.

Leah Sdoucos started to work with her husband, music producer John Sdoucos, as a teenager in the 1960s. She grew up in the music business. In 1980, she moved to California and went in another direction, and is now retired from a successful business. As she told me, heart and soul is still with her time booking acts for the college circuit. She has particularly poignant memories of working with Barry and The Remains. Even today it is painful to recall what might have been for the best Boston group of that era. Their careers went south after opening for the final Beatles tour in 1966.

Charles Giuliano Overall, the Boston scene in the 1960s never had the national reputation it deserved. You respond with a list that you characterized as The Beantown All Stars.

John Sdoucos In no particular order: Peter Wolf, Steve Mindich [publisher], Nate Cobb [*Boston Globe*], Charles Giuliano, Ernie Santosuosso [*Boston Globe*], Barry and The Remains, James Taylor, Boston, Bonnie Raitt, J. Geils, James Montgomery, Fred Taylor [Jazz Workshop/ Paul's Mall], Leah Sdoucos, George Wein, Kathy Kane [Associate Mayor under Kevin White], George Papadopoulos [Unicorn], Al Perry, and the folks at WBCN, the WBZ people like Larry Glick, Donna Summers, Kevin White, the Berklee College of Music guys, Herb Pomeroy and his musicians Johnny Neves, Varty Haroutunian, Ray Santisi [piano], the whole Storyville scene, WBUR's Ken Squier, Father Norman J. O'Connor, Joe Bucci, Lennie Sogaloff [club owner], Aerosmith, The Cars, The Barbarians, The Lost, Modern Lovers, Charlie McKenzie [manager of Boston], oh boy, and I could go on. Those are just some of the Beantown All Stars.

When producing and traveling around the country I hear about Boston music, its groups, the Newport Jazz Festival. We started that at Storyville when Elaine Lorrilard came in and said, "Can you do something for us poor rich folks in Newport?" George [Wein] said, "Yes, I've been walking around with this idea for a couple of years. I would like to bring jazz down there, but I want to do it festival style."

So we started the first one, then Newport Folk Festival. Boston has been a real impact on the national music scene.

CG My focus is on events from 1968 to the 1980s, which I am describing as an overlooked golden age for Boston. You were a part of that.

JS I guess so. It got me off and running. Fred Taylor and I discovered Joe Bucci [August 9, 1927 to September 30, 2008] the organ player who was playing like

Count Basie in a joint in Lynn. I was going to Boston University and working at Storyville [Wein's jazz club in Copley Square]. I was a junior at the school of communications, which was on Exeter Street and Storyville was right around the corner. I was doing promotion for George. Fred was hanging out and had that famous tape recorder.

So we recorded Bucci, got him going, and landed a record deal [*Wild About Basie!* Capitol Records]. Fred and I set up at 739 Boylston Street, where the Marathon bomb went off a couple of years ago. That was our office. He was HT Productions and I was Music Productions.

Out of the same office, he was booking bands locally and I was working with Wein. It was a productive time for me. We went to Newport in 1954. He invented the festival and I made everyone aware of it. My job was to run all over New England to radio and TV stations and newspapers.

Ultimately, I went national while Fred stayed local. We both got a lot out of Boston. So did George.

CG When did Harry Paul become a part of the Newport organization?

JS His job was advertising. He placed ads. I was the guy running around doing promotion. Harry had a budget and placed ads in newspapers and radio stations. My job was to hit the street. I would go to a radio station and they would say, "You're doing more for Dave Brubeck than Columbia Records." I was making sure they were playing his stuff because he was a part of the festival.

CG Early on it seems that your primary focus was jazz?

JS I grew up at Storyville where I was introduced to Wein by none other that Father O'Connor.

[Father Norman James O'Connor, nicknamed "The Jazz Priest" (November 20, 1921 to June 29, 2003) was a Roman Catholic priest known for playing and promoting jazz music. On a number of live Newport recording he is heard introducing musicians.]

We were both producing a jazz radio show. Ken Squier was my announcer on WBUR. Father O'Connor was also producing a jazz show. I would get jazz artists who were appearing around town and Storyville was one of the places I would go to.

George invited me to work for him. I made sure that customers who came in were well taken care of. I can still see it now. Elaine and Louis Lorrilard came in. There were settees at the back of the club and George was talking about jazz with them. I was the kid who would stand by listening. They wanted jazz in Newport because that's where they lived.

CG There is a strong BU connection. Others at BU include Wein, Taylor, yourself, WGBH DJ, Ron Della Chiesa, Steve Mindich, David Bieber. I was there for graduate school.

JS George was ahead of us, and in fact taught a course on jazz. Faye Dunaway and I were in some of the same classes. What a beauty.

CG She married Peter Wolf and inspired the song "The Lady Makes Demands."
When did you start managing groups? Did you manage The Hallucinations? [1965–1968 with lead singer Peter Wolf, who then joined J. Geils Band.]

JS At that time we were everything. We managed and booked The Remains, The Hallucinations, Moulty and The Barbarians. They had a hit with "Are You a Boy or Are You a Girl." Leah [Sdoucos] and I managed The Remains.

CG Talk about The Remains. In my interview with Jon Landau he recalled them as one of the best of the Boston bands.
[The Remains were a mid-1960s rock group led by Barry Tashian. Although they never achieved national success, they were popular in New England, and were one of the opening acts on The Beatles' final US tour in 1966.]

JS They were Boston University kids. That's how we got connected. We were booking and managing them. We got them on some shows with The Beatles. They were going in different directions and broke up. Barry got more into producing. I've got his number and we talk every couple of years.

CG Arguably, Barry and the Remains and The Hallucinations were just too early. In the mid to late 1960s there wasn't the national focus on emerging bands that would come later. Then things got even more muddled with the fiasco of The Bosstown Sound. The Remains got attention opening for the Beatles but it didn't equate to establishing a national reputation.

JS Later we were booking Aerosmith before they broke out. James Taylor was hanging out in the office looking for gigs. I got him going. There's another one. I got him his first gig at The Charity Ward in Cambridge. I said, "James there's 35 bucks for it." That was his first gig ever. He came back and said, "John they stiffed me and only gave me 25 bucks." I pulled ten bucks out of my pocket to make up the difference. Then I got him going for a couple hundred bucks here and there. We started him on the college circuit. We had colleges all over the Northeast, down into Virginia and Pennsylvania. You name it. There were five or six colleges in Worcester.

We got him up to $500 then $1500 and $2500. All the way up to the days of James and Carole King. Fred [Taylor] and I were instrumental in getting a lot of people and projects started.

CG I heard him at one of those early Cambridge club appearances. I talked with him after the gig but he had a curfew. Then the album came out on Apple. I remember Ken Emerson, who worked with me at *Avatar* and later *Boston After Dark*, trashing that album which I loved. I respected Ken, but felt he got that dead wrong. Critics can be like that.

My friend Rick Robbins knew Arlo Guthrie from Stockbridge School. We went together to the Newport Folk Festival. I spent an afternoon in Arlo's room at the Viking Hotel. He and James were rehearsing Taylor's "Country Road." During Arlo's set he brought James on for a duet. Those are intimate moments you never forget.

JS There were a lot of things we never got credit for. We were ripping and running. We were doing everything.

CG Did you book the Hallucinations?

JS Absolutely, we had them all over the place. Do you remember the cellars in Kenmore Square where everyone played?

CG The Rathskeller better known as The Rat.

JS Not the Dugout across from BU. The Rat, my God. We put everybody and anybody we could in there: The Hallucinations, The Remains.

CG Let's talk about Summerthing. Did it start in 1968, and were you in on the beginning?

JS I was doing its bookings like the Clancy Brothers in Southie. We had Smokey

Robinson in Roxbury. That led the next year to Concerts on the Common. Mrs. Forbes came to me one day and said, "The Boston Arts Festival needs help." Just like George Wein I said, "I've got an idea." I told her we needed a location like The Boston Common. We can put some acts there and set it up with controls to collect admissions and see that the profits go to The Boston Arts Festival.

Thank goodness for people like Herb Gleason who was the attorney for the city. We went to the city and got an okay but had to go to Beacon Hill as well. We met with governor Mike Dukakis. The Hill and Irish politicians were against it. "All those people are going to come and ruin the city, blah blah."

We finally got that established for 1970. That's when we met. In 1969 I was involved with John Shearer who got Schaefer Beer to sponsor concerts at Harvard Stadium. I was involved because they were going to help us with Summerthing, which never happened.

My job was to see that acts got in, on, and out. I can still see Janis Joplin coming up the stairs. There are about 20 steps to the stage. She's coming up with, not one, but two bottles of cheap Kentucky bourbon. She had a bottle in each hand, Charles. I looked at her and said, "Hey babe, no, no, no, you can't come on stage with booze."

Looking at me she did a swoop and said, "I'm sorry" with the left hand passes me a bottle and keeps on going to the stage clutching one in her right hand. Can you see the picture, Charles?

CG I was at that concert. What do you remember about that performance?

JS Ragtag.

CG I covered Miles Davis at Harvard Stadium just after the release of *Bitches Brew*. Later that week, I caught him with the same group at Lennie's on the Turnpike. The band was Jack DeJohnette, drums, Michael Henderson, bass, Gary Bartz, soprano sax, John McLaughlin sat in. He had Keith Jarrett and Chick Corea playing early Fender Rhodes keyboards.

That night, after the gig, in the Green Room Miles asked me, "I got Keith and Chick but can't keep them both. Who should I get rid of?" He fired Chick, which in hindsight seems like a mistake. It's known that Keith hated playing an electric piano where Chick later went far with developing technology.

JS We worked with Lennie's. You mentioned Jon Landau. He hung out at our office. He was at Brandeis. I had a lot of those kids hanging out. Don Law ran the social committee that arranged acts for BU concerts. Don worked for us for a while. People would work with us then leave the office, like the manager for Dionne Warwick. We were doing a lot of dates with her. Landau asked, "Whenever you do Bruce Springsteen can I get in?" We said, "Absolutely." We were doing a lot of gigs. There were a lot of dates all over the place in his early career. We had him in a couple of clubs in Connecticut, Worcester.

Bruce loved to play pinball. He would say, "John you have to book me in clubs with pinball machines." That's how Landau got to hang out with him. They became friends. That's the evolution. That's the process. Nobody all of a sudden becomes a manager.

CG What kind of money were you getting for Springsteen?

JS Probably in the five hundreds range. Not $500,000 like now. Less zeros. We booked club dates then colleges. We got maybe $1500. We were booking The Kingsmen.

[The Kingsmen were a 1960s band from Portland, Oregon best known for their 1963 recording of Richard Berry's "Louie Louie." It was Number 2 spot on the Billboard charts for six weeks.]

The college circuit was important. When groups outgrew clubs they couldn't jump to arenas. There had to be an intermediary step. We were getting calls from major New York agencies. They were bringing in the British Invasion. They were asking for gigs to keep them on tour across the country. As New England went so went rock 'n' roll.

Frank Barsalona [March 31, 1938–November 22, 2012] of Premier Talent had one of the world's biggest rock agencies at the time. He would call me about the British acts and say, "John you've got to keep these acts going in the colleges in the Northeast."

CG What were some of the groups? Jeff Beck [with Rod Stewart and Ron Wood]?

JS Absolutely, many times. The Youngbloods many times. The Who, absolutely, we did them all. Boston was important as the jump-off point. Maybe because of us, the bookings, people like myself, and yourself.

CG A factor in why Boston was a locus for counterculture and youth marketing is the ratio of college students relative to overall population.

[Greater Boston is ranked tenth in population among US metropolitan statistical areas, home to 4,732,161 people as of the 2014 US Census estimate, and sixth among combined statistical areas, with a population of 8,099,575. It has a density of 13,841 people per square mile (5,344/square kilometer), and Greater Boston is the 4th most densely populated region in the United States, after New York Metro Area, Greater Los Angeles and South Florida Metro Area. The student population of Boston is estimated at 250,000 with 20,709 across the river in Cambridge. There are also a number of schools and colleges within an hour's drive of Boston.]

JS It's America's college town. Students come there from all over the world. Take Clark University in Worcester. They had a capacity of 750 to 850 seats. That was a nicely scaled venue and a step up from clubs. We had Jimi Hendrix and Janis Joplin there.

CG Coming back to Summerthing in 1968. Entertainment went into neighborhoods. It was targeted to specific communities like Irish Americans in Southie and African Americans in Roxbury, Hyde Park. That was a strategy of City Hall to bring a pacifying element into troubled neighborhoods during an era of social and political unrest. Music was seen as a vehicle for unification. When you were approached, what were politicians saying to you? Why would you put Smokey Robinson into a neighborhood?

JS Well for just the reasons you describe, to try to calm things down. It showed the neighborhoods that the city cared. Some of the selectmen, however, were opposed to the events. We didn't have any riots, other than Uptown in the Park. Do you remember those concerts at White Stadium? I produced them.

CG I saw a Sly Stone concert and mini riot there.

JS Yeah, there you go. They were breaking in on us if you want to call that a riot.

CG Okay, perhaps rampage is a better word.

JS They just broke in on us. That's why we stopped the series. The Elma Lewis School was to be the benefactor. We did a couple of events over two years.

CG At that time I was caught up in several riots. In addition to the Sly "rampage," the Newport Jazz Festival riot [1971], as well as an anti war protest/riot in Harvard Square. The Square was getting trashed routinely, including after the Janis Joplin concert at Harvard Stadium.

Let's talk about when Kathy Kane [she died at 78 in 2013] took you to meet Kevin White [September 25, 1929–January 27, 2012] about the 1970 series Concerts on the Common.

JS We were ready to go and Kathy said, "Kevin wants to talk to us." She was a dream, Ms. Everything. Kathy wanted to see that The Boston Arts Festival survived. We became friends.

CG I knew Kathy and Louis when the Institute of Contemporary Art, then all but dead, got restarted under Drew Hyde regrouping at the abandoned former venue on Soldier's Field Road. Drew worked with architect Edwin Childs and Adele Seronde through Summerthing. He got to know Kevin and the Kanes. Louis was a trustee of the ICA at that time. The Kanes were dedicated to the arts. He later founded Au Bon Pain.

JS Kathy and I went into White's office. We approached his desk. He looked up at us and said, "John Sdoucos, if you fuck this up, it's yours. If it scores, then it's mine."

I threw him an old Army highball. We did an about face and split. That was it.

CG So who got to own it, you or Kevin?

JS (*laughing*) We made sure he got good credit. It was on the Common. I have a large aerial photo of the site, which had snow fences. It shows people inside and outside.

CG What were you paying acts?

JS The most was $2,500. Chuck Berry. OMG! He had his car parked on Charles Street, not far away. It was my idea to package B.B. King, Bo Diddley, and Chuck Berry. Now here's Chuck standing in the wings. He hadn't been paid and we paid as we go.

He said, "Hey man I got to get my bread now." I said, "Don't worry." I paid everyone cash and they put it in their stocking. Do you remember those days? He said, "No man, I gottah get paid now." I said, "Charles you're going on in about ten minutes."

I don't know where I got it, but there was some money stashed and I gave it to him. I said what you are going to do now. He said, "Don't worry." He went into the wings and I followed him. He jumped off the stage and booked it all the way to Charles Street. He got to his car with me following him. He opened the trunk and took out the tire iron. He used it to remove a hubcap. In broad daylight he stashed the money. People walking by figured it was a black guy changing a tire. Then he hightailed it back to the stage. That was Chuck Berry.

CG After one of the events on the Common, I watched the cleanup crew. They had a huge pyramid from raking the field. There were hundreds of bottles of Boone's Farm Apple Wine. Costa del Sol was another version of cheap wine. That was a product of M.S. Walker based in Boston. They sponsored a series of rock concerts of local bands at the Hatch Shell.

My editor, Sam Hirsch, insisted that I write a Sunday piece. After the interview, the owner asked if I would like a few samples. He gave me an assorted case of gin, tequila, vodka, and bourbon. Not long after, I threw a party. When I got back to the office, with a smile Sam asked, "Did he take care of you?" There was a lot of that. Cameron Dewar, an old hand at the drama desk, regaled me with tales of how, back in the day, at Christmas, the office would be piled high with cases of booze. Payola scandals changed that by the time I was on the beat.

There was always beer and wine backstage during the concerts. After your Allman Brothers date, I was feeling mellow. The norm was to file right after a concert. But I hooked up and found myself in a North End apartment cracking a couple more bottles. Nearing deadline, remembering the gig, I begged her to take me to the office. Wearing a bikini and a big sombrero she draped over me as I wrote the review.

At my desk that morning you called but couldn't stop laughing. "What the heck happened to you, man?" you asked. I didn't know what you meant until I read the paper. The headline was "25,000 Fans See the Allman Brothers." It seemed that I added a zero. Also the second graph more or less repeated the first one. Nobody other than you said a word to me. A rule of journalism is, no matter what, never blow a deadline. Many a story gets saved at the rim.

JS I have a great photo of that gig taken from a nearby rooftop. I will try to find it.

CG There is a long history of racism in Boston particularly the issue of bussing which divided the city. Did you have anything to do with the James Brown Boston Garden concert during the weekend when Martin Luther King, Jr. was assassinated?

JS Yes. Kevin White called me and said, "You can't do this; there's going to be a riot." I said, "Your Honor, if you don't do it we will have a riot." I distinctly remember my words to him. I did the booking for the James Brown concert. He said, "We're going to have all those people down there and it's going to cause a riot." He said, "Those people."

I said, "If we don't do it we will have a riot." It clicked with him and to his credit he was a quick study. With him it didn't take long for a yes or no answer."

CG WGBH broadcast the live concert and looped it all weekend. The city remained calm and mourned a great loss through the soulful performance of James Brown.

Mayor White had a way of grabbing the spotlight. It was getting late at Boston Garden when he came onstage and announced, "The Stones have been busted in Rhode Island." There was a howl of protest from the audience. After an interval he called for our attention then stated, "But I got them out." It was a long wait, but the Stones finally went on for a great concert.

My attorney friend Marty Kaplan tells a different version of getting the Stones out of jail. There had been an altercation and Keith clocked a photographer. Several quick deals went down, but as usual, Kevin took the bow.

(We contacted the Boston attorney who had a different insight into the incident.)

Martin Kaplan relates true story of Stones bust in Rhode Island

The Rolling Stones had a system of protecting themselves by retaining major law firms in every American city where they performed. It was the Stones' 1972 *Exile on Main Street* tour.

I got a call from Allen Arrow, a prominent music industry attorney. They wanted to hire a law firm to have people available in the event of any need for legal services. They didn't want to get hit with emergency bills.

The deal was to bill our hourly rate and there will be two free tickets for each night. You will have a partner for each performance to be reached in the event of an emergency and someone else at home.

The first night, I sent my partner Bob Fast, who was more senior. Then I got a panicky call at home. Fast said, "We need help. The Stones have been arrested in Warwick, Rhode Island."

On the way from Toronto to Boston, their plane was diverted because of fog. They were in a hanger waiting for a limo. Security let their guard down, and the media got too close. Keith slugged one of the photographers. It was the fault of security for not preventing that.

Cops arrived and arrested Keith, as well as Mick, who joined in. They were just trying to defend their privacy. So now, they're sitting in the clink and needed help.

Immediately, I called Jim St. Clair. His wife told me he was having dinner at The Bay Club. I got him on the phone and he said, "Let me get you the name of a top lawyer in Rhode Island." I called and the attorney said, "Meet me at the police station in Warwick."

So my wife and I raced there. Of course there was a crowd and reporters. It had become a media circus. The cops were saying, "We have to follow procedure." The cops turned them on to a local attorney who had a good relationship to them. We spoke with him and the attorney I had hired. I was talking to the police chief to get them out.

All of a sudden the chief said, "They're out of here. Put them in the limo."

I got into the parade of many cars following the limo. It was racing and I was behind, not letting anyone get in between. Reaching the Garden, I pulled the keys and left the car saying to security, "I'm the Stones attorney," and just left it there.

They were supposed to be there at eight but it was more like eleven or so. [They arrived and went on at one a.m. after a very long opening set by Stevie Wonder.] I had seen them sitting in a cell.

When I got to the Garden, Fast told me what happened. He was in a room with Joe Jordan, a high-ranking Boston Police officer. Jordan got on the phone with the police chief of Warwick. Jordan said, "I've got fourteen thousand kids waiting here for the Stones. I don't want a riot if they don't show up. So let's make a deal. You let them out right now and I owe you a favor. If you don't let them out I'll get you." The chief in Warwick said, "They're out of here."

Kevin White went onstage and said, "I have bad news and good news." [Actually, "The Stones have been busted, but I have sprung them!"] White kept the MBTA running until a half hour after the concert.

There were no problems, and my wife and I went the next night. That's the story, and Kevin White, who took credit, really had nothing to do with it. He wasn't on the phone with the people in Warwick as he claimed. Problems don't get solved by politicians talking to cops. It works from police chief to police chief. Why on earth would a Rhode Island police chief do a favor for Kevin White? Cops work with and trust each other.

The criminal charges were dropped, but the photographer sued for assault and battery. The Stones would not pay a dime. After a couple of years of back and forth the Stones did not apologize, but signed a letter to the plaintiff stating, "We regret the incident that happened." We were paid at our hourly rate, which was fine, but gave our firm the great memory of having gotten the Stones out of jail.

[It was reported that "Kevin White suggested the Stones give a private concert to his family and supporters to thank him for his help. He never got it."]

JS We had a similar problem getting Cream from Rhode Island to a gig at Brandeis. They went on at four a.m. We sent vehicles to get them. I was on the phone to the social committee chairman. At two a.m. I asked if they wanted to cancel. They hung in and it paid off.

CG That's the concert that Jon Landau covered for the *Brandeis Justice*. Another version of it ran in *Rolling Stone*. Famously, he trashed the group.

JS Then there was the opening of the *Jesus Christ Superstar* tour.

CG You were working late in the office with no time to drive to the gig during rush hour. You hired a chopper and invited me to join you. I vividly recall flying low and noting all the swimming pools in the suburbs. We landed in a football field, and getting out, we caused a fuss. The headline of my piece, a national scoop, was "Holy Smoke in Holyoke." I remember that there were nuns at the concert.

JS *Jesus Christ Superstar* is coming out again with John Legend.

Looking through my files I found your obit for Richie Havens. It talks about interviewing him after a performance of Concerts on the Common. We worked a lot with Richie, who was a great guy. You mentioned in the review that he had taken out his choppers and mostly mumbled. It was crossover as we managed and booked Richie. It was anything and everything.

CG What started as Concerts on the Common switched to the edge of Boylston

Street and became The Sunset Series.

JS By then I was on to other things. I get things started and then do something else.

CG As I recall George Davis took over.

JS He was Kathy's assistant. The Sunset Series started in 1970, but he wants to take credit for it. I booked the acts and produced the shows. He was that kind of a guy who wheedled in and wheedled out. He was an okay guy, but wanted to take credit. After 1970, a year or two later, I turned it over and let them run it.

CG Acts I covered there were Willie Nelson, Go-Gos, Milton Nascimento, Wayne Shorter, Pat Metheny, Julio Iglesias, Marvin Gaye, Dionne Warwick, Gladys Knight, Chaka Khan, John Denver, Whitney Houston, James Taylor, Joni Mitchell, Miles Davis, Johnny Mathis, Linda Ronstadt, Melissa Manchester, Oscar Peterson, Cyndi Lauper, Hall and Oates, and others.

There was another venue and a few concerts. It was on the Common and close to Beacon Street. I saw the Chambers Brothers there.

JS That could have been '69 and not '70. We did a lot with them.

CG Jimi Hendrix was supposed to play the Common.

JS Yeah, I remember, remind me what happened?

CG He died just before the gig.

JS We booked that date. There is a lot of this I have to look up. It's hard to keep track there were so many things we were involved with and still are.

Leah Sdoucos Recalls Barry and The Remains

Charles Giuliano Who was the musician you were promoting who recorded "Night Moves"?

Leah Sdoucos That was Ralph Graham. We negotiated a record deal for him with RCA. He put out an album called *Wisdom* produced by Leon Pendalis. Unfortunately, RCA was not the kind of company that knew how to promote a talent that major. Ultimately, the album didn't go anywhere, so they dropped him. I moved to California in 1980 and started to do other things.

CG Let's talk about the Boston scene.

LS I began with John (Sdoucos) working for George [Wein]. We were doing press and public relations for the Newport Jazz and Folk Festivals. John and I have worked together since 1963. I was then about eighteen or nineteen. John was brilliant and I was a quick learner. We could work together or separately and come out with the same wonderful result. Ultimately, we fell in love and got married.

We decided that we wanted to develop talent and produce programming. We explored the concert system in colleges throughout the Northeast. We were the first ones to do that. Then Buck Spurr of Lordly and Dame picked up on what we were doing. They became our competitors. Primarily Lordly and Dame was a speaker's bureau. We were Music Productions.

CG What acts were you working with?

LS Every single major artist in the recording industry. We worked with all of the major music agencies. Actually, we kept the agencies in business.

There were two categories. First were artists we were really pushing because we were in control of them. We had Barry and The Remains. It proved to be a bad time for us. A couple of guys came in from New York. We felt that they should not have done the Beatles tour, which proved to be true.

CG Why was that?

LS Nobody would know or care who they were. The fans just wanted The Beatles. They were screaming and yelling and had no idea who was on stage. It was a terrible thing. Barry [Tashian] after that said, "I'm out of here. I'm gone from this business." He moved to Nashville to sing in coffee houses, get married, and have children.

CG In hindsight one thinks, hey, they opened for The Beatles.

LS Yes, but it didn't work for their career. They didn't have adequate A&R representation at Epic Records to pick the right material for them. They were competing with groups like The Young Rascals.

CG When was that, and did you see any of the concerts with The Beatles?

LS It was the final Beatles tour in 1966, and sure, I saw lots of their concerts, but not with The Beatles. There is a documentary about The Remains called *The Lost Band*. [Boston Film Festival, World Premiere, 2008] That's been shown in small theaters all over the country including here in LA. I got to see Barry and Billy [Briggs]. The documentary shows clips of them on The Beatles tour and they look lost. People are walking by them as if, who the hell are you?

CG What were other Boston bands that you managed?

LS Tavares, they had some hits and signed with Capital Records. They were Cape Verdean brothers from Providence then New Bedford.

We were booking Steven Tyler. Aerosmith were guys who went to Boston University.

CG Was Frank Connelly managing them?

LS Not at that time. We never saw him. We dealt directly with the band.

CG Maxanne Sartori from WBCN took me to see them at The Surf in Revere. She was very excited about them. In the dressing room, Tyler was doing handstands. Onstage they seemed too much like the Stones.

LS We all thought that at the time. Even if they were a Stones throw off, they were a local band and we could all do very well. Working locally would be good for us and for them. In the early days, he was wearing all kinds of makeup emulating the KISS guys. I vividly recall a gig in a large renovated garage in Framingham. I was backstage with them and he said to me, "Please, please can you put on my makeup?" So I said sure, and stood there painstakingly putting on his makeup. When I see him on American Idol, I think, "Steven, if you only knew who was watching you on TV." That's what it was like for all of us.

During that whole time period, we developed and maintained acts. We lost a lot and we made a lot. When they came out with "Dream On" they became superstars. The minute I heard that song, I said, that's it.

John and I introduced Steven Tyler to Steve Leber. [He managed Aerosmith and AC/DC. Leber helped organize the 1971 *Concert for Bangladesh* at Madison Square Garden, which featured Bob Dylan, Eric Clapton and George Harrison. It raised money for UNICEF.]

We put people together that actually we should have kept to ourselves.

CG Did you manage Richie Havens?

LS For a while John may have, but I wasn't involved. Back in the beginning we were responsible for the initial exposure of people like James Taylor. We booked acts like him in local bars and coffee houses in Cambridge. We started them off on national careers. He was working for $35 a night but lost $10 and didn't know where he lost it.

We were booking the Isley Brothers a lot. After the gig, they would come to our apartment. It was 1965 and we had just gotten married. Other than a bedroom set, we had no furniture and they would sit on the floor with us. We would drink and talk until five in the morning.

Also, we were working with Moulty and the Barbarians. [Their hit was "Are You a Boy or Are You a Girl," 1965] They could have done more with their careers, but it never happened for them. Moulty was not an easy person to get along with and he made enemies along the way.

CG I had a friend, Susan Sessions [later married to Dr. Gonzo, William J. Cardoso], who followed the band. She took me to one of their gigs. They were from Provincetown, as I recall. It seems you were into rock before the Boston Tea Party.

LS Absolutely. Ruth Clemmont, who worked with Dave Maynard, had a club in Kenmore Square. Originally, it was called The Bronze Door and became Where It's At. We put Barry and The Remains in there. The audience rushed the stage. That's when we knew that we had a hit group on our hands. It was a wild night. That club did a lot for local groups developing as artists. That was around 1966.

CG What were the venues that those early groups were playing at?

LS There weren't very many. There were coffee houses and colleges. There were a few individuals taking chances, like Ruth Clemmont, providing groups with a stage. We were involved with booking colleges. That was before the club scene. Our focus was becoming independent concert producers for colleges. For us it was very successful. We branched out from Boston to upstate New York and into Pennsylvania. Had we kept going, we would have done even better.

One event tells a lot about how John's mind worked. He booked The Grateful Dead at Boston University.

CG I was there.

LS Do you remember the opening act? He had a chimpanzee and it was a sensation. As I mentioned we were booking the Isley Brothers. Melanie was a big act for us. At the time, she was managed by David Geffen. We did a lot of work with Odetta and Ray Charles. There were a lot of jazz musicians.

CG Did you book Chuck Berry?

LS Oh sure, of course.

CG Did you pay him before he went on stage?

LS I don't know. It was up to the schools to take care of that. When we were doing Summerthing the entire Motown roster was a part of that. It was usual for Tina Turner or Diana Ross to sit on the floor of our house and have dinner with us. [As David Wilson recalled.]

Programs like Summerthing happen now all over the country. But ours was the first one. It was a way to entertain people free of charge. They would come to the park. It was community outreach in terms of the city giving something. It was very successful, and why they didn't continue is beyond me. The concerts were in neighborhood parks. We had Smoky Robinson, Gladys Knight, Dianna Ross, Tina Turner, Martha and the Vandellas, Patti LaBelle. It was the 1960s when Motown was in its infancy.

Thinking of that era, Barry and the Remains should have been huge stars. They were doing so well. The bass player, Vern Miller, was one of the top three in America at that time. They were that good. Frankly speaking, I almost came apart over this. I cried my eyes out, I was so upset about the whole thing.

These two guys from New York came in and they literally stole The Remains. They sold them a bill of goods. "Leah and John are nice people. They have done all they can and aren't capable of doing anything more. Please, come with us and we'll make you stars." That was the beginning of the end of The Remains.

To this day I remember it so vividly, and it impacted me personally. I was never the same after that. I looked at John and said, "It's over for them. These guys have made the biggest mistake of their careers." He looked at me and said,

"How do you know that?" I said, "John, nobody is going to remember the opening act for the Beatles. They don't have a good record company or solid material. They'll put out a couple of records that go nowhere then it's over for them." That's exactly what happened. If they stayed with us we would have made the slow, methodical moves. They could have been another Aerosmith.

Hats off to Sdoucos. Photo courtesy of Sdoucos.

Left to right, entrepreneurs Fred Taylor, Sdoucos, and George Wein. Photo courtesy of Sdoucos.

Sdoucos produced concerts for Mayor Kevin White here with Leonard Bernstein.
Photo by Charles Giuliano.

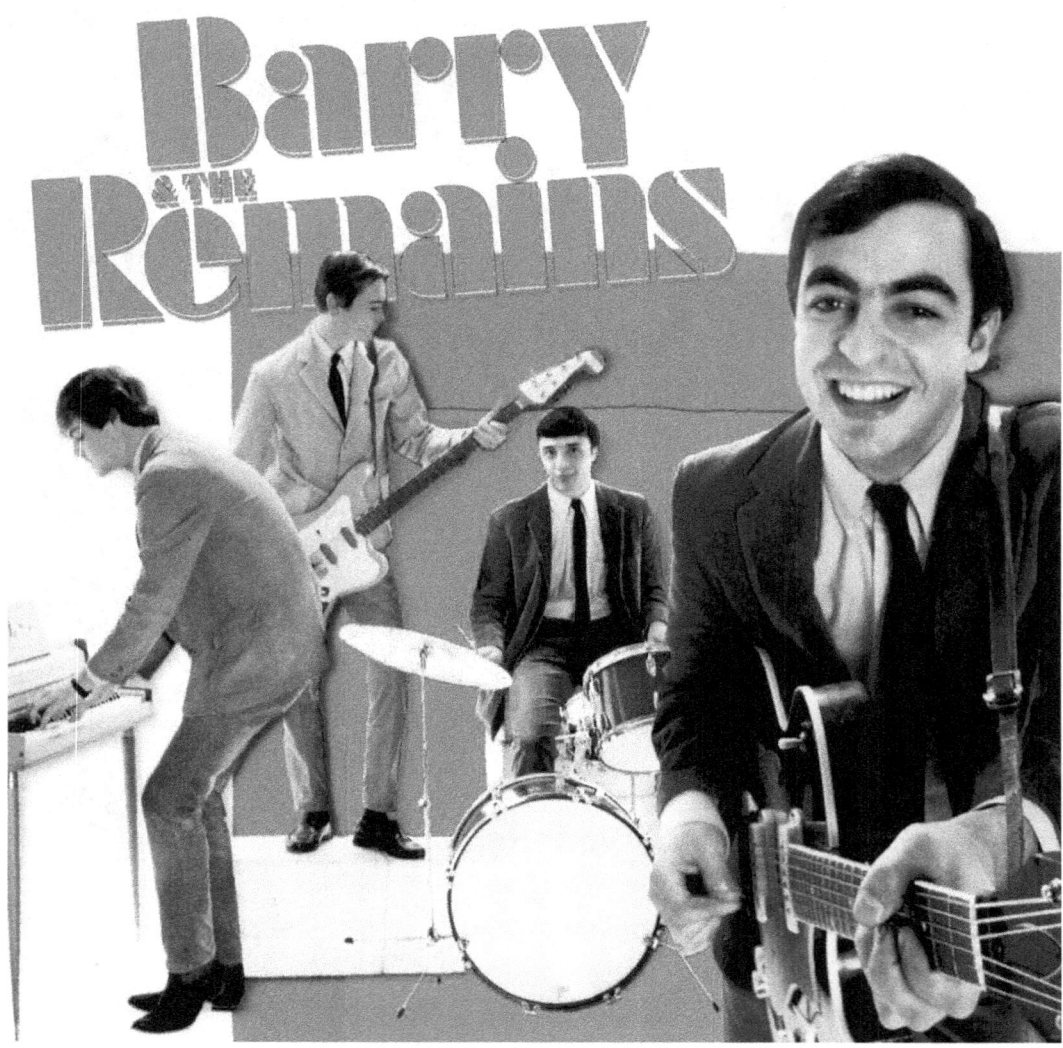

John and Leah managed Barry and the Remains.

The Barbarians were a promising early band.

They got James Taylor a club date for $35 dollars. Photo by Charles Giuliano.

One of the last performances by Marvin Gaye was on Boston Common. Photo by Charles Giuliano.

Chuck Berry demanded cash before going on stage. Photo by Charles Giuliano.

They managed Richie Havens. Photo by Charles Giuliano.

Havens in later years. Photo by Charles Giuliano.

Bonnie Raitt performed on Boston Common. Photo by Charles Giuliano.

Janis Joplin let it all hang out at Harvard Stadium

I was hired by the daily *Boston Herald Traveler* in 1970 to cover jazz and rock.

The music of the era, a golden age, was woven into a tapestry with warp and woof comprised of social and political change resulting from protest against war in Vietnam.

The music was agitator and catalyst, as well a means of unification and pacification.

Through the national syndication of underground papers, targeting a massive youth market, on April 28, 1969, Columbia Records ran a controversial ad that stated: "The Man Can't Bust Our Music."

That didn't sit well with the suits at corporate headquarter on the upper floors of Black Rock. It implied that corporate America condoned and encouraged illegal activities from drug use to radical protests.

Caught between Black Rock and a hard place, Columbia Records pulled its ads from the underground press. Other record companies followed suit. Without that financial resource, most underground papers folded. They were replaced by more moderate "alternative weeklies" like the Boston/Cambridge market of *Boston After Dark/Boston Phoenix*, *Cambridge Phoenix* and *The Real Paper*. With professional journalistic standards, they won back entertainment industry advertising.

Seeking a share of the youth market through mainstream media, *Boston Globe* and *Boston Herald Traveler* created staff positions to cover what my editor, theater critic Samuel Hirsch, regarded as "popular music." There was a big news hole to fill with daily reviews and a Sunday feature in the pull-out "Show Guide."

There was a lot to cover from jazz clubs to rock venues. By then, the most popular rock acts evolved from clubs to the old Boston Garden, stadiums, and festivals. On my watch, covering the music transformed from casual to corporate. Early on, one had backstage passes and access to the greenroom. At some point that phased out. Today, music managers see their job as controlling access and limiting the media. *Rolling Stone* opened the door to that by allowing final edits to top acts.

On many levels, it was the best job in the world. Then it got dark. I was dismayed to find myself writing rock obituaries.

It started with Al Wilson [July 4, 1943–September 3, 1970] of the blues band Canned Heat; then Jimi Hendrix [November 27, 1942–September 18, 1970]; not long after, Janis Joplin [January 19, 1943–October 4, 1970]. That was the class of 1970, with an average age of 27–28. A year later, we lost Jim Morrison [December 8, 1943–July 3, 1971].

Signing on at the *Herald Traveler* the job was not what I had anticipated. The sense of loss and sadness was personal. On August 12, I had covered what proved to be the final performance of Janis Joplin at Harvard Stadium. Later she was in California recording her final, posthumous album *Pearl*. Given the state she was in during that appearance, an overdose came as no surprise.

During an earlier time in New York, I hung out in the greenroom of The Cheetah with a musician I knew as Jimmy James. He did all those iconic riffs with a Broadway soul band, Curtis Knight and the Flames. Gerry Berkery and I visited him at a flophouse hotel to give him some photos we took. His low-key manner was very different from the Jimi we knew on stage.

Just prior to death by suffocation, inhaling vomit, Hendrix seemed exhausted during a *Tonight Show* appearance. He was scheduled for a performance in Boston that never happened.

Years later during spring break in Paris, I visited the grave of Morrison at Père Lachaise Cemetery. That inspired a conceptual art installation and photo collage exhibition. I created a tombstone and stuffed trash bags interspersed with strands of swamp reeds. On the floor of the gallery I scattered Chinese hell money and scattered a can of coins I had saved. My art school colleagues just scratched their heads.

The first stadium rock event I covered was *Sound Blast '66* at Yankee Stadium. It included several acts from the Cowsills, the Byrds, Little Stevie Wonder, and headliner Ray Charles. Several years ago I wrote a feature on that event for the Yankee's magazine.

The late 1960s was a time of festivals from Woodstock to Newport. During long, hot summers, cities sponsored neighborhood events and festivals like Boston's Summerthing under Mayor Kevin White in 1968. The annual music events were staged at different locations on Boston Garden.

In 1970, Schaefer Beer co-sponsored a summer concert series at Harvard Stadium along with the city of Boston's Summerthing. The stadium has thirty-five thousand seats, but concerts were limited to ten thousand at $2 per person. The lineup included The Grateful Dead, Miles Davis, Ike and Tina Turner, Van Morrison, B.B. King, and The Supremes, as well as Janis Joplin.

It was the end of Joplin's tour with a Canadian band: John Till, guitar; Richard Bell, piano; Ken Pearson, organ; Clark Pierson, drums; Brad Campbell, bass. They were the musicians who backed her on *Pearl*.

The concert was brief and chaotic. They performed "Tell Mama," "Half Moon," "Mercedes Benz," "My Baby," "Try," "Maybe," "Summertime," and "Full Tilt."

I was 29 that summer, just a year older that the exquisite corpses I wrote about. One may say, "I remember when rock was young." This is what I wrote nearly 50 years ago:

Janis Joplin at the Stadium

Boston Herald Traveler, August 14, 1970

At 5 PM the Janis Joplin concert at Harvard Stadium started. Holyoke Center merchants busily put up sheets of plywood over their often-shattered plate glass windows.

By 7:30 PM Janis Joplin pulled in backstage demanding a quick fix of J&B to warm up her act.

After two and a half hours of schlock rock, sandwiched between tons of beefy security, Janis staggered onto the Erector Set stage. Gonzo, she sipped from a paper cup, snapped her fingers for a cigarette, and stared bleary eyed at the fans, occasionally rotating her million dollar hips.

Producer John Sharer shook his head on stage as equipment men struggled to set up a sound system. For the second time this summer, valuable speakers and amps had been ripped off by midnight movers.

"It's been like this since 9 AM," he said. "The phone hasn't stopped ringing and by noon we sold out."

Huffing and puffing in tie-dyed, wine red, velvet pants, a black lace blouse, gold thread vest, and a feather dangling from her hair, Janis was impatient, yelling, "Let's go, come on toots. Let's get the show on the road. Stop ego tripping and get it on."

Sarcastically, a fan quipped, "She'll be sober by the time they get her on."

Finally, at 10:30 PM, Janis bounded on as a spot pinned her, revealing a face with all the charm of a Green Bay Packer and a head start on a double chin.

Janis attacked a song with the vengeance of the Vietcong. She squats down and grabs the mic, belting a song into the bleachers. She seems intensely nervous, almost frantic before each song. Cupping her hands together and listening to what the band is giving her.

In the middle of a song it's all flat out, wide open delivery which leaves her huffing and fighting for breath as the fans scream for more. Like a fighter who has been in the ring too long, Janis knows that she has to deliver even when she's on the ropes. She never spares herself as each round is for a title shot when you're the queen of rock.

Between songs, relaxing a bit, with the crowd with her, she launched into a bit of Port Arthur philosophy. It purples the ears and leaves little that is decently quotable. Janis makes no bones about it as she launched into "Try Just a Little Bit Harder." What she can't remember she makes up.

She tells the band "five chords in D" and then improvises "Oh Give Me an Old Mercedes Benz Cause My Friends All Got Porches."

Always a pro, she conducts the band in an off-handed manner with a thrust of the hip. Her phrasing is always fine as she strains through a raspy, version of Gershwin's "Summertime."

Fending off calls for "Ball and Chain" Janis compromised with "Piece of My Heart" and another great hit, "Maybe."

After a struggle with a big band, which just dragged her and produced poor record sales for her *Kozmic Blues* album, Janis returned to a small combo. Her band is Canadian with organ, piano, lead guitar, bass and drums. They provide just enough backing for her without getting in the way.

Somewhat sobered by her efforts Janis and police escort departed by 11:30. 35,000 fans marched peacefully over the bridge to Harvard Square past an army of police seemingly armed for the Tet Offensive. They sported helmets, grenade launchers, gas, dogs, machine guns and walkie talkies. (end of HT review)

Given that the sound system was set up under pressure, the technical quality of the performance was limited. The bootleg LP that surfaced provides flawed documentation of what proved to be her last live performance. It documents bawdy comments that I was unable to report for a "family newspaper."

Before "Try a Little Harder" she said, "When I lived in San Francisco, I used to live in a hotel and every day I would go out on the street looking for a little talent. But there was this chick on the second floor who seemed to be getting all the action. One day I woke up early and camped out by her door. I found out that she hit the streets at 10 a.m. or four hours before I did. Then I told myself that I had to try a little harder."

After Janis's death a news editor with the look and demeanor of a U.S. Marine assigned me to write a Sunday piece providing young readers with a heads up about emulating the bad habits of rock stars.

Doing as ordered, I took the assignment in a different direction. Searching the paper's morgue I looked for envelopes of clippings with headings that said "Drugs" and "Stars." There were lots of stories going back for several decades.

While reporting on the demise of Wilson, Hendrix, and Joplin I dug into Hollywood and the big band era.

My Sunday feature "Drugs and the Stars" ran on October 18, 1970. There was a litany those who died young; early Hollywood stars Marie "The Body" McDonald, Carol Landis, Jean Harlow, 26, Marilyn Monroe, 36, jazz stars Charlie "Bird" Parker, 35, Billie Holiday, 44.

There were numerous celebrity busts. Drummer Gene Krupa served 90 days for smoking pot in 1943. When actor Robert Mitchum was busted in 1948, he told that judge that he smoked up to three marijuana cigarettes a day.

I concluded the piece that they had succumbed to the pressures of their professions and had "only tried to entertain us" urging readers to remember them with compassion.

That Monday morning, passing that editor, he snarled but said nothing. I had done my job.

From then to now nothing has changed. Whom the gods love, continue to die young. One might quickly mention Tim Hardin, Curt Cobain, Whitney Houston, Michael Jackson Amy Winehouse, and the suicides of Philip Seymour Hoffman, Robin Williams, and Anthony Bourdain. All of these losses continue to feel personal.

Wicked Woman is a bootleg LP of August 12, 1970, Harvard Stadium concert. Giuliano archive.

The *In Concert* double LP was released posthumously in 1972. Giuliano archive.

White label promo copy of *Pearl*. Joplin died October 4, 1970, while recording it. Giuliano archive.

Jon Landau covered and then managed Bruce Springsteen

Jon Landau covered and then managed Bruce Springsteen.

"It's four in the morning and raining. I'm 27 today, feeling old, listening to my records, and remembering that things were different a decade ago…"

An hour later, by the light of dawn, on May 22, 1974, Jon Landau had completed a 1,985-word essay that in another era might have been written by Jean-Jacques Rousseau.

It is significant that he was 27 at the time. In the genre of rock it's a tipping point when artists have enough experience to create their best work but also feel the pressure of mortality. It is the cusp separating sanguine poetry, passions of youth, and shifts to mature work and sustainability.

Brian Jones of the Rolling Stones died at 27 in 1969. The class of 1970 added three more: Al Wilson of Canned Heat, Jimi Hendrix, and Janis Joplin. A year later Jim Morrison joined the elite of whom the gods loved.

By the 17th paragraph of the essay he wrote 430 words, which comprise the most famous and transformative review in the history of rock. After two albums with marginal sales Bruce Springsteen was on the verge of being dropped by Columbia Records. Following the review, Landau became, initially, a confidante, and then co-producer and manager. What Landau wrote was a turning point for their remarkable careers.

I sent questions which he answered by email. What did he see that was different about that May 9, 1974 performance when Springsteen opened for Bonnie Raitt at the Harvard Square Theatre? He had seen Springsteen perform in clubs prior to that night, including a week-long gig at Charley's in Harvard Square.

The dialogue with Landau is "front-loaded" with the iconic excerpt from his column in *The Real Paper*.

"But tonight there is someone I can write of the way I used to write, without reservations of any kind. Last Thursday, at the Harvard Square theatre, I saw my rock 'n' roll past flash before my eyes. And I saw something else: I saw rock and roll future and its name is Bruce Springsteen. And on a night when I needed to feel young, he made me feel like I was hearing music for the very first time.

"When his two-hour set ended I could only think, can anyone really be this good; can anyone say this much to me, can rock 'n' roll still speak with this kind of power and glory? And then I felt the sores on my thighs where I had been pounding my hands in time for the entire concert and knew that the answer was yes.

"Springsteen does it all. He is a rock 'n' roll punk, a Latin street poet, a ballet dancer, an actor, a joker, bar band leader, hot-shit rhythm guitar player, extraordinary singer, and a truly great rock 'n' roll composer. He leads a band like he has been doing it forever. I racked my brains but simply can't think of a white artist who does so many things so superbly. There is no one I would rather watch on a stage today. He opened with his fabulous party record "The E Street Shuffle" -- but he slowed it down so graphically that it seemed a new song and it worked as well as the old. He took his overpowering story of a suicide, "For You," and sang it with just piano accompaniment and a voice that rang out to the very last row of the Harvard Square theatre. He did three new songs, all of them street trash rockers, one even with a "Telstar" guitar introduction and an Eddie Cochran rhythm pattern. We missed hearing his "Four Winds Blow," done to a fare-thee-well at his sensational week-long gig at Charley's but "Rosalita" never sounded better and "Kitty's Back," one of the great contemporary shuffles, rocked me out of my chair, as I personally led the crowd to its feet and kept them there.

"Bruce Springsteen is a wonder to look at. Skinny, dressed like a reject from Sha Na Na, he parades in front of his all-star rhythm band like a cross between Chuck Berry, early Bob Dylan, and Marlon Brando. Every gesture, every syllable adds something to his ultimate goal -- to liberate our spirit while he liberates his by baring his soul through his music. Many try, few succeed, none more than he today..."

Charles Giuliano You grew up in Lexington. As a teenager did you go to clubs in Boston and Cambridge? What were you listening to? You were involved with bands. Were you doing just covers or any original material? How were you learning about music both as listener and to perform? The scene was mostly folk and jazz. Did you ever go to clubs like The Sugar Shack?

Jon Landau I had been playing the guitar since I was very young and grew up on Folkways and folk music mixed with Top 40 Radio. I loved Pete Seeger, the Weavers, the New Lost City Ramblers, Leadbelly and at the same time Little Richard, Elvis, Buddy Holly, a little later Jackie Wilson, all of it.

While at Lexington High School in the very early sixties I started going to Club 47 on a regular basis, which was a seminal experience. It felt very special to be sitting in that audience watching Keith and Rooney, the Charles River Valley Boys, Geoff Muldaur, the Loving Spoonful (that came later) and my personal favorite, Jim Kweskin. He was totally committed to his own unique taste in folk and early 20th century pop songs, but delivered them with the excitement and energy of rock music. To this day I can easily picture him performing his classic "Somebody Stole My Girl."

In I think 1962, I saw Bob Dylan give his first solo concert in Boston at Jordan Hall. Talk about life changers, that evening surely changed what I thought about everything.

CG We are graduates of Brandeis University but did not overlap. I was a studio and art history major. You took courses from Leo Bronstein and perhaps others. How did that develop into your later interest in collecting Old Masters? Do you have any interest in modern and contemporary art? You are known for music but it appears that you have a passion for fine arts. Did these interests manifest simultaneously or emerge over time?

JL While at Brandeis I took the famous Persian Manuscript course with the truly memorable Leo Bronstein and another art course or two. However, I left Brandeis with no real interest in visual art. Years later, some friends and relatives started sharing their interests in different areas of 20th century American art and I simply got hooked. Ever since then, I have been looking at great Western art (primarily) and began to collect works in the late seventies.

I started with an interest in American Modernism—Marsden Hartley, Arthur

Dove, John Marin, Alfred Maurer, and Arnold Friedman. Over time my taste kept moving back and I began to add works from the pre-Impressionists in France, by artists such as Courbet, Corot, Delacroix, and Gericault.

Finally, in the 1990s, I found my way back to the Renaissance and Baroque and have been collecting painting and sculpture from those periods for the last 25 years. Visual art has long been equal to my passion for music, and it is an extraordinary privilege to be able to live with some of the greatest examples of what has gone before.

CG Brandeis produced a number of writers during the counter culture era of Boston/Cambridge. Did you write for *The Justice*? If so, who was the editor? Mine was Arnie Reisman, who later recruited me and other Brandeis writers to *Boston After Dark*.

JL I wrote for *The Justice* as an occasional music critic. In 1967, I started writing for the newly created *Rolling Stone*. I occasionally wrote something for the *Justice* that I would then rewrite for RS, such as my infamous pan of a Cream concert performed at Brandeis' athletic center.

CG When David Wilson, editor of *Broadside*, was away on leave, you proposed a series/column. When Wilson returned, for reasons he can't articulate, he cancelled the idea. Do you recall what it was about and was anything published? Would that have been your first submission to a music publication? What would have been a date?

JL When in high school going to Club 47, *Broadside* was a give away at the folk clubs. Never lacking in confidence, I got in touch with Dave or some others and proposed that I write a piece for them. So, my first published work was published when I was a Lexington High School junior. After publishing a piece or two, I was discontinued, I'm sure because the pieces weren't very good.

CG As Reisman recalls, you either approached or were recommended as another potential Brandeis writer. He states that *Boston After Dark* published several articles, but you left the paper. What were you writing about? Were you covering local clubs and performances? Was the music scene of interest to you? Did you check on bands at the Tea Party then in the South End? Did you see the Hallucinations? Or the Jeff Beck and Led Zeppelin gigs?

JL I played the guitar in bands all through my Brandeis years. As a freshman I ran into a slightly bohemian and exotic character with whom I became lifelong friends. His name was Peter Wolf. He went on to form the Hallucinations.

My band was called the Jelly Roll (a la the Loving Spoonful) and I tried to follow the path that the Hallucinations were charting locally. Unfortunately, we weren't so good and I found stage work very difficult. So I continued with my growing career as a critic, both nationally for *Rolling Stone* and locally for *The Phoenix* and then *The Real Paper*.

I saw (and often reviewed) all the legendary Boston Tea Party Shows, including Jeff Beck (with Rod Stewart as the singer), Ten Years After, Procol Harum, the Byrds, BB King, Butterfield/Bloomfield, Van Morrison, and so much more. That was a great moment in rock music and the excitement at those shows was overwhelming. I would just add that the greatest rock band live that I saw in this period was actually a quartet from Boston University—Barry and the Remains. It's a shame that they didn't become better known in their day because they were absolute masters.

CG Ray Riepen was building a media empire. He started The Tea Party, taking over the South End lease from the Fort Hill community. Then he talked T. Mitchell Hastings into morphing WBCN from classical to rock programming. He was a partner in *The Cambridge Phoenix*. As Harper Barnes puts it, when he came on board as editor, you were one of his first hires. That occurred at the insistence of Riepen. The implication is that he knew of you through his involvement with rock. Riepen's reasoning to Barnes was that you would help to lure music industry advertising. Can you tell us about Riepen who was such an entrepreneur/visionary but cashed in his chips and left town? He has shown up at WBCN gatherings over the years.

JL Ray was a truly charismatic entrepreneur with great ambitions and ideas. He was a person of large gestures, and I was always impressed by him. I have never had anything to do with advertising where ever I have written, and I was utterly uncontrollable in my views on music, which I regarded as sacred. However, Ray believed I was a draw for advertisers and no doubt exploited my presence to get ads, which was fine with me, as long as no one interfered with my writing—and no one did. Harper Barnes, meanwhile, was one of the truly soulful editors you will ever meet and was always deeply helpful as an editor.

CG Can you give your version of how you left *Boston After Dark*, the hiatus, and then joined the staff of *Cambridge Phoenix*? As Riepen implies, you were making connections with the music industry. Your reviews helped to promote groups and sell their vinyl. You were also working with groups like MC5. I remember their gig at the Tea Party. That predates your transition from writer/critic to management and producer.

JL Charles, I am a little confused by the chronology of the time, but my general memory is that the owner of the *Phoenix* sold or merged with *Boston After Dark*—they were competitors, and the staff of what had been *The Phoenix* started *The Real Paper*, which went on for quite a little while. I went with *The Real Paper* at that time.

At that moment, I was also trying to become a record producer and to eventually move from journalism to making records. While I, of course, never reviewed anything that I worked on, it was difficult trying to wear two hats, which is why I eventually gave up the journalism. The MC5, who I produced in 1969, were an incredible group of people and the four months I spent living in their home in Ann Arbor, Michigan, were amazingly influential in how I approached things going forward right up to the present day. I just learned so much from them, for which I remain incredibly grateful.

CG As Barnes put it, he was bringing professional journalism to talented but unformed writers. In that sense, he describes you as different. You wrote a piece about the Muscle Shoals recording studio. He edited it to Mussel Shoals. It seems that you politely told him not to touch your copy. He told me that was fine because it "was so clean."

JL Harper's memory is sharper on this point than my own. However, I was incredibly proprietary about my copy, and it would take a lot to convince me to make changes. Harper was a great diplomat and had more success at getting to make changes than any other editor I worked with back then.

CG It seemed that for *Cambridge Phoenix* and later *Real Paper* you had an enormous readership. Can you recall your relationship with other writers? Some of them you later recruited to *Rolling Stone* when you became an editor. Was Steve Davis one of them? Were you interested in the social/political/cultural ambiance or were there other interests?

JL Stephen Davis was a terrific writer who I brought over to *Rolling Stone*, as I did with Timothy Crouse, Joe Klein, Dave Marsh, and many others.

CG Of course everything changed with the Bruce Springsteen review. I recall gigs at Charley's at the edge of Harvard Square. Fred Taylor states that he had booked Springsteen at Paul's Mall opening for David Bromberg. It was on the cusp of when he signed with Columbia. We saw the Netflix version of the Broadway play. It conveyed the long hard years leading to that night in Harvard Square. What did you see that led to the transition you were an intimate part of?

JL Charles, I believe the best answer to that question is in the article itself. Suffice it to say that in the 45 years or so since I wrote that article, the relationship that it led to with Bruce has been one of the great joys of my life in music.

CG In 1972, you published *It's Too Late to Stop Now: A Rock and Roll Journal*. Is there any possibility that you will write another book?

JL Stay tuned…

Rock critic Jon Landau. Photo by Jeff Albertson.

Landau attending a 2013 Brandeis reunion. Photo by Charles Giuliano.

Steve Nelson booked the British Invasion for the Boston Tea Party

In 1967 Harvard Law graduate Steve Nelson became manager of a rock club The Boston Tea Party. When he left after a year, it was a key stop on tours by new American and British bands. Forty years later he co-founded the website Music Museum of New England to preserve the region's musical history. His memoir *Gettin' Home: An Odyssey Through The '60s* recalls those times.

Since the late 1960s, we have shared and debated mutual interests from culture to politics. Not long after Astrid and I settled in the Berkshires, Steve and Jan left Gloucester and moved to the town of Washington, Massachusetts. As neighbors and friends the dialogues continue.

Charles Giuliano The Boston Tea Party was a rock club which only existed from 1967 to 1970, but has since become legendary. Give us a sense of what it was like back then.

Steve Nelson Well, it became legendary because of the who's who of '60s rock bands and blues greats who played there. Just to cite one example, Led Zeppelin did four nights at the Tea Party on their first U.S. tour in January '69. They only had about an hour's worth of material. On opening night, the crowd went crazy and wouldn't let them stop, so they just kept jamming. The band recalls this as the key gig in the transformation of their performance style to long sets that they became noted for.

The building in which the Tea Party was originally located was an old gothic brick pile in the South End of Boston, at the corner of Berkeley and Appleton Streets. It had a big Star of David window on the top floor, so at the time, we assumed it was an old synagogue. It was actually a Unitarian meetinghouse built in 1872–73. The land for the building was donated by a Boston businessman, John Gardner. He developed much of the South End after it was filled in, like the Back Bay was. His son Jack married a prominent socialite, Isabella Stewart.

The meetinghouse was dedicated to the memory of Theodore Parker [1810–1860], a controversial reformist Unitarian minister with ties to Emerson, Thoreau and the Transcendentalists. Parker was an abolitionist and early advocate for women's suffrage.

In a speech in 1858, he said that "Democracy is direct self-government over all the people, by all the people, for all the people," which was echoed by Lincoln in his Gettysburg Address. Parker also talked about how the curve of history "bends toward justice," as Martin Luther King later famously said.

People who hung out at the Tea Party in the sixties were for civil rights and women's rights and against the Vietnam War, so Parker's spirit was alive at the Tea Party

Just before the Tea Party came in, it was briefly a folk coffeehouse called the Moondial.

The crowd at the Tea Party was an incredible mix of people. Hippies and college students, of course. But since we didn't have a liquor license, a lot of the local teenyboppers, black and white, were from the South End and nearby Roxbury. In the early days, people came to dance. A local motorcycle gang, The Devil's Desciples (sic), hung around out front and in the balcony.

As the notoriety of the place grew, it started attracting a somewhat older crowd, professors and professionals, even a smattering of local celebrities, journalists, and other people curious about what was going on. After a while it was too crowded to dance and became primarily a listening experience, especially as bigger-name acts were booked.

CG We can't discuss the Tea Party without talking about Ray Riepen, who owned it. You knew and worked for him. How does he fit into the counterculture?

SN We wouldn't be having this dialogue if it weren't for Ray. He was a lawyer from Kansas City who came to Cambridge for a year to get a master's degree at Harvard Law School. It was kind of a gut program [unlike the regular three-year law program] which gave him time to get involved with other things. A friend of his from Missouri, Jessie Benton, was living in the Fort Hill commune. She asked Ray to get her a divorce so she could marry Mel Lyman.

CG Jessie was the daughter of the famed regionalist painter Thomas Hart Benton. They were descended from the first governor of Kansas. The artist was among the foremost of his generation. He was also the teacher of Jackson Pollock, who regarded him as a mentor and friend. Pollock summered with the Benton family on Martha's Vineyard. A major painting by Benton depicting "Streetcar Named Desire" was sold by the estate to the Whitney Museum of American Art for the benefit of the Fort Hill community.

SN Another of the Hill people, George Pepper, was starting the Film Makers Cinematheque at the former Unitarian meetinghouse on Berkeley Street. They were going to show underground movies by the likes of Andy Warhol, Stan Brakhage, and Jonas Mekas.

CG Mekas ran the original Film-Makers' Cinematheque in New York, and also wrote a column for the *Village Voice*. Mel knew Jonas, who befriended and wrote about him. Mel was influenced by the underground film movement. He acquired some equipment and made films in which he mentored Hill residents through their LSD trips. Today, some of those films would be regarded as Svengali-like and offensive.

SN I never met Mel and wasn't aware of the connection you mentioned to Jonas and the Cinematheque in New York. That was completely separate operation from the one in Boston, which Pepper ran. He decided that the movies would be shown during the week, and on Friday and Saturday nights, they'd have rock bands and dancing like at the Avalon Ballroom in San Francisco.

Ray got involved in setting up the dance concerts in partnership with David Hahn, a hippie MIT grad who was living on Fort Hill at the time. He owned a three-decker across from the stone tower atop the Hill and at one time had run a bus line in Honduras. He sold used army jeeps and military transports.

Together Ray and David scraped up $3,000 and opened The Boston Tea Party at the meeting hall. You can see the connection between the film and music in the sign over the front door with the names of both the Cinematheque and the Tea Party. At first the Tea Party just booked local groups like The Lost [with Willie Alexander, an icon of the Boston punk scene] and The Hallucinations [Peter Wolf's first band]. Over time they began to bring in name groups from out of town.

CG From what I understand, neither Ray nor David had any experience running a club. I had some media dealings with Riepen and found him to be arrogant and sarcastic. I have a lingering memory of ashes all over his lawyer's three-piece, pin-stripe suit from chain smoking.

SN They didn't know anything about the club business, but were riding a cultural wave, and quickly had a real success on their hands. Ray brought his legal and business acumen to the venture. David was more the creative guy involved with bookings and designing some of the posters promoting shows. The Tea Party was the place to be if you were hip and into music. It only cost two-fifty or three dollars to get in and was jumping every weekend.

CG When and how did you get involved with the Tea Party?

SN In late May 1967, about four months after the club opened, I went to see The Velvet Underground. It was a big turning point for the club, the band, and me. It was the VU's first gig without Warhol and the Exploding Plastic Inevitable, a multimedia freak show that usually accompanied them. Nico was still supposed to be playing with the group. When she showed up late the first night, Lou Reed wouldn't let her on stage. Bye-bye Nico.

That really marked the beginning of the Velvet's career, if I can call it that, as a four-piece rock band. It was also the start of their close relationship with the Tea Party. If you look at the back cover of their *White Light/White Heat* LP, there's a shot of the band sitting on the front steps of the club. The letters "ARTY" from the Tea Party sign is in the upper right-hand corner of the photo. For The Velvet Underground, the Tea Party became, as Lou said on stage during a gig in December 1968, "our favorite place to play in the whole country."

That May gig was a special one for me too, because I was turning 26, which meant I was no longer a candidate for the draft. It was the height of the Vietnam War. So to celebrate, I went to the Tea Party to see the Velvets. I had first seen them play a year earlier in New York at a private party thrown by George Plimpton at The Village Gate. It was a benefit for his magazine, *The Paris Review*.

That was when I first met Ray, at the Tea Party. We were introduced as two Harvard Law School guys. I had done the full three-year program there. At the end of the night, he gave me a ride to Cambridge, where we both lived, in this big brown Mercedes limo he chauffeured himself around in.

Several weeks later, he got in touch with me and said that he and David Hahn were going to split. One of them was going to buy out the other. Ray asked, if he bought out David, would I be interested in becoming the manager of the Tea Party? He figured that with my law background and connection to the "scene" and being into the music that I could do the job. I knew nothing about the music biz or running a club. Of course, Ray hadn't either when he opened the Tea Party.

I found out later that the only other person he approached about the job was Jim Rooney, the manager of Club 47 and an acoustic guitar player. He was in a duo with Bill Keith, the pioneering banjo player from Boston who had been one of Bill Monroe's Blue Grass Boys. Jim was really a folkie at heart and didn't want to abandon Club 47. It was struggling to keep its doors open, despite being a cornerstone of the 1960s folk revival.

So when Ray bought out David, he hired me to run the Tea Party. That was a dream job for me. I was a rock 'n' roller since my teenage days in New York listening to great '50s DJs like Alan Fried and Dr. Jive. Even though Ray and I were both lawyers, we made an odd couple. I showed up for my first day of work, with Country Joe & The Fish headlining, in bellbottoms, beads, and a wild mop of hair a la Dylan. Ray was ever the lawyer from Kansas City, with a short haircut slicked down and neatly parted. He was always in a suit and tie even when at the Tea Party.

I took care of the day-to-day club business and the creative side, booking the bands and promoting shows. He kept his eye on the bigger picture, because he knew he was really onto something. The whole sixties counterculture thing was exploding, and Ray was looking to get a bigger piece of it.

CG We met not long after you went to work at the club. At the time, I was briefly the design director of *Boston After Dark*. I recall you coming into our office to place an ad for the Tea Party. It annoyed me that you insisted on laying out your own ads. I thought who the heck is this guy?

SN Yeah, I walked in the door, and took over a workspace, just like that. And when I opened the cheap plastic attaché case I was carrying, there were no file folders or papers. There was just stuff to do graphic layouts: a T-square, blue pencils, an Exacto knife, rubber cement, and lots of Letraset. That was press-on type we used back then to make mechanicals. You stood there looking at me, and your jaw dropped when you saw that stuff. But hey, I was having fun!

But more than that, I was very conscious of trying to develop an image for the Tea Party. The intent was to set it apart from the psychedelic look of its California counterparts like the Fillmore and Avalon Ballrooms. The work the poster artists were doing, like Stanley Mouse and Alton Kelley, was spectacular. I didn't want to do a second-rate version of that, which is what the Tea Party had been doing when I came on board.

I gave up doing the graphics pretty quickly since I really wasn't a designer, I brought in Bob Driscoll to do posters and ads. He created an entirely new unpsychedelic look, spare with lots of white space, very graphic New York/Cambridge, Design Research-y. Absolutely brilliant, his posters are highly collectible.

Ray, in the meantime, was spending part of his time dealing with hostility from Boston politicos and bureaucrats. For them, the Tea Party was anathema, what with the longhairs who frequented the joint and its racially-mixed crowd. One night during a show in January '68 the house lights suddenly go on and dozens of cops swarm into the place, led by Boston Licensing Commissioner [and future 14-term City Councilor] Albert O'Neil.

CG The notorious "Dapper" O'Neil was a throwback to another era who had worked for Boston's infamous Mayor James Michael Curley.

SN Dapper was always looking to create a stir and get a headline in the paper. He brought along a *Boston Herald-Traveler* reporter figuring he was about to make a big drug bust. The cops didn't find any dope, and all he got us on was an expired license to dispense soft drinks.

Still, we had to make an appearance in court, where Ray went into this country lawyer routine, "No your honor, we don't approve of drugs. Shucks, all we're doing at the Tea Party is giving the kids something to do." The judge turned to Dapper and made him apologize to us right there in court. He was fuming; you could see his florid face turn even redder.

Dapper got his story in the *Herald*. The headline read "Soda Pop Raid Fizzles."

CG Despite the hostility of the powers-that-be in the city, the club is not only surviving after less than a year in business. It was more popular than ever and packed every Friday and Saturday night. Seeing what was going on in Beantown, MGM Records decided that there's money to be made from its music scene.

SN Alan Lorber was a record producer, arranger, and A&R man who had worked earlier in the sixties with artists like Neil Sedaka, Connie Francis, and Jackie Wilson, taking them from basic '50s rock 'n' roll roots into a more orchestrated sound. He thought Boston was ripe for the picking and signed several Boston bands to MGM: Ultimate Spinach, Orpheus, and The Beacon Street Union. Other producers quickly jumped in the game and signed other acts.

CG During that period I was living in Roxbury and mostly involved with Avatar. It was tough getting by paying even modest rent. We only occasionally went to the Tea Party. I recall a promo event for Ultimate Spinach which was pretty hokey. I saw The Hallucinations and Julie Driscoll. When I moved from Roxbury to Harvard Square there were free Sunday concerts on the Cambridge Common. They were organized by Bob Gordon of Polyarts and Kenny Greenblatt, with the support of the Episcopal church across the street.

SN That came later. Lorber's notion was that Boston could be promoted as the next big thing after San Francisco. Suffice it to say that there was no such thing as a Boston sound. The worst part was that many of the bands who did sign deals had some talent but weren't ready for prime time. Their records, typically, were typically poorly produced.

The Bagatelle was a good example. They were a great live act, a 9-piece mixed-race R&B band, with three lead singers sharing solos with great harmonies. They did a mix of covers like "Soul Man" and originals, some penned by Willie Alexander [formerly of The Lost].

Their producer was Tom Wilson, a black Harvard grad and Cambridge resident who had worked with jazz greats Sun Ra and Cecil Taylor. Then he produced Bob Dylan, Frank Zappa and the Mothers of Invention, and The Velvet Underground. He was probably most famous for taking Simon & Garfunkel's folky acoustic duo of "The Sounds of Silence" on their first LP and, unknown to Paul and Art, overdubbing electric instruments to turn it into a smash folk-rock hit that made them stars.

I guess Tom figured he'd do the same for The Bagatelle, overdubbing their tracks. It didn't work, and the band broke up a while later. Tom also produced Boston band Ill Wind, but with no overdubbing. Their sole LP, *Flashes*, never went anywhere at the time, thanks to a defective first pressing and poor support from the label. Now it's considered a psychedelic classic.

The whole Boston Sound hype soon collapsed. None of the bands had a hit record, although Spinach and Orpheus did each put out three LPs. They had moderately successful but short careers. For most of them, it was one record and done.

In *Rolling Stone*, Jon Landau dismissed the whole thing under the headline "The Sound of Boston: Kerplop." But I might add that he had some nice things to say about the Tea Party. He called it "consistently well-run" adding that it was "popular with out-of-town groups because of the professional treatment they receive." And that really was what made the Tea Party a success, being a great place for musicians and audiences.

CG As I recall, the hype for a time created a stigma for rock bands from the city. As Dave Wilson and I have discussed, there was a thriving folk scene with many clubs and coffee houses. With its enormous critical mass of college students in the Boston area, there was vast potential audience for rock. The gradual emergence of a great rock scene and locally-grown bands was inevitable.

SN Boston turned out to be a major incubator of musical talent. The original J. Geils Blues Band played the Tea Party, and then debuted their new lineup there when lead singer Peter Wolf and drummer Stephen Jo Bladd joined them from The Hallucinations. Steven Tyler, Joe Perry, and Tom Hamilton of Aerosmith talk about having seen shows at the Tea Party and being inspired to start a band, as did Barry Goudreau and Sibby Hashian of the band Boston.

The Cars came along a little later, but their drummer, David Robinson, first played in the The Modern Lovers with Jonathan Richman, who as a teenager was a rabid Velvet Underground fan, and never missed their gigs at the Tea Party.

CG I had an interesting relationship with The Modern Lovers. In 1973, my Cambridge neighbor Arthur Gallagher was looking for a band to bring to Bermuda to perform during spring break. His family owned a hotel called the Inverurie. I suggested The Modern Lovers. The band performed every night that week. The turnout at the hotel was sparse. But the word spread, and some kids returned every night and brought their friends. By the end of the week, we had a pretty good house.

The band has long been regarded as forerunners of punk. During the Bermuda gig, they had a solid rock sound that included the anthem "Roadrunner." Later Richman wanted to go in more of an acoustic folk direction. I recall him playing a cappella in the recessed entrance of the Coop in Harvard Square. He clapped his hands and slapped himself to create a rhythm.

The Modern Lovers broke up but were a seminal band. Jonathan had a solo career and created the music for the film *There's Something About Mary*. Drummer David Robinson joined The Cars. Keyboard player Jerry Harrison joined Talking Heads. The bass player Ernie Brooks worked with other musicians.

Let's get back to the Bosstown Sound.

SN In retrospect, it's ironic that before Alan Lorber "discovered" Boston, MGM already had on its Verve subsidiary label the most important band associated with the Tea Party at that time, The Velvet Underground. After John Cale played his last gig with the Velvets at the Tea Party in September 1968, the band's ties to Boston grew closer when they added local musician Doug Yule. He had played the Tea Party with the Boston band The Grass Menagerie. But MGM never had a clue what to do with the VU and damaged the band's chances for success with its inept distribution and promotion.

CG Did the Bosstown Sound promotion leave any scars on the Tea Party, since you booked many of the bands who got caught up in it?

SN Not really, even though we were in the middle of it. It was the bands who were the victims of the "Bosstown" massacre and in most cases didn't survive it.

The Tea Party, on the other hand, was doing so well that in the spring of '68 we decided to add to our normal Friday-Saturday schedule a series of one-night-only Thursday gigs, with the likes of The Yardbirds, B.B. King, Procol Harum, and Traffic. The first one was on April 4, headlined by Muddy Waters and his band, featuring Otis Spann and Little Walter, with The Hallucinations opening.

Muddy had played many gigs at Club 47. Struggling financially, and unable to compete with the much-larger Tea Party for bookings, the 47 had shut down just days before. I was thrilled to have Muddy play for us, although I did feel bad about helping to put the 47 under. But there was no time for guilt trips that day, because we got word that Dr. Martin Luther King, Jr. had been assassinated. There were riots in the streets of many American cities, including Boston, but inside the Tea Party the racially-mixed crowd was totally peaceful, and Muddy sang the bluest blues I've ever heard, more of a wake really than a concert.

CG Actually Boston was unique regarding riots when Dr. King was assassinated. James Brown was booked to play Boston Garden the next night, Friday. Mayor Kevin White asked public television station WGBH to air the concert to encourage people to stay home. That weekend it was rerun several times. White acknowledged Brown at the show for helping to keep the city calm. I was living in Roxbury and watched it on a small black-and-white TV. We were living in a black neighborhood, but there were no incidents. I recall hearing the JB broadcast playing in adjacent apartments.

SN The Garden was actually going to cancel the concert. But Tom Atkins, Boston's first black City Councilor, convinced the Mayor that it would only make matters worse if thousands of people arrived at the Garden to find the show called off. So it was decided that afternoon to let it go on and televise it.

At the Tea Party that Friday night, the headliner was The Amboy Dukes, featuring guitar hotshot Ted Nugent. Under normal circumstances that would have drawn a full house, but not surprisingly, the crowd was sparse. I always made a point of catching part of our shows, but that night someone brought in a TV. Several of us stayed in my office and watched the Garden concert. It was a riveting experience, because in those days you never saw anything on TV like a live James Brown concert. No wonder the streets of Boston were virtually deserted, with everyone home glued to the tube.

For the Tea Party, it was a time of change. We were open three nights, and then four. The crowds, now almost all white after MLK's assassination, weren't dancing much anymore, just listening to the music. The club's reputation in the music business was growing, and it had become a must-play stop for bands on tour, especially many of the new wave of blues rock acts coming over from the UK.

CG You mentioned earlier that Ray Riepen, the lawyer from Kansas City who started and owned the Tea Party, was looking for ways to build on its success as the place to go in Boston. Where did that lead him?

SN I was pretty much running the club on my own, from booking the bands to promoting the shows to taking care of business during the day. I personally took the receipts to the bank deposit box at the end of the night.

That freed up Ray to look for new opportunities. He saw that the kind of music being played at the Tea Party and being sold on millions of stereo LPs was, except for hit singles from those albums, not heard on commercial radio stations, which were only mono AM anyway. The record labels had no way to promote the stereo LPs sitting in record store racks.

But there was a new kind of programming you could hear on some of the college stations in the Boston area. It came to be called freeform radio. The DJs didn't work from a fixed playlist of Top Forty singles. They played whatever they were into, including cuts from LPs that never made it onto AM. They had to be knowledgeable about music to make it work.

CG In 1968, Ray persuaded T. Mitchell Hastings to put freeform rock programming on the stereo FM station he owned in Boston, WBCN.

SN In April 1967, the legendary San Francisco DJ Tom Donahue first brought the freeform album-oriented format to a commercial FM station, KMPX. That was one more piece of the puzzle which fell in place for Ray, a commercial station going freeform. By early 1968, he was deep into negotiations with Hastings to air rock programming on BCN. He had owned stations in a number of cities.

By 1968, his chain of stations was bankrupt, and WBCN replaced classical music with easy listening and literally begged on air for sponsors to buy spots. Hastings was not comfortable with rock and the counterculture, but he was desperate. He cut a deal with Ray to let him program the graveyard shift from 10:30 p.m. to 5:30 a.m.

In keeping with the Boston Tea Party name, I came up with "The American Revolution" as the brand for the new programming on BCN, which went live on March 15, 1968. At 10:30 that night, people snoozing at home to the sound of easy listening were jolted awake by Cream playing "I Feel Free." News about the new format went crazy viral by word of mouth. By May firstt, rock had taken over BCN 24 hours a day, and you could walk around Boston or Cambridge neighborhoods where lots of young people lived, and hear the station blasting out of open windows. It was music to Ray's ears, no doubt.

CG I remember Ray back then, he had this impish little smile, like "I know something and you don't." But with the huge overnight success of WBCN, he must have been grinning from ear to ear.

SN When BCN first went rock, Peter Wolf was on the air from 2:00 a.m. to 5:30, the "Woofa Goofa" doing the jive patter he became famous for and spinning R&B tunes for "the little ladies of the night." He was still with his first band, The Hallucinations, who were practically the Tea Party house band. In fact, in the very early days of rock on WBCN, the 10:30 to 2:00 shift originated remotely from what we called "the back room" at the Tea Party, which was a combination dressing room and hangout space. Hastings was nervous about people seeing longhairs going into the building on 171 Newbury Street where BCN's studio was. So a portable two-turntable board was installed at the Tea Party, the output connected remotely to Newbury. The record library initially consisted of a few cartons of LPs.

T. Mitchell was okay with Wolf doing his shift at the studio in the wee hours when no one was around. What that meant was that before Wolf's shift we'd leave a few LPs with the on-air jock, throw the rest into the Tea Party's VW bus, and someone would drive them the few blocks to Newbury Street. We would take the elevator to the third floor and then carry them up two flights of stairs to the fifth-floor studio for Wolf's show. Obviously, that arrangement didn't last long. The record library grew enormously as labels sent BCN everything they issued in hopes of getting airplay. They were also, as expected, among the first advertisers. When ad dollars started pouring in, Hastings quickly got over his hang-up about having hippies hanging around.

CG With all that going on, though, you left the Tea Party that summer. Why?

SN When I got hired by Ray in the summer of '67, we had a one-year deal paying me $1,000 a month, plus use of the club's VW bus. For a neophyte in the club business, it wasn't bad money at the time. As a music fan it put me in the center of the hottest spot in town. When I came on board, the Tea Party was still pretty much just a local club, but a year later it had become internationally famous. That was not all my doing by any means. We were riding this huge cultural wave, but I knew how to ride it and took the Tea Party to a new level. Plus, WBCN had taken off. So I told Ray I wanted more money and a piece of the action, but he wasn't buying.

Then one day, my friend Kenny Greenblatt, who left his job as a teacher in the suburbs and would later become a mainstay of the BCN sales department, said to me, in his unique baritone voice, "Hey Stevie, let's go hitchhike around Europe." Well, I never intended to have a career in club management, and Ray was giving me grief, not only about the new deal I wanted, but also about my bookings. He was particularly annoyed that I paid The Jeff Beck Group, with Rod Stewart and Ron Wood, the princely sum of $2,000 for four nights in late June. They packed the place, and Ray made a bundle. That was the last straw for me, so in the hippie spirit of the times, I just said farewell and a few weeks later flew to London with Kenny.

After a few rainy days there, we wound up taking an overnight ferry to Sweden. On board we met this Swedish rock band returning from a recording session in New York. We were blown away when they told us their producer was Tom Wilson, whom Kenny and I knew from Cambridge. The band invited us to stay with them in Gothenburg, which we did for a few weeks.

One night we went to an after-hours club, and who did we run into but Jimmy Page. I had just booked him at the Tea Party in April for what turned out to be the Yardbirds last American tour. So it was "Hey man! What's happening? What are you doing in Sweden?" He was playing a few dates there and in Denmark with his new band, then called the New Yardbirds, before debuting it in London. He introduced me and Kenny to his new lead singer, a guy with a big mop of curly blond hair named Robert Plant. We had just missed one of the first-ever performances of the band soon renamed Led Zeppelin.

Sweden starts to get cold in September, so we went to Ibiza for several weeks before going home. Within a couple of days of returning to Cambridge, I was approached by some people who were starting a new club. The Ark was under construction in an old taxi garage on Lansdowne Street behind Fenway Park. It was supposedly going to have a much bigger and nicer space than the Tea Party. I agreed to become the booking manager. It opened with a big promotional splash and klieg lights in January 1969. Spirit, a hot new band from California, headlined, opening with Tea Party regulars The Beacon Street Union.

The club was the baby of Charlie Thibeau, a businessman from the 'burbs who wanted to be cool, which to him included driving an Excalibur, an expensive and showy replica of a 1930s Mercedes roadster with a Corvette engine. He poured a lot of money into The Ark, especially into multimedia effects, but knew nothing about music. He thought people would come to the club for the trippy environment, and that the music was secondary. So it wasn't long before he started complaining about my bookings and money we were paying the bands. I didn't need that again, so I bailed, and wound up opening my own place, The Woodrose Ballroom, in western Mass.

CG When The Ark opened I was the design director for *Boston After Dark*. I created the half-page ad and illustration for the opening. I well remember the event and hung out there after that. John Kostik of Omniversal Design created a metal pod over the space that was supposed to be the control booth, but it didn't prove to be functional. There were groovy ramps and curved walls but they didn't put in a wooden dance floor. There was a gallery near the entrance that displayed the visionary paintings of Paul Laffoley. Today he is regarded as one of the most important Boston artists of his generation.

SN Ray Riepen and Don Law, who took over as manager of the Tea Party when I left, had been looking for a larger venue so they could bring in bigger acts and bigger crowds. By July the Ark sank and the Tea Party moved into its space at 15 Lansdowne Street, where it remained until it closed down at year's end 1970. If you look back at the bookings of who played at the Lansdowne venue—yes, The Who played there—it was an astonishing lineup of performers who went on to become famous, infamous, and even legendary. By the time the Tea Party was shuttered, band performance fees had risen to the point that the club could no longer afford to book the bands it helped put on the map.

CG I became a regular when Don took over the Tea Party on Lansdowne Street. I interviewed him for a story in *Boston After Dark*. That created a relationship with him and full access to the club. There was a side entrance and Don had his office next to it. There was a guy at the door. Don would check you out. From there was a staircase to the greenroom on the second floor. You could just walk in and hang out with bands like The Allman Brothers, The Grateful Dead, and Fleetwood Mac.

There was a men's room where you could sneak a joint. Rock critic Tim Crouse and I were taking a toke when Joe Cocker barged in and asked for a hit. Later, on stage he sang "I Get High with a Little Help from My Friends." He mentioned us. There was the infamous New Year's Eve gig with the Dead when they served spiked acid punch. Jerry Garcia was a hoot to hang out with.

SN The Dead did a New Year's gig every year in San Francisco, except for that one Tea Party show on December 31, 1969. So that says a lot about the club's stature in the rock world by then.

CG There were a couple of times when the greenroom was off-limits. There was no access during a gig by The Who. Another occasion was the Delaney and Bonnie tour with Eric Clapton in February 1970. Fleetwood Mac was on the bill. There was a long delay during which there was a jam session with Peter Green of Mac, Clapton, and Joe Walsh of the James Brothers. When Delaney and Bonnie finally performed they were sloppy and smacked up.

Later that year, I got a call from an LA publicist, Norm Winter, to go talk to this new British star having his first East Coast gig at the Tea Party. I knocked on his door at a motel near Fenway Park. The guy who answered the door, soaking wet holding a towel around his waist, was Elton John.

We had lunch and he ordered the Executive Club sandwich. I asked what was happening in London. He answered, "Me." Taken aback, I came to realize that he was absolutely right.

There were maybe a hundred people at the club on opening night. I wrote his first US review and interview for *The Herald Traveler*. Whenever he was in town, Elton phoned and invited me backstage. He flew me to LA when Rocket Records was launched with a party at Universal Studios.

Norm and I hung out with a side trip to San Francisco, which proved to quite decadent. We were up to no good. Flying back to LA, via Burbank, we visited his friend Nudie. I had mad money for the trip, but Norm wouldn't let me spend it. So I paid cash for my orange, sequined cowboy suit. It was custom made for a singer who never had that second hit. When I tried it on the fit was perfect. Norm talked me into it, "It's your logo man." I wore it that night at the Troubadour for The Pointer Sisters but in Hollywood nobody seemed to notice. Back home it was a different story. You took a photo of me and Jan at the Castle Hill promo party I organized. It's the cover of my book *Total Gonzo Poems*.

SN That Elton John gig on Halloween weekend was one of the last shows at the Tea Party, which closed two months later.

CG After the Tea Party, rock acts had progressed from clubs to arenas, and access to bands got a lot tougher.

SN It got a lot tougher for audiences, too, with no more three- or four-dollar shows. There was no affordable place to hang out and hear the top bands. The Boston Tea Party was the center of gravity for the music scene in Boston from 1967 to 1970, for fans and musicians. It was our temple of rock. The communal gathering place that was the Tea Party, the energy and oneness of the crowd and the band, was now just a treasured memory. Almost too good to have been true, like something we'd dreamed up while passing a joint. Hey, man, remember the night that....

Steve Nelson and B. B. Photo by David Laing.

Velvet Undergound Poster by Steve Nelson.

Johnny Winter Tea Party Poster. Bieber archives.

The Boston Tea Party Building. Photo by Charles Giuliano.

Steve Nelson with Peter Wolf. Photo by Charles Giuliano.

Me in my Nucie's suit with Jan Nelson. Photo by Steve Nelson.

The Tea Party Sign. Photo by Steve Nelson.

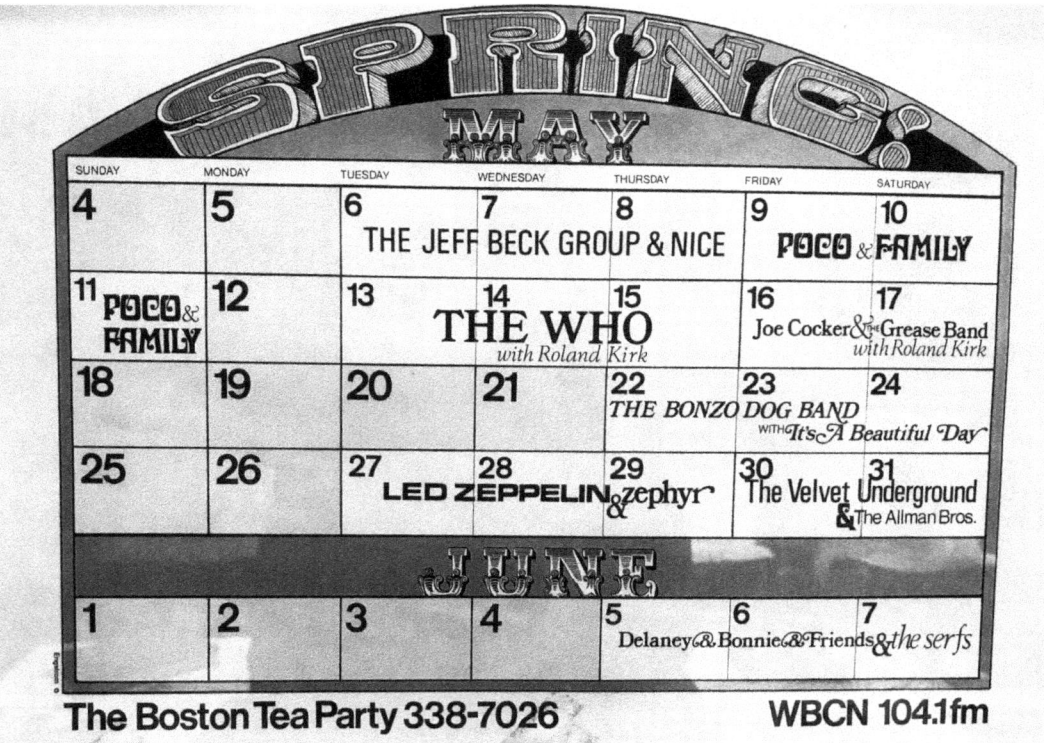

Tea Party Schedule. Bieber archives.

Wolf and Shapiro jam at the Tea Party. Photo by Charles Giuliano.

From left, Willie Alexander, Paul Shapiro, and John Lincoln Wright. Photo by Charles Giuliano.

Ron Della Chiesa, The Voice of the BSO, started with WBCN

On the jazz/cabaret scene WGBH, DJ Ron Della Chiesa was a frequent running buddy. With a box of LPs, from time to time, I was his guest on *Music America*.

A graduate of the Boston University School of Journalism, he started a career in broadcasting in the early days of WBCN, before the nearly bankrupt FM station switched to an all-rock format. Ron has interesting tales of working for the eccentric radio visionary and pioneer T. Mitchell Hastings.

Charles Giuliano I am contacting you about an ongoing series of dialogues on the arts and media in Boston from the 1960s on. Last week I spoke with George Wein about Storyville and the Newport Jazz Festivals.

Ron Della Chiesa I hosted those for years. He always had me there opening night at the Casino. Unfortunately, now that I'm doing the BSO broadcasts, I'm at Tanglewood. We went through so many great evenings at the Casino with Bobby Short, Count Basie, Dianna Krall, Tony Bennett. It was wonderful.

CG You're working on a book?

RD I hope to have it out by the end of the year. It's called *Radio My Way* [published in 2011].

CG Somebody called me and asked for permission to use a photo of you.

RD That's right, with Dick Johnson. So you'll be in the book with Dick.

CG This past winter I worked on my photo archives scanning and tweaking images with Photoshop. The images go back decades and many were shot with available light in nightclubs. I have a great shot of Illinois Jacquet at Lulu White's.

RD I remember that gig so well. I knew Jacquet.

CG Of course, you knew everyone. You were close to Dave McKenna and Teddy Wilson.

RD Very close to Dave. I used to hang out with Teddy Wilson. He said, "Ron you have so many lovely women around you." Teddy was a very elegant, urbane guy. He was something else.

CG You had a schizophrenic life.

RD Yeah, I did. That's a good way of describing it.

CG You're involved with classical music but also dedicated to jazz.

RD No question about it; I crossed over. It had to do with my early days, which I talk about in the book. My father was a renaissance man, a painter and artist. I was an only child. He played opera at home. That was my introduction to music, listening to tenors Gigli, Caruso on the old Victrola. I listened to the NBC broadcasts with Toscanini. That's how I came into the world. I took some trumpet lessons for a while. The jazz thing kind of grew out of that and then the film thing and Broadway. Little did I know that I would end up hosting the Boston Symphony Orchestra. I've been doing it for 20 years now with the same crew and engineer.

CG Who preceded you?

RD William Pierce. Remember him that very Brahmin guy?

CG We were in the GBH studio one time to do a *Music America* broadcast. He walked in. You turned to me in a whisper and said, "That's the voice of the BSO." Who knew it would be you one day.

RD Before him, of course, there was Milton Cross. He was the voice of the Met

Opera and one of my early idols. He was on for 50 years, and then, when I went on to GBH, I met William Pierce, who was right out of that school—that avuncular style. He was a very erudite gentleman.

CG Another of your colleagues was Robert J. Lurtsema.

RD Absolutely. I knew him very well. He was the master of the pause.

CG I recall you telling me of a time when he was delayed getting in for his show. He called you and said, "Ron, start the birds."

RD You've got a good memory, Charles. That's absolutely true. He said, "Do not go on the air if I'm late. If you go on the air people will think something has happened to me." So I put the birds on and they ran for about twenty minutes. That was in the middle of a huge blizzard and he made it in. I'll never forget him standing there looking like the abominable snowman.

Just to digress I have turned 73. I was at your 40th birthday party. We were all in your Cambridge apartment [5 Line Street around the corner from Savenor's Market] and you raised your glass and offered a toast, "Here's to death." So we made it. Right?

CG Who knew.

RD Joyce and I are very comfortably living in Dorchester. We left the South End after some 25 years.

CG I helped you move in. We moved your record collection with your friend Walter. Then we had dinner in Cambridge at the Turtle Café, which Joyce was running.

RD You did. Do you still have your vinyl?

CG I have 7,500 LPs.

RD Where do you store them?

CG We had shelves built in the loft and they are in the bedroom alphabetized in categories. The past two winters, I have been transferring them to the hard drive in iTunes. Then I can make mixes and burn CDs. I have been sharing them with friends and turning them on to my taste in jazz. It's a slow process, but very rewarding to listen again to all that music and have it stored and accessible.

Let's talk about your early years in broadcasting and WBCN.

RD My beginnings at BCN started in 1961. I had just come out of the army and graduated from Boston University School of Communication. I worked at a shipyard in Quincy during the day. At night I had a part-time gig. Arnie Ginsburg hired me to work at WBOS. It was an ethnic radio station on Comm Ave up from BU where Cadillac Olds used to be. It was a really antiquated studio. You went up a fire escape to get in there. I did the ethnic radio shows from six to ten at night, and Arnie Ginsburg came on with his Night Trane show as Woo Woo Ginsburg.

CG He was Boston's first rock DJ. My sister, who was three years older than me, was a fan and called in requests.

RD He was the first. Arnie is on the cover of a new book on Boston radio. In 1961 I got an offer to go to BCN. The program director at that time was Don Otto. He was a BU alumnus. I sent him a tape and resume. My father drove me in because I wasn't sure about getting around in Boston. I worked Christmas Day for the first time. It was at 171 Newbury Street in Boston on the fourth floor in an attic studio. They had a little record library and everything was confined to one room. The UPI machine was outside the studio. It was all classical. It was created by T. Mitchell Hastings, a pioneer in FM. He knew Major Armstrong. I don't think he knew Marconi. But he went way back there. He had a vision of a classical music network all across the country. He had HCN in Hartford, NCN in New York, XCN, I think was in Providence. He even owned MTW, which was on top of Mt. Washington in New Hampshire.

We didn't have satellite but we had bicycles. We recorded everything on huge ten-inch reels. We would just send them to different stations in what we called the bicycles system. Sometimes the problem was that the announcer didn't stop the tape, so you could hear local weather. It was what we called a cluster fuck. I was riding through Connecticut and it was like July. Just as I came in contact with the HCN signal out of Hartford I hear "God Rest Ye Merry Gentlemen" They were playing Christmas music. They had the wrong tapes up and nobody was there.

Hastings was a visionary, and he did go through some difficult times financially. Then a guy named Ray Riepen, this was around 1968, started something called The American Revolution. They hired Charles Laquidara, Sam

Copper, Mississippi, all those guys came in.

CG The first DJ was Peter Wolf.

RD Peter was actually on the air from the Tea Party and I introduced him. We were a mixed format. We played classical during the day, and then we would go to the Tea Party at night.

CG He had a midnight show.

RD Yeah, I introduced him. I'd be playing Stravinsky and then we switched over to him.

CG Hastings didn't want rock on Newbury Street. He was afraid about having hippies walking into the building.

RD At that time everyone was high, smoking shit, it was wild. We were very conservative. So we went from the most conservative format to the most radical format. At that time, I had started part time at GBH in the television booth. I would replace William Pierce when he went to Symphony. Then I crossed over into radio full time. It was perfect timing, as I had no future at BCN. That wasn't my bag. In 1968 I joined GBH full time.

CG Let's got back to Hastings. You told me that he was experimenting with different formats from sports to all talk.

RD No, he never went all talk. He always stayed with music, but he went into easy listening.

CG Didn't he do religious?

RD Yeah, in the mornings. The religious programs paid the bills. He had a guy named John DeBrine from the Ruggles Street Baptist Church who did a thing called *Songtime*. Then he had a thing with Brother Mandus who was a faith healer from Blackpool, England. A lot of screw ups would happen. You would get the back side of a four-track machine. You would start with "Our Father" and get beeennnnweeere. Things would happen there. But that paid the bills. His mission was to be the Classical Music Network so we were still all classical.

CG You told me about how he hired a program director who divided all of the albums into boxes labeled Fast, Medium, and Slow.

RD That's right. His name was Marlon Taylor. He took all the albums by André Kostelanetz, Percy Faith, Montovani. Later JIB developed that into an Easy Listening format. He had a flow chart system and the selections were marked slow, medium slow, medium fast. There was a card you pulled out and you had to follow a medium with an ms (medium slow) and so on. Naturally it was just a complete disaster. Hastings experimented with that for about a year. He also tried an early automation system. It was developed around 1966. It was a carousel rack. It played tapes and was a kind of automatic device. It inevitably screwed up and stopped, so there would be dead air for hours. Hastings bought that at one of the early radio trade shows in Vegas. Later on, when BCN went to rock, they bastardized and ripped that machine apart and used it to play eight track tapes. There was a guy who slept at the station, and Hastings paid him a day rate and a sleep rate.

CG Did you like Hastings?

RD I did. He was a kind man, but he was really out there. He believed in Edgar Cayce and the Lost Continent of Atlantis. He was in touch with the spiritual world. He was a visionary and in many ways a genius. He developed one of the first FM car radios—a stereo car radio. He went to Harvard.

CG Of course his ship came in when BCN went all rock.

RD He tried to find a niche for me. He wanted me to be the public service director, but I could see that wasn't going anywhere. They weren't doing any public service. Just smoking a lot of shit and having a ball.

CG Did you have any interaction with Ray Riepen?

RD A little bit. He was kind of a shitkicker from down South.

CG Kansas.

RD He could see how vulnerable things were, and he could see the writing on the wall. Mitchell's station was in a financial quagmire. I remember when we didn't get paid for a couple of weeks. He knew there as an opening for this kind of music.

CG What happened to the stations?

RD They were sold off individually.

CG So BCN was the last one.

RD Yeah, but Mitch was a part of the station until Infinity Broadcasting bought the station.

CG That's when they had the strike.

RD That's right, but I was long gone by then. Kenny Greenblatt was around and Jack Carney. Charles Laquidara who is now retired and living in Hawaii, living like a king.

CG Mark Parenteau has been on a government vacation.

RD A lot of this is in my book by the way. I talk about those early days.

CG Who is publishing it?

RD Pearson Publishing. They mostly do textbooks. I had a friend there, Bill Bart. He was a big jazz fan, and he decided to put it out. I have a co-writer, and her name is Erica Ferencik. She writes fiction. I met her and we bonded. A year and a half ago, we collaborated because, as you know, I'm not a writer. She writes like I would if I could write. She's very funny and writes great satire. We collaborated for about a year and a half on this thing. She taped a lot of me, and interviews I used on GBH. Everybody from Pavarotti to Jacquet, Mel Tormé, Dizzy. All the people who came to my studio, I recorded them. I made cassettes, and I kept a lot of those. The book has 44 profiles. I could have done three hundred, but I had to narrow it down. It's a broad spectrum of people I interviewed, even Chuck Jones is in there. He's the guy who created Bugs Bunny. David Raksin. He wrote [the scores for] *Laura*, [and] *The Bad and the Beautiful*, one of the foremost film composers. Gunther Schuller is in there. Harry Ellis Dickson.

CG So it goes back and forth between jazz and classical.

RD Yeah, it reflects what I did during an era of Boston radio, so it is all encompassing. It's an eclectic mix.

CG What is your current status at WGBH?

RD I'm the voice of the BSO and I work for them part time. It's year round. When the symphony season ends, we go right in and do four or five pops broadcasts. Then we go to Tanglewood and do 26 broadcasts. That's where I saw you the last time.

CG Tony Bennett.

RD We do that, and then after Tanglewood, pick right up again.

CG So you don't have a daily radio show.

RD I do on WPLM on weekends. I do a Saturday night show called *Strictly Sinatra*. It's been on for 15 years now.

CG Isn't that the old Bill Marlow gig?

RD I pick up where Bill left off, and I do *Music America*, which is basically the Great *American Songbook*. So I have ten hours of airtime on one of the last independently owned radio stations [WPLM 99.1 FM and WPLM 1390 AM]. They stream on the Internet Easy 99.1. I do that show out of my house. I tape it and send it down. That's commercially sponsored.

CG You also have the cruises.

RD We host our annual Tribute to Sinatra cruise. We just finished our fifth one to the Caribbean. I do a series of big band swing concerts. On June 24, I will hire a band and a couple of singers and get to meet my audience. At my age, there's not too many people doing that.

CG What's Ron Junior up to?

RD He lives in Idaho and we have five grandchildren. He works for the Idaho Transportation Department. He's 39 and it's been quite an experience.

CG Can we talk about the era of *Music America* at GBH. I was fortunate to come on as a frequent guest, and we played albums I brought along and talked about the music. We were also hanging out at Lulu White's in the South End, the Merry Go Round, in Copley Square, Lennie's on the Turnpike, Sandy's Jazz Revival in Beverly, Fenton Hollander's Jazz Boat on Boston Harbor, the *Boston Globe* Jazz Festival. I believe we met after Jazz Workshop and Paul's Mall had closed.

RD Right. Freddy Taylor hadn't started Scullers yet. Lulu White's, that club was run by what was his name?

CG Chester English. They also had Chef Chandler.

RD Willard Chandler was the chef. The place was wide open. They would serve drinks to three and four in the morning. Jane Lanouette was doing the PR. She now works with Allied Advertising. They had some of the great musicians coming in there: Bill Evans, Dave McKenna, Scott Hamilton, Illinois Jacquet.

CG Jo Jones was the house drummer. Wasn't he living there?

RD He might have been. Willard Chandler had an old barber's chair in the back room. He would sit there with a chef's hat on. He was a throwback to another era.

CG Chandler had been previously involved in a scandal with another club in the South End. Wasn't there are gangland slaying like the St. Valentine's Massacre? An undercover reporter was killed in that event. I knew *Herald* reporters who covered the mob. They were the only reporters I knew who packed heat. Larry Novak who was pals with Bill Cardoso was a part of that scene.

RD Right, Chandler's, which was a club owned by Howie Winter, of the infamous Winter Hill mob. There's a whole book out about him. I don't remember that one, but what about the Blackfriar's Massacre?

[The 1978 Blackfriars Massacre was an American Mafia massacre that occurred on June 28, 1978, in Downtown Boston. The massacre claimed four criminals known to the police and a former Channel 7 [now WHDH-TV] Boston television investigative news anchorman and reporter, John A. Kelly. The massacre was allegedly over the sale of cocaine, and the shooters that carried out the murders have never been caught.]

I don't think Chandler was involved with that.

CG He had some weird side gigs.

RD He sure did. Chandler started as a chef with the old Hartford New Haven Railroad.

CG He served a mean gumbo.

RD He did, man. They had very good food and jazz there. I remember one night I had my son Ron there and Sonny Stitt came over. He asked my son what he liked, and Ron said, "I like 'Bye Bye Blackbird.'" He was about eight at the time. Stitt played about a half hour of that tune for him; he played every possible variation. A nursery rhyme. Things like that stand out. The club was wide open.

CG Let's talk about Dave McKenna because you were very close to him.

RD I heard Dave play for the first time at the Columns in West Dennis. Dick Johnson introduced us. We bonded because we all liked the same things: the Red Sox, he loved to eat, and Italian food. He was just something else. When he settled in at the Copley Plaza that was a whole era, ten years.

CG He would come in for a couple of months at a time.

RD Even longer than that. He would go out on the road. Teddy Wilson would come in, or Jean Harris, other piano players, but it really was McKenna's room.

CG Before that it was the Merry-Go-Round Room run by Clinton Creasy.

RD He was a hair stylist in Cambridge. Yes, that was the previous era. The great cabaret acts performed there: Bobby Short, Mabel Mercer, Carmen McRae, Blossom Dearie, Mary Lou Williams. You could sit and revolve around or stay put. George Shearing would be smiling at some guy floating by. The Shearing Quintet played there. It was a classy room. The room had a long history. I think it started in the '30s or '40s. They dismantled that whole mechanism. It was a big deal to take it out of there. The Merry-Go-Round was a very unique room in the country.

CG Chester English tried cabaret at Lulu's. Do you remember a gig with Madam Bricktop?

RD Yes. The legendary Madam Bricktop from Paris. She sang "Miss Otis Regrets" by Cole Porter. Her piano player was Hugh Shannon. He was big in New York for cocktail piano. McKenna used to say, "I play cocktail." I would say no, Dave, you don't play cocktail. He was his own man with that left hand, that walking bass line.

CG Let's talk about some of the standard Boston jazz musicians of that time: Ray Santisi, piano; Al Dawson, drums; John Neves, bass.

RD Herb Pomeroy. The Herb Pomeroy Big Band played at the Stables.

CG Do you go back to that era?

RD I do. I was at BU at the time and cut classes to go and hear their rehearsals. That band had everyone in it: Lenny Johnson, Joe Gordon, Varty Haroutunian, Jimmy Mosher, Dick Johnson, Charlie Mariano, Jimmy Zetano, John Neves, Jean DeStasio, trombone, (Remember him?), Dave Chapman, one of the great lead alto players. They're all gone now. Not only did he have a big band, he scaled it down to an octet at times. I cut my teeth on that.

CG Did you go to Storyville?

RD Oh yeah. I was a member of the Teenage Jazz Club. George Wein started that. I was then at Quincy High School. Around 1956–1957, we would go in on a Sunday afternoon. George would have these great musicians play for us and we would drink Coke. I heard the Sauter-Finegan Orchestra there. I listened regularly to Symphony Sid. Most of the time he was stoned.

[Sid Torin (born Sidney Tarnopol on December 14, 1909–died September 14, 1984) went with his friend Norman Furman to Boston about 1952. Furman had become general manager of WBMS, which had been doing classical music (the call letters reportedly stood for "World's Best Music Station"). He changed the format and hired Sid, who did a gospel show and a jazz show. But Sid had a unique arrangement with Furman—he worked at WBMS in the daytime, and at night, he worked for WCOP, where he did live jazz shows, just like he had done in New York. During the mid-1950s, Sid could be heard live from the Hi-Hat, a nightclub owned by Julian Rhodes, in a part of Boston known for live jazz—the area near the intersection of Massachusetts and Columbus Avenues.]

CG I heard Symphony Sid as a teenager in Boston, and then later, when I lived in New York. By then he was into an all-Latin Jazz format with Tito Puente, Willie Bobo, Mongo Santamaria.

RD Sid Torin ended his last days down in the Florida Keys.

CG He was the most legendary jazz DJ in America.

RD Then Tony Cennamo came along.

[Tony Cennamo, September 30, 1933–June 8, 2010, was for 25 years a jazz disc jockey on Boston University's WBUR. When he had a morning show in the 1970s and 1980s, he began his show with Oliver Nelson's "Stolen Moments".]

He did a long stint in the morning from six to eleven. Cennamo had a long run of ten years or so when he was the king of the morning.

CG More than king, I thought of Tony as something of a dictator. He had a very purist definition of jazz, which was not generous and inclusive to those who didn't conform to his dictates. Like Wynton Marsalis and other jazz purists, he regarded many of the great white performers as imitators.

That was the mantra that Ken Burns followed when he did his PBS Jazz series advised by Marsalis and the critic Stanley Crouch. The great white musicians were notable for their absence.

Cennamo stated that "Jazz is Monk, Ornette, Duke, Bird, Dizzy, Miles, Trane, Toshiko, Pee Wee Russell, and Gil Evans, Mingus the imaginative, the juices flowing, not the bland, watered down, the whitewash of a thousand Xeroxed copies. Jazz is not safe and doesn't hide in Symphony Hall…Most new forms of jazz music are initiated by black musicians. White players (with few exceptions) copy; black musicians invent!"

It was easy to end up on the wrong side of him.

RD He and I had a falling out.

CG With everyone.

RD We used to hang out, then I started to play a mixed format. He was a purist, whereas I played Rosie Clooney and Mel Tormé, and started to move into film music. He felt that was betraying the cause. I didn't do a jazz show. *Music America* was very eclectic.

CG Do you think the Boston musicians we talked about ever got the recognition and respect they deserved?

RD Dick Johnson certainly did. He took over the Artie Shaw band. Artie had turned his clarinet into a lamp. Dick sent an album to Artie, and he said this is damn good clarinet playing, would you like to front my band? That's how that happened. Herb Pomeroy did, as did Al Dawson. Charlie Mariano played a lot in Europe.

CG Al Dawson was considered to be one of the great drummers but he didn't like to tour. He went on the road with Brubeck. Did you ever go to Connolly's in Roxbury?

RD Absolutely. The Sunday afternoon jam sessions with Jimmy Tyler.

CG Jimmy "Bottoms Up" Tyler.

RD Hillary Rose was the organist. That was the house group, and they would bring in Coleman Hawkins, Ray Nance, Paul Gonsalvez, Johnny Hodges. A lot of guys from the Ellington band played there.

CG I think Tony Williams was the house drummer.

RD I thought Joe Riddik was.

CG Sam Rivers played there.

RD The only guys going as purists in Boston radio today are Steve Schwartz and Eric Jackson. Eric is celebrating his 30th anniversary this month.

CG Do you remember when we were having lunch with Fenton Hollander. He was wondering what to do next with the jazz boat and I said, "Jazz is dead."

RD I do remember that. He took over the Regattabar at the Charles Hotel. He later dropped out of that when they brought in New York management. He's out of the business as far as I know.

CG I put him in the jazz business. He rented a harbor boat and put on a concert with a string quartet.

RD The Jazz Boat.

CG No, this was before that. He was doing classical music. I wrote a review for the *Herald* which he used to promote his series. He invited me to dinner, and I said what would really go over would be to combine jazz and the harbor cruise. I recommended the New Black Eagle Jazz Band. Not only did it take off, he added more boats.

RD Was that before he took over the Regattabar.

CG Well before that. Many of the clubs used house bands and brought in headliners. Frequently the pianist was Ran Santisi or Muzzy.

RD Ray played with everyone including the Herb Pomeroy Band. That's when I first heard him. Also, he had quite a few students. He still plays regularly at a place called The Club Caravan in Revere. It was an old wise-guy hangout. Most of those guys are now dead or in jail. Ray is a very soft-spoken guy with a wonderful repertoire. Another great pianist was Bob Winter. He plays regularly with the Jazz Pops Ensemble. It was an offshoot of the Boston Pops, a quartet. John Williams loved that group. Bob is still playing piano with the Pops and Keith Lockhart.

CG The Pops drummer was Fred Buda.

RD He's retired now, but he was the booking agent for all the theaters around town.

CG Let's talk about Lennie's on the Turnpike.

RD He's not doing well, but I talked with him occasionally. He would show up for gigs at Scullers. He had that room up there. It was a great place. Buddy Rich was his man. He brought in a lot of great jazz musicians.

CG I heard Miles at Lennie's.

RD Did you hear Miles when he played a gig in Cambridge at a club, I think it was called Johnny's?

CG Maybe. I heard Miles lots of times.

RD Do you remember Bo Jo's Record Store in Harvard Square?

CG No.

RD A well-known record store. Apparently the owner OD'd listening to Coltrane with headsets on. It's quite a story. I dreamt about that the other day. Didn't mean to get sidetracked.

CG Who did you see at Lennie's? There was a time when he was pushing a local kid who did standup before the band came on. Of course that was Jay Leno. Who knew?

RD I always went to see Buddy Rich. The first time I interviewed him, I was intimidated. He could be a tough guy on the bandstand—screaming and hollering. I went one-on-one with him in the dressing room. He was completely stripped down to his underwear. I still have that interview from 1966. He was very nice to me.

CG I had a similar experience with Rich at Lennie's. My uncle Jim Flynn took me to see Duke Ellington at Storyville when I was a teenager. Later, when I was the jazz critic at the *Herald Traveler* I returned the favor and invited him to come with me to hear Buddy at Lennie's. After the set we went into the dressing room. Just as you say, there was Buddy skipped to his skivvies holding court. A very elegantly dressed George Frazier was in the room. He was the legendary *Globe* columnist and former *Esquire Magazine* jazz writer. We were in awe, and Buddy paid close attention. But George was juiced and just mumbled now and then. So the dialogue was all between me and Buddy. He was at that time a frequent guest of Johnny Carson on the *Tonight Show* and we mostly focused on that. On the drive back to Boston my uncle was thrilled. "You cut George Frazier," he said. "Buddy Rich was talking to you not George Frazier." But it was really no contest. After that night Frazier disappeared for a couple of weeks on a bender in a motel in Southie.

RD He had a habit of doing that. They used to put him up at that motel on the Expressway. You can still go by it. He had a great line in one of his columns. He said, "I'm in a place right now for forty-nine dollars for three people. If we can get another person we can make it a quartet." They would dry him out there. He wrote great columns when he was hung over.

CG Another one of his habits was finnan haddie at Locke Ober's. That's all he would order.

RD He wrote some great stuff including liner notes for albums. For a Miles album he just wrote about his wardrobe. He didn't write a word about what he played. The whole thing was about Miles as a fashion plate. That's a great story. So Charlie, are you going to do a book? I think you should. Absolutely. We're at that age. As I said to Joyce, at least I want to leave something for the grandkids to know what the hell I did.

CG Let's talk about Sandy's Jazz Revival in Beverly. The club of Sandy Berman.

RD Oh man. Sandy's Jazz Revival. Do you know what Stan Getz said? He came on stage one night and said, "I'm glad to be here, everybody. Sandy is an empty suit, but I like his mother."

CG Rose.

RD He would stand at the door and play disc jockey. He was a frustrated DJ. Sandy had a raging battle with Cennamo. Late at night he would be on with James Isaacs and they would call him Sandy Boreman. He would call me up and say, "Did you hear those guys?" He was notoriously cheap and tried to get the best deals possible from musicians. I used to send recording crews from GBH up there every week. Sometimes he wouldn't tell the guys that he was going to record. I was the producer and would have to go in and tell the guys.

Dexter Gordon had just come back from Copenhagen. He came in and saw all the recording equipment. Sandy said to me, "Can you go up and talk to Dexter?" I said, "Why didn't you talk to them?" He said, "I forgot." Did you ever go to that dressing room which was above the club? I climbed up the stairs and Dexter was sitting there. Long, tall Dexter, huge guy. He was like a basketball player like Bill Russell.

He's sitting there with a joint, and he looks at me and says, "Hey baby, what's happening with this recording equipment, man. I don't dig this at all." I said, "Didn't Sandy tell you that we were going to do this for WGBH? A public radio station." He said, "No, man, nobody laid it on me." He looked at me and took a long, long look and a huge toke. On the exhale he handed me the joint and said, "That's cool, baby" and that was it.

CG Years ago near the end of my gig at the *Herald* I had the chance to take a cheap flight and have a week in Copenhagen. In the newspaper business you can be out of the office, but you have to come back with a story for your regular Sunday section feature. So I was looking around Copenhagen. It turns out there were two expatriate jazz musicians Ben Webster and Dexter Gordon. Webster was out of town but I phoned Dexter. He answered and said, "What's happening, baby."

We met for lunch. He was sweating and had the shakes. I was treating, and he ordered a shot of aquavit to get straight. It comes frozen and is poured like syrup. I joined him for three shots and he gave me an incredible interview. There was a jazz club called Montmartre.

RD Yes, he recorded there.

CG Walking out of the restaurant it was like I was on LSD. I was hallucinating. Later it was that gig at Sandy's, which you mentioned. I was there with the late great

Barry Savenor. He always had pimp weed and was turning Dexter on in that room upstairs. I said to Dexter, "Hey remember me? We had lunch in Copenhagen." He took a big toke, looked at me and said, "No, I don't remember, baby."

So it got to be a riff. Every time I talked with him I would say, "Hey Dexter, remember me?" It was always the same answer, "No, baby." But I really dug the guy and it was a hoot to hang with him. Dexter was a stone cold hipster and he could play ballads like an angel. You could feel the words of the lyrics in his horn. Each song ended with that tripped out salute of the vertical sax offered up as a sacrifice to the musical gods, perhaps some bebop Apollo or the shade of Bird.

RD He was nominated for Best Actor in the Academy Awards. For *'Round Midnight*, which was probably the best jazz film ever made. Rollins gets all the accolades today. He's the only one still out there. He goes into those long extended improvs for forty-five minutes.

CG I saw Rollins at Tanglewood a couple of years ago. He can still play like a bitch but was hobbling around the stage. We're all getting wasted, Ron.

RD I hear you, man. I go to the health club every day and work out.

CG You were a runner for many years.

RD Yeah, I did six marathons. Three in New York and three in Boston. I started late in life. In my late 40s, early 50s.

Do you remember Sammy Price? Boogie-woogie piano player? He played at the Copley Plaza, too, on the other side the bar. I used to hang there; you did too.

CG When GBH cancelled *Music America* how did you feel about that?

RD I was caught between the group that wanted to save it and go out with them, or hang around and do classical music and save my gig. I had mixed emotions, but in the long run, I reinvented myself after doing that show for 20 years. There was an editorial in the *Globe*—all kinds of stuff. People wanted their money back. They still come up to me and say I miss you in the afternoon. GBH wanted to be consistent with classical music all day.

CG You were such an incredible resource. Everyone who came through town did your show.

RD Carol Channing came in. Everyone from Carol Channing to Dizzy. Sammy Cahn, who did "Teach Me Tonight" and all those great songs for Sinatra. Jimmy Van Heusen. He was a big part of the *American Songbook*. Mort Sahl would come in. Gene Shepherd, another one of my favorites.

CG How about Professor Irwin Corey?

RD Oh yeah. He's still alive. Fred Taylor told me he's in his 90s. Mort Sahl is around.

CG Dick Gregory?

RD I don't know where he is. You hung out with a lot of these people. You hung in to the bitter end. That's how we ended up going to some of those bizarre parties.

CG All behind me now. Just memories.

RD Exactly. Do you still have your slides and photo archive? I brought some slides to a friend's, and we looked at them with a projector.

CG Do you have much material?

RD Oh yeah, I have a basement loaded with archives. I think I'm going to donate it to BU. When Joyce and I got together 30 years ago, we started taking slides together. But now it's all digital. The Kodacolor holds up real well.

CG That's when Joyce had the Turtle Café in Innman Square.

RD She had jazz there. Santisi played—Bob Winter, Dave McKenna, Gray Sargent, who's on the road with Tony Bennett.

CG I'll be anxious to see your book when it comes out.

RD I had to get a lot of permissions. They don't want to put anything out now unless everything is cleared. It's different than fiction where you can write anything you want.

CG If you do an interview, do you have to get permission?

RD No, if I put it into my quotes and use some of theirs. You are allowed to use so much of it, you know.

CG You can't put out a transcription?

RD Not a whole transcription. It's my spin on my interviews, which is how we get around that. Terry Gross did a book called *All I Did Was Ask*. There's no narrative about her life. It's all about fifty interviews line by line.

CG How did she do that?

RD When you're on her show you sign for permission. She gets the release right away, which is the way to do it. For your photos, it's all your stuff. You don't need any permissions. So I would put something out. A drummer friend of mine, who is our age, is putting out a book called *Natural Causes* because all his friends are dropping off.

CG Ron, when they have your funeral, will they play jazz or classical music.

RD I think classical.

CG Really. So Pavarotti not "The Saints Come Marching In."

RD I think it will be the Intermezzo from Puccini's *Manon Lescaut*. It opens the third act. If you listen very carefully, John Williams used a direct quote for *Star Wars*. I hear a lot of things that are lifted when I'm listening.

CG Let's connect at Tanglewood this summer.

RD Right. We lived in another era, Charles

Ron Della Chiesa in the WGBH studio. Photo by Charles Giuliano.

Ron hosted a live broadcast of Tony Bennett and Dave McKenna. Photo by Charles Giuliano.

Ron broke into radio working for T. Mitchell Hastings at WBCN. Photo by Charles Giuliano.

Teddy Wilson alternated with McKenna at the Copley Plaza. Photo by Charles Giuliano.

Ron introducing drumming prodigy Terri Lyne Carrington. Photo by Charles Giuliano.

Ron with jazz entrepreneur Lennie Sogaloff. Photo by Charles Giuliano.

Ron with club owner Sandy Berman. Photo by Charles Giuliano.

Club owner Chester English of Lulu White's. Photo by Charles Giuliano.

Al Perry settled differences between talent and management for WBCN

While many during the Golden Age of WBCN had their heads in the clouds, former station manager Al Perry had his feet on the ground. Somebody had to stay straight and pay the bills.

In the volatile mix of on-air personalities and management, Perry was a fixer. He describes an era when the station was so poor that it recycled tapes of now-rare and priceless on-air interviews and live performances.

For the past couple of years, during crunch time, he worked closely with Bill Lichtenstein bringing to fruition the documentary *WBCN: The American Revolution.*

Charles Giuliano In terms of the counterculture in Boston from the late 1960s to the 1980s, why has it not gotten the recognition that it deserves?

Al Perry *Rolling Stone* was based in San Francisco and always writing about KSAN. Tom Donahue, who ran the station, was very progressive. He was a nice guy and I had the occasion to meet him in DC. In New York, there was WNEW with a transmitter on top of the Empire State Building.

Neither of these stations was along the lines of WBCN and what we got involved with. KSAN with Donahue was a little more political than WNEW.

Part of the problem was that we were in Boston and not in New York or LA.

That had a lot to do with it.

The Who loved playing at The Boston Tea Party. They could be drafted if they overstayed their visas, so they would play Boston on the way in and on the way out. There was a 30-day window before they could get drafted into the service.

They were working on *Tommy* and Townsend sent an acetate to MCA meant for WBCN. Somebody at MCA in New York took it to WNEW. When Townsend was in New York and heard it on the radio, he asked, "How did they get that?" The guy at MCA said, "You sent it to us and we gave it to them." Townsend said, "I sent it to be given to WBCN in Boston, and that's to be done immediately."

We got it by Greyhound Bus that day, as there was no FedEx at the time.

It was the mentality of MCA saying, we have to take this to WNEW. The Who were on Decca/MCA at the time.

CG While doing research, I came across a reference that Queen broke out on WBCN.

AP I would attribute that to Maxanne [Sartori]. Queen was among her favorite, favorite bands. Aerosmith was another. Freddy Lewis [original manager of J. Geils and Cars] was working for Elektra Records. He was the promo guy behind Queen. He was close to Maxanne and likely came to the station and played it for her. That kind of thing happened a lot and she went with it.

CG When were you with WBCN?

AP I was there in 1967 and the change to rock in 1968, through the fall of 1976.

CG When were you program director?

AP I was never the program director. I was station manager, sales manager, and announcer.

CG You have seen *WBCN and the American Revolution*. To what extent does the film reflect your own views?

AP Very much so. I loved music and the arts. A lot of that came from my good friend Dennis Metrano (1942–2015). We were very close early on. When he moved to Newburyport we didn't stay in touch as much. When we had a WBCN anniversary party at the Hard Rock Café, I insisted that he come.

CG Dennis picked me up in a limo and we arrived in style for a memorable evening.

AP I was actually in the military, and Dennis was in Boston. I would be home for a few days to see my parents. My mother would say, "What's up?" I told her, "I'm going to see Dennis." He played a lot of great music for me which had a real influence.

I was never in Vietnam, but having been in the service, I saw the stupidity of it all.

CG Former Boston promo guy Roger Lifeset has emphasized how much music was breaking with WBCN. He was with Warner Brothers while Paul Ahern was promoting bands for Atlantic Records.

AP Maxanne broke Aerosmith. Carole King flew out of stores when we pushed *Tapestry*. [Released in 1971, it sold 25 million copies.] Emerson, Lake and Palmer is another band that broke on WBCN. Also we backed The Who, Rod Stewart. [In 1971 John Garabedian, of Boston's WMEX, broke "Maggie May" on Mercury Records.] J.J. Jackson, an African American DJ for WBCN went on to great success. He broke Jethro Tull.

There was always that spice of jazz, which we were allowed to play. We even had some classical music, which Charles Laquidara loved. We played Roland Kirk and people like that. He was being paired with rock bands at The Tea Party.

If a promo guy walked in with a new Muddy Waters or John Lee Hooker album, it was on a turntable immediately.

CG You were in management for a station in which the DJs determine the suitability of what ads were aired. What kind of financial problems did that create?

AP We had to convince people to let us do their commercials our own way, in a manner that appealed to our audience. In the movie, someone comments that "You had ads that people actually listened to." The problem was what to do with Coca Cola, shampoos, and creams that were being promoted at the time. We really didn't want those ads.

CG Was WBCN profitable?

AP The station never lost money when I was there. We didn't make a lot of money but it was profitable.

CG What was your role in the WBCN strike?

AP I wasn't there at the time [three weeks in 1979], but I helped Kenny Greenblatt [sales department], who was trying to make calls. In the annals of radio strikes, it was one of the few successful ones.

CG Why did you leave in 1976?

AP I was getting a lot of pressure from [owner] T. Mitchell Hastings. He was the primary stockholder at the time. Ray Riepen was gone, and Mitch was basically in charge. He wanted out. Obviously, we didn't want to see it sold. He wanted to sell WBCN, and we just weren't getting along. It was time for me to get out of there. After that, I worked for various record companies. Music was what I knew.

CG What are highlights of your time with the station?

AP I kept a lot of great people employed. Norm Winer was program director, but I played a role in any live broadcast that we did. Previously, I had worked with Fred Taylor, so it was intuitive to do live broadcasts from Jazz Workshop and Paul's Mall.

When the staff formed a union, I was involved with negotiations from a management standpoint. Having been an announcer, as well as in sales and management, I was sympathetic to what they needed in order to continue. I fought for them.

CG Were you involved in the live broadcasts from Intermedia?

AP One of the biggest ones was with J. Geils and Canned Heat. Norm was friendly with Marty Mull and we did a hilarious broadcast. What happened was the Youngbloods. They were playing for Freddy Taylor at Paul's Mall. They wanted to do a live broadcast but we weren't set up for that at the time. They came to the station and performed in the front office. They played for a couple of hours. The next day I got many calls from people I respected in the music industry.

A couple of days later, Norm and I sat down and discussed it. Norm was friendly with Intermedia Studios, so we put in a telephone line from Newbury Street to WBCN on Stuart Street. That's how it started, and then we moved to the Mall and Workshop.

CG Were you present during the live broadcast when Patti Smith unleashed a screed of obscenities?

AP (*Laughing*) Yes, I was. Norm and I were sitting there in the Jazz Workshop. She started in and I said, "Norm, I'm going home."

The movie talks about obscenities on the air. By then I had written enough letters explaining incidents to the FCC.

Andrew Kopkind and Little John did *The Lavender Hour* and were working in the news department. When we were working on the contract, Andy said, "Al we need to talk about something." There was a gay woman, Elaine Noble, representing the Back Bay. She wanted to introduce a bill about not being fired for sexual preference. He said if we can get some wording in our contract, it would be very useful for her. So the language was put into our contract, which was pretty early on in 1972 or 1973.

CG Did you have problems with Duane Glasscock?

AP I had left. Charles had left and they wanted him back. I said to him, "Why don't you go back under a different name?" He came up with Glasscock. That was a pretty big show let me tell you.

CG How were the ratings for the station?

AP They were never great. They were okay. They were pretty good. Then WCOZ came along, and we took a bath. It took awhile to get our rating back.

CG In what way was WBCN different from other stations?

AP If you take the notion of free form, a DJ could pick fifteen or twenty albums to start a show. On a Top 40 station you couldn't pick your own music. We didn't have it laid out on paper to play this or that.

CG Were you around when Maxanne and women came aboard?

AP It came about because there was a backlash that there were no women on air. We were using terms like chicks and the local women's movement protested. Debbie Ulman, a very talented person, had been on the air off and on. But we needed someone full time. A friend of Sam Kopper knew of Maxanne in Seattle. We were happy to have her.

CG Were you around during the time of Ray Riepen?

AP He was my mentor. He was always a good guy to me. He was an interesting guy, always full of new ideas. He was very forward and liberal thinking.

CG It's hard to imagine a liberal lawyer from Kansas.

AP He was well read and well educated.

CG What was the dynamic between Riepen and Hastings?

AP Before Ray even got the first rock record played at WBCN he had found the ability to buy stock. There were a lot of old Yankees and friends of Hasting on the board. They didn't want to see him lose everything. They were encouraged by what Ray was proposing. I wasn't in the room, but I think they convinced Hastings to give it a chance. Even though he thought the on-air talent looked like shit, which it did.

CG You were there and how did Hastings deal with the changes?

AP He enjoyed the fact that money was coming in. New England Merchants Bank wasn't beating him up every week. He owed money, and there was a lot of pressure on him. Now and then, he got foolish on me and wanted to spend money we didn't have. He had a grand vision, for example, of putting a super stereo system in his car. It was thousands of dollars and the company would pay for it.

CG Eventually the station went commercial, broadcasting Patriots games, running national ads, and hiring Howard Stern.

AP It was a tough decision. Very few of us working for the station at the time wanted to see the move to the Prudential Building. We knew that it would cost more money. That meant changing patterns of commercial acceptance.

CG Who was behind the move to the Prudential?

AP T. Mitchell. It was his dream to be on the fiftieth floor. I was happy with where we were.

CG Did you have a stronger signal from the top of the Pru?

AP The signal was on top of the original John Hancock building, the smaller

25-story Hancock. When they were building the new one it was going to block the signal in many ways, so we had to make a choice. We had to think about moving the signal somewhere.

CG What was the listenership when you were there?

AP It was pretty large. There is no question that Arbitron, now Nielsen, didn't do a very good job of rating 18 to 24-year-olds. They weren't looking at college students unless they were living in an apartment. We did an off-handed survey of college listeners. I should have kept that stuff, but it was pretty big; among college students it was massive.

CG It seems that all the sales were local and that you weren't getting national ads.

AP Clive Davis, the head of Columbia Records during the heyday of Bob Dylan, was one of the few record company executives who realized that they weren't going to be selling 45s much longer. They were going to be selling LPs. We got a lot of buys from labels when we played their albums. That's primarily what Kenny Greenblatt did. He was our liaison to various labels.

There was a sizeable income that came our way because of what we played. Now and then there was a buy for something a record company wanted us to play but we wouldn't play it.

Allen Freed of Sack Theaters told [sales person] Jack Carney that "You know, WBCN is where I put all my money to promote youth movies."

We were happy to have a radio station where we could do what we wanted to do.

You talked to [promo guy] Roger Lifeset. He moved to the other coast, and from that vantage point, can look back and appreciate what the station meant to people.

CG How radical were Danny Schechter and the news department compared to other stations?

AP Danny was a guy you could go to, say what you want to say, and he wouldn't chop it up. People like Abbie Hoffman and Angela Davis knew that they could do an interview and it would get on the air. They trusted him. He was a good voice for them.

CG What was the impact of his news coverage on local and national politics?

AP I was very much involved in the bussing era. Many times I found myself and other media people sitting in [Mayor] Kevin White's office. How could we explain this to people and keep the city calm? We had our moments.

We were in pretty tough shape when Nixon invaded Cambodia. The students erupted. Then we didn't have a choice but to go along with them. The phones never stopped ringing, and people were at the station all night long. It was intense and I don't think that was happening at other radio stations.

CG What are you doing these days?

AP I'm retired living with my wife in Cambridge. For the past couple of years, I have been spending a lot of time with Bill [Lichtenstein] working on the movie. It's been crunch time for him. I helped him with fundraising ideas. I donated some of my memorabilia to be auctioned off. We would have dinner and talk through the process. It's been difficult.

You know what he went through to get the Jeff Albertson and Peter Simon images. Back then nobody was walking around taking pictures with iPhones or putting things on tape. It's been a long process.

There are some great storytellers in the film; Ray [Riepen], Tommy Hadges, Charles [Laquidara].

CG He says that when the project got started [2006] there was no WBCN archive to work with. What happened to all that material like tapes of live interviews and performances?

AP I had a little bit of stuff, like bumper stickers. I might have an occasional tape of a live Muddy Waters broadcast or something. But I didn't have a lot of that stuff. When Bill put the word out, listeners came forward with things.

We used to do a show now and then on Sunday nights called *The Underground Tapes*. They were live tapes and various things people had given to us. Obviously there were the *Dylan Basement Tapes*. There was Buffalo Springfield stuff. We would do a four-hour show.

I went into Cheap Thrills in Harvard Square on a Saturday. I said, "I need to buy some blank tape." The clerk said, "We don't have any. Since you guys announced the show we've been sold out." So people were taping this stuff.

In the film, you saw that part about Duane Allman and Jerry Garcia showing up and doing a live session. It was taped, but we were so poor, that the next day, that tape must have been used for something else.

CG If you were doing live shows, wouldn't one expect that the station was archiving that unique material?

AP Not necessarily so. We were poor in some way.

CG What were salaries like?

AP Nobody was making lots of money. Back them maybe somebody like Charles made twenty grand. If they were frugal maybe they could buy a used VW.

CG Jim Parry was a neighbor of mine in the Murder Building [University Road] in Cambridge. It was cheap rent for his apartment filled with stacks of records. I know for a fact that he wasn't into spending money. Jim was unique in that he listened to, rated, and logged every album he received. He had a recycled stack that now and then I bought from.

AP I'm glad we had this conversation because I read your stuff. I wanted to thank you for what you wrote about Dennis [Metrano] because we were close.

CG So you hung out at Daisy [Buchanan's, a bar on Newbury Street where Metrano was the bartender. It was a music business after-work hangout.]

AP Oh, yeah. I lived on Gloucester Street, which was just around the corner. Dennis was a very talented guy. When I was in the service he had a six-foot standup promo cutout of Bob Dylan in his apartment. What would that be worth today?

CG I'm sure Bieber has one.

Al Perry settled disputes between talent and management at WBCN. Photo by Jeff Alberson.

Perry in his office. Photo by Jeff Albertson.

WBCB studio portrait with Al wearing a tie. Photo by David Bieber.

Dennis and RCA promo guy Don Delacey. Photo by Charles Giuliano.

Bartender and rock critic Dennis Metrano. Photo by Charles Giuliano.

Dennis and Al grew up together. Photo by Charles Giuliano.

Charles Laquidara concocted mayhem and mishegoss at WBCN

From 1968 to 2000, first on WBCN and then for the last five years with WZLX, Charles Laquidara was one of the most beloved, outspoken, and controversial DJ's during a golden era of counterculture in Boston.

During the week, he hosted a morning show *The Big Mattress*, which started as a parody of AM shows like New York's *Imus in the Morning*. On Saturday mornings, all hell broke loose when the alter ego of Laquidara, Duane Ingalls Glasscock, unleashed his roiling and outrageous mishegoss.

Arbitron/Nielsen ratings of two to four are regarded as good to excellent. Those for Glasscock were unprecedented at 13. At his peak, Laquidara was one of the nation's top DJ's and part of why, for a time, WBCN-FM dominated key demographics in Boston radio.

It is argued that Howard Stern, while a student at Boston University, tuned into *The Big Mattress*. There are aspects of his radio format that resemble Laquidara's.

In 1973, Stern worked as a DJ for WTBU on a show called King Schmaltz Bagel Hour. WTBU was the first of several stations to fire Stern, after he ran a segment titled "Making the Bishop Blush."

Eventually, Stern's syndicated show bumped *The Big Mattress* causing Laquidara to move to WZLX.

During two lengthy phone calls to his home in Maui, Laquidara stated that he got out of 'BCN and Boston radio in the nick of time. In 2000, he left in his prime and avoided the ugly endgame of decline and fall of all that was glorious about Boston's unique counterculture media.

Charles Giuliano Aloha.

Charles Laquidara I'm just burning an English muffin here.

CG I'm sure you've burned something else over time.

CL Really. What time is it there? It's only 9 a.m. here.

CG As you suggested I'm calling at 3 p.m. To what extent have you been impacted by the eruption of a volcano. I understand that you're on Maui but have there been any issues?

[A new lava flow opened in the Puna district of Hawaii Island the afternoon of Thursday, May 3, 2018.]

CL None whatsoever. It depends on which way the wind blows. Since the eruption, the trade winds have been blowing in the other direction. When those winds switch, as some day they will, they're called Kona winds because Kona is a big area for tourism on the big island. So when the winds switch and come this way, then we'll probably get some issues. We may get some ash, which irritates the eyes. Who knows what nature is up to, but we'll see.

CG How do you get from island to island? Or do you?

CL What usually happens here is people tend to stay in their own areas. People up-country tend to stay away from the city life of downtown Maui and towns that are more populated.

CG It doesn't sound like you're suffering.

CL (*Laughs*) No Charlie, one of the interesting things is that me being an atheist for years and years—I'm very, very grateful for, what's that theory, the butterfly effect? There was a movie about it but wasn't very clear.

[*The Butterfly Effect* is a 2004 film written and directed by Eric Bress and J. Mackye Gruber, starring Ashton Kutcher and Amy Smart.]

What it means is that if you knew that every single thing you did and every single thing that everyone else does, minute by minute—it's not a theory really, it's true—everything you do affects everyone else in some way or another. Whatever led you to be married or take the job you have? Whatever phone call you didn't take which led to…? Everything depends on decisions that you make. If you take a left on a road, you may pick up a hitchhiker who decides your future; or that hitchhiker gets lost in the woods. It goes on and on. If you really knew how many changes that butterfly effect has, you might never want to leave the house, or get up from your chair, because it impacts everything you do, if you think about it: how you got your job; how you met somebody; what one friend did to change your whole life.

[In chaos theory, the butterfly effect is the sensitive dependence on initial conditions in which a small change in one state of a deterministic nonlinear system can result in large differences in a later state. The term, coined by Edward Lorenz, is derived from the metaphorical example of the details of a tornado (the exact time of formation, the exact path taken) being influenced by minor perturbations such as the flapping of the wings of a distant butterfly several weeks earlier. Lorenz discovered the effect when he observed that runs of his weather model with initial condition data that was rounded in a seemingly inconsequential manner would fail to reproduce the results of runs with the unrounded initial condition data. A very small change in initial conditions had created a significantly different outcome.]

CG It sounds like the butterfly effect has been good to you.

CL I'm thankful when I watch the sunsets out here every night. I realize how lucky I am. That's all it is, luck. To be living in Hawaii for most of my life, twenty years now. I've spent more time here than even in Massachusetts.

CG You moved there in 2000.

CL I moved here officially in 2000, but my wife Doreen and I bought a home here a couple of years before that. Yeah, I've been here awhile.

CG I went to a website that has rumors about Charles Laquidara. (*Laughing*) There appear to be a lot of them.

CL Is there a Charles Laquidara rumors page?

CG Yes. Like, what's his sexual orientation? What drugs does he take? Stuff like that.

CL Are you friggin' kidding me? I would love to see it. Can you send me a link? Give me an example of what they said, and I'll tell you whether it's true or not. What do they say about my sexual orientation? That I'm gay or ACDC?

CG As I recall a reader can check a box and there are a number of options.

CL So it's like a survey.

CG I thought it was your site because it's very graphic and colorful with lots of different boxes. You said to me, "Go to my site and play a little bit," which I've done. I also came up with this, which had some of the same feeling as your official site.

CL There's a lot of Laquidara shit out there. But there's nothing I can do about it. There are a lot of sites that praise me more than I'm worth. That's what you get when you work on WBCN.

CG Can you quantify your fan base? It was demonstrated to me when you linked to my site and within a couple of days I got 3,000 hits [For a mention in an article].

CL It's weird. When I left radio in August 2000, I put it all behind me, and said, I'll just go to Hawaii. I just think back on those days and again 'BCN, not me, and the fact I was lucky enough to work there 'BCN's magic, mythology, tradition, whatever you want to call it, is so powerful that these people out there all kind of stuck around. They didn't forget. So they see my name on Facebook and go OMG, 'BCN. Most of what I do is what anyone with a public persona does right now—from having a dialogue with 20 people, or having a Facebook page with thirty-five thousand people. It's all about Trump, which is the most amazing phenomenon I've ever heard of in my life. My Facebook page is 90 percent political.

It pissed off a lot of the 'BCN people who are conservative. Boston has a very big base of conservative listeners. Boston itself is liberal, but when you go to the suburbs, or inner city, like Southie, it changes. So I've got I don't know how many people on Facebook. But almost half of them are very conservative. They hate my politics. There are a few dozen people who are always arguing with me and putting up their bullshit Fox News and doing all that stuff.

My very intelligent conservative friends, even though they know that Trump is a clown, they go along with the conservative stuff because that's the state of America right now.

Some of my former listeners say, "Charles why don't you stick to the music? You turned into a leftie."

In fact, for most of my 'BCN days except for the end, they told me to back off on the politics because they wanted me to get good ratings. Every now and then I made a statement on the radio that would get me in trouble. They allowed me to do one huge thing and that was a boycott of Shell Oil. That went very well because any time anyone, a celebrity or politician, would come into the studio we would have them read a short audio bit that would ask listeners to boycott Shell Oil and tear up their Shell Oil credit card. Actually, it turned out to be pretty successful and I even got my picture in *Time Magazine*. It was a wicked ugly picture and I looked like Charles Manson, at least I made *Time Magazine*. It could have been worse a few years later *Rolling Stone Magazine* did a feature on me and called me Tony Laquidara through the whole fucking article.

[In 1986 the *New York Times* reported, in part, that "Union officials joined leaders of the movement against South Africa's policy of racial separation today to call for a consumer boycott of Shell Oil Company products. Organizers said the boycott was the opening of a new campaign to get companies to withdraw their investments from South Africa. 'Shell is the first company on our list,' said Randall Robinson, co-chairman of the Free South Africa Movement, 'It is not the last.' The Washington-based group has organized protests at the South African Embassy here for more than a year to press South Africa to dismantle the country's official policy of racial separation… Owen F. Bieber, president of the United Automobile Workers, said union members would be urged to cut their Shell credit cards in half and mail them to the American Federation of Labor and Congress of Industrial Organizations…The action came at the request of the International Confederation of Free Trade Unions…Organizers said Shell, a wholly-owned subsidiary of the Royal Dutch/Shell Group, was chosen for the boycott because of the parent company's heavy involvement in the South African economy, where it has petroleum and mining operations. Labor leaders also accused Shell of "mistreating" its South African miners.]

CG Was this kind of on-air activism reflected in the music for your program?

CL The problem with the music, no matter who it is, Bruce Springsteen, Bono, Paul McCartney, all of them, Bob Dylan, they were all liberals. The conservatives showed an incredible ability to love Paul McCartney and Bob Dylan, Bono, Sting, and everybody— Leonard Cohen, but they still kept their conservative views. I don't know what the heck they do, what these Trump lovers do with lyrics. The lyrics hit them in the brain, but I don't know what it does to them. They don't get it.

Do me a favor spell my name right and fact check for spellings. I used to be an English teacher and mistakes drive me nuts. Good luck with spelling mishegoss.

CG No problem. I graduated from Brandeis, so I use a lot of Yiddish.

CL My son went to Brandeis. What year did you graduate? He was born in 1980.

CG 1963. I read that it took you four years to do two years at RISD?

CL My dad was a barber, so I was lucky to even get into RISD. I guess one day they decided that there would be some kind of Italian quota. So they let me in. Yeah, I had to work for a year.

CG Were you considering being an artist?

CL I wanted to be a political cartoonist.

CG I emailed you that you did cartoons for a parody I wrote of Hunter Thompson and gonzo journalism. It was for a one-off *Phoenix* tabloid project that David Bieber put together. [Spring, 1977, *Rolling Boulder*, "Fear and Loathing in the Carter White House," supplement of *The Boston Phoenix*.]

CL Did you send me those illustrations or just tell me about them?

CG Bieber has them in his vast archive, but he is very difficult to contact. A friend who "works with him" says that it is impossible to reach him. He has a warehouse which is being considered to be a museum, but it's a work in progress.

[David Bieber was a publicist for WBCN, the *Boston Phoenix*, WFNX, and other media outlets. When writing a thesis on pop music as a student of the Boston University School of Journalism he compiled back issues of *Billboard Magazine* as part of his research. That snowballed. Bieber has signed a 20-year lease at the Norwood Space Center, which will serve as the home to over one million items of pop culture memorabilia. Though not open to the public, he curated the rock-theme installation for Boston Verb Hotel.

CL If the cartoons ever show up ship them off to me. That would be great.

CG I was surprised when Bieber used you as the illustrator for that *Phoenix* supplement. Prior to then I had no idea that you did graphic art. Also in an email I mentioned that I saw you perform at the Loeb Drama Center in *That Championship Season*. [A 1972 play by Jason Miller. It was the recipient of the 1973 Pulitzer Prize for Drama.]

CL Again Charlie, I don't know if there is a word for someone who is pretending to be humble and is actually bullshitting, but all my success was about finding the right people. For *That Championship Season*, Tommy Thompson was a fantastic director. Whatever qualities, I had he brought it out. I was not that good an actor, but Tommy was such a great director.

Do you remember Pat Collins back in the day? She worked for the *Globe*.

CG No, she was a TV critic.

[She started in Boston media and became a three-time Emmy winner for WWOR-TV. Collins was an entertainment editor and film critic for *Good Morning America*, *The CBS Morning News*, and from 1972–1977, hosted the *Pat Collins Show*, which won two Emmys on WCBS-TV.)

CL She was like Louella Parsons. She saw my name on the marquee and figured I was just that DJ from a hippie rock station. She gave me a great review.

CG All these years later, I recall that production and your performance. That speaks well to your acting.

Famously, you did a screen test for *The Boston Strangler*. [The 1968 film starred Tony Curtis.] That could have been a butterfly.

CL For sure. What happened was, I didn't do a screen test. I was working in the print shop of 20th Century Fox. I saw the script for *The Boston Strangler* and I stole it. I made a copy and took it home. I asked some of my actor friends to help me, like Charlotte Stewart from *Little House on the Prairie*. She played one of the women that Albert DeSalvo killed. We used a videotape recorder, which was unheard of at the time. It was a new invention. Jerry Lewis was starting to use it in films that he was directing.

We rented one, and I did an audition scene. At the time, I was dating the secretary of the producer of the show. She let me into his office when he was out to lunch. I set up a video recorder in his office. When he came in, the shades were drawn down. He called her on the intercom and said, "What the heck is going on?" She said, "There's this fellow from the print shop and he has something he wants to show you."

I actually have a copy of that scene in *Daze in the Life: A Slightly Disjointed Multimedia Memoir*.

I played the Boston Strangler for about 20 seconds. He said, "Where have you been?" He was all excited. He was going to cast me right away and talk to the director. He set me up for a screen test. So there I was in the middle of the stage a few weeks later with all of the producers and directors of 20th Century Fox. I can't do cold readings and I thought that was the end of it.

CG You went on to better things. On your website I saw you as The Godfaddah. You did the scene when Don Corleone dies in the tomato patch.

CL (*Laughs*) Yeah I did *The Godfather* in Hawaii.

CG You took over from Peter Wolf [as WBCN DJ].

CL Yes, but it's interesting how history changes depending on who experiences it and how they remember it. According to Steve Segal, The Seagull, Steven Clean, who says he was the program director at the time. I had just moved to Boston from California because my mom was sick. I called 'BCN and was invited to the station. Peter Wolf had just started working with a band. He was doing late night at 'BCN, according to Steve Segal, Peter had a gig with the J. Geils band, which had just formed. So he asked if Charlie "Master Blaster" Daniels could take Peter's slot. Do you remember him?

CG Of course, he was the MC for the Tea Party.

CL He asked Charlie Daniels to substitute for him [Wolf]. So he went on air, and said whatever girls might want to come down and give him pleasure, or whatever it was, it was not cool. Segal said to Peter, you have to make up your mind whether you want to be a DJ or with that band [J. Geils]. So Peter quit.

About the same time Tommy Hadges was working daytime. According to Segal, Hadges decided that he wanted to go to dental school. We called him Captain Novocain. He decided to go back and finish up at Tufts. So there were openings at night and during the day. Steve decided to put Jim Parry on at night and me during the day.

But if you talk to Joe Rogers, Sam Kopper, Al Perry, Tommy Hadges, you'll get an entirely different version or bunch of versions of this.

[Hadges and Joe Rodgers were students of Tufts who were DJ's for M.I.T.'s WTBS. They were recruited to WBCN by its rock entrepreneur Ray Riepen. Together they launched rock as a new format for the station on March 15, 1968, playing "I Feel Free" by Cream. The staff also included Wolf, Sam Kopper, Al Perry, and Jim Parry.]

Segal's take is totally different from the legend. You can decide which of the two the right story is. History is written by the winners. Both Kopper and Segal are alive with different versions. That was winter of 1968 when I came to 'BCN.

CG Can you talk about T. Mitchell Hastings, founder of WBCN, and Ray Riepen, who convinced him to switch to a rock format?

CL Yeah, but there are so many different things to talk about. What I can say about T. Mitchell Hastings is that he was a weird guy, an eccentric. He was just trying to make money for the station and he thought that there was money in rock 'n' roll, so he let the people do what they ended up doing. It turned out to be very profitable. He sold the station for a lot of money. He could have made ten times that if he waited.

[Theodore Mitchell Hastings, Jr. was an engineer genius who launched WBCN FM on April 24, 1958. It was, originally, a classical music radio station. Prior to broadcasting he invented an FM radio for the car and an early pocket FM transistor radio. Until then there was little access to FM radio and minimal commercial potential. He formed the General Broadcasting Corporation, later to be known as Concert Network Inc. Hastings acquired, then changed the call letters to: WNCN New York City; WHCN Hartford; WXCN Providence; WRCN on Long Island and WBCN Boston. Hastings and his wife were followers of the clairvoyant Edgar Cayce, whose predictions influenced questionable business decisions. That resulted in selling stations with only WBCN left when Ray Riepen convinced him to experiment with rock radio. He remained as general manager and owner. In 1973 he moved the studio to the top of the Prudential Tower. He sold the station to Hemisphere Broadcasting in 1979. That sparked a strike against new management.]

There's a story that Norm Winer, Old Saxophone Joe, could tell you. One day he was in Mitch's office, and in the middle of a conversation, he said, "excuse me," leaned over a shopping bag with new socks and changed his socks. Hastings didn't wash his socks he just bought new ones that went up to the knee.

As far as Riepen goes, I can't say enough great things about Ray Riepen.

CG Oh really!

CL We had ups and downs. I pissed him off a lot. The drum solo story you might have heard of.

CG Of course.

[Ray Riepen, a Kansas lawyer who enrolled for post grad work at Harvard Law School, was driving around listening to his station. Laquidara was playing a drum solo. Riepen called and told him "no more drum solos they're boring to listeners." Charles hung up and played nothing but drum solos for the rest of his show. Riepen, initially with David Hahn, also started the Boston Tea Party and had a piece of the *Cambridge Phoenix* an alternative weekly. Facing labor disputes, he sold his interests and left town. It is rumored that he bought an abandoned mining town in the West. He has remained under the media radar. A resident of Kansas, he has attended the occasional WBCN reunion.]

CL He hired Arnie Ginsburg and his main job was to fire me, which he did.

[Arnie "Woo-Woo" Ginsburg (born August 5, 1926) was an American disc jockey in the Boston radio market from the mid-1950s to the 1970s. Following this period, he was a business manager, president and owner of WVJV-TV, and later an executive with Pyramid Broadcasting and program manager of their Boston station WXKS/1430.]

The legend is that when he fired me, they formed a union and that's how we beat the Infinity Broadcasting people from New York when they bought the station.

[The staff went on a three-week strike against WBCN in 1979, when Hastings sold it to Michael Wiener and Gerald Carrus.]

Through Riepen, Ginsburg fired me, but Hastings went over his head and hired me back.

When Ginsburg fired me, Danny Schechter put together a union saying if they can fire Laquidara they can fire anybody.

["Danny Schechter, the news dissector," as he was known, died at 72 in 2015.]

I think Danny and the fellow who was news director before him, Bo Burlingham, would have different versions of how our union was formed.

Both stories sound good and it's a matter of finding the right one. I don't know, Charlie…everything is so foggy that whatever you write will be okay.

CG I'm trying to put together an overview of what was happening in the 1970s.

There is the sense that compared to what was going on in New York and San Francisco the counterculture in Boston has gotten relatively little respect. In that context WBCN was a dominant radio station of the era. Everything was new. There was no template. You guys were inventing it as you went along. How did that evolve, in your case, into *The Big Mattress*?

CL The time you are talking about, the 1970s, 'BCN was very popular with college students, the millennials, or whatever you called them back then.

There is a movie coming out in a week or two by Bill Lichtenstein called *WBCN and the American Revolution*. It addresses the era and issues you are asking about.

CG How did that evolve, in your case, into *The Big Mattress*?

CL The major shift of prime time FM listening was not morning drive time. Nobody listened then. They were listening to WBZ, RKO, or whatever. They were on their way to work getting the news, weather, traffic, whatever. The most popular shift for 'BCN was 6 p.m. That's when people were stirring their rice, cooking, smoking dope, and getting ready for the evening. So that was prime time when I was working. Dinah Vaprin at the time was working mornings. We had these weekly DJ meetings.

This was the time of Bread and Roses and the women's movement was getting active. Dinah Vaprin was down at the front of the room. She raised her hand and said, "How come women always get the shit shifts? Why do women get stuck in the morning?"

I said, "Dinah, there's no such thing as a bad shift at WBCN." (*Laughing*) At the time I thought that may be the biggest mistake of my life. She turned and said,

"Okay fucker, you take mornings." So I said, "Okay, I will."

I left the meeting and said to the program director, Norm Winer, "What the fuck did I do?" He said, "Sorry, but you're now on mornings." (*Both laughing*) So it was weird. What was I going to do with the morning shift?

So I said why don't we do a parody of AM morning shows and do all this stupid stuff? Let's just have some fun. At that time, morning radio was like that guy in New York who wears a cowboy hat.

CG *Imus in the Morning*. [The show ended after 50 years in 2018.]

CL He put out a vinyl record of wakeup calls. I said, damn, that's what we're going to do on 'BCN. So Charlie, I swear to God, everyone in Boston and radioland forgot about Imus and they give me credit for those calls, which is very interesting, that I get credit for inventing the radio wakeup call. But, really, it was Don Imus.

Anyway, we used it and took it to a different level. Imus did a lot of scripting and most of them, I'm pretty certain, were acted out in advance. But I'm not sure. My calls were not rehearsed, and sometimes we didn't have delay and might have risked our FCC license once in awhile.

CG To what extent did *Big Mattress* pull together aspects of your background? In some respects you became what today we would call a performance artist.

CL I could give a little credit for my success, first of all, to the fact that I was a big, testosterone-laden, Italian bullshitter. Fuggedaboutit. Screw your mother. Going to RISD. I remember being turned down by a girl because it was a time in the '60s when rich girls were having coming out parties. "Coming Out" had a different meaning then than today. They were debutantes. I remember being totally in love with one of my classmates. She was a debutante. Her dad wouldn't let her go out with me because I was a barber's kid. I remember driving away from her house crying and playing Verdi's *Aida* full volume on my car radio.

It was that kind of time and having that experience of being with all these wonderful artists who were so much more creative than I, being so lucky to be at Rhode Island School of Design and meeting all these incredible true artists who went on to great things.

Then going to Pasadena Playhouse, with all of its great actors. My girlfriend, Deanne McKinstry, was a great singer, a soprano. One of my best friends, Danny Truhitte, got one of the lead parts in the movie *The Sound of Music*. He was the one who sang "Sixteen Going on Seventeen." Danny came to Milford, Mass, to visit me. We brought my parents to see *Sound of Music* and they didn't know he was in it.

All these stories are in *Daze in the Life* and you can use them for your article.

CG Unfortunately, there are so many stories that you are the *War and Peace* of radio. So I'm trying to catch the highlights.

CL It is true, but there are certain things I can point you to check out. There's the story of me flying with The Blue Angels. You're right, there's a lot of stuff.

CG It fascinated me that you had an early gig as a classical radio DJ. There was a particular interest in opera. To what extent is that a part of your Italian heritage?

CL None. None whatsoever. That came when I was living in Pasadena and when I went to RISD. This was before rock 'n' roll, which didn't come in until the late '50s. Doo-Wop and that. What we were romancing to was Pat Boone, Johnny Mathis, maybe once in a while they would play a black guy on the radio.

CG For me it was The Platters.

CL Absolutely. "The Great Pretender" (1955) and songs like "Silhouette" [The Rays, 1957]. And "Why Do Fools Fall in Love" [Frankie Lymon and the Teenagers, 1956] But there was no rock 'n' roll as we know it today.

There I was at RISD with all those artists and rich kids. Some were working class like me. But I wanted to fit in. I remember going to a party—and they really knew how to party—my first year there. Here I am, just turned 18, fresh out of high school from Milford, Mass., a dinky suburb of Boston, with a Boston accent. There I was at a RISD party. I didn't know anybody. I didn't get laid until I was 20, later at Pasadena Playhouse. Most of the Catholic girls I grew up with, you got nowhere. You couldn't get below the third button before they were grabbing the crucifix.

So here I am at this wild RISD party with everyone dancing. I didn't know the basic rule that you have to immediately find someone you know. Or someone you can talk to and go to them. That's your place of comfort.

CG I had a somewhat similar experience. I went to these pre-deb parties, The Beacon Assemblies, with kids from private schools. Coming from a public school I didn't know anyone. The guys were slow and awkward and hung together talking about school and sports. Being alone, I went over and asked girls to dance. I was a good dancer, so that cut the ice and they liked me. By the second or third occasion they were hitting on me. At that point, I didn't give a fig about being friends with the guys.

CL It's called "Partying for Dummies." When you find that place you're secure and can go grab a drink or whatever, with a cigarette in one hand, and you're all set. People come to you because you look like you're cool. But at RISD I didn't know that yet.

I was standing by myself in a corner and a girl came up to me. She was half in the bag and said, "Can I ask you a personal question." I said, "yeah," and she asked, "Are you gay?" She was really hot, and I said, "Yeah, can you help me out?" (*Both laughing*) It did not work. I didn't fit in at all.

CG Did you read "Partying for Dummies?"

CL No, I just made that up.

CG We should write it. That would be a best seller. Eventually, who could you relate to at RISD?

CL One of my friends was a classical music aficionado; he turned me onto all kinds of great music. Verdi's "Requiem." Music as powerful as "O Fortuna" from *Carmina Burana*. He turned me onto all kinds of stuff like Rachmaninoff's Second Piano Concerto, Tchaikovsky's First Piano Concerto and all this beautiful music that took me to other places. One of the first classical albums I bought was Rachmaninoff's Second Piano Concerto. The cover was so beautiful. It was a photo of a young couple walking along a stone wall with the ocean behind them. The way they were dressed was so intriguing. I loved that album and cover so much I talked about it on Facebook way back when it first started.

I told the story of how to this day I remember that album. I went on the Internet and got a picture of it. That couple walking along the wall in Czechoslovakia on a cold day late in the afternoon. I played it over and over. I was thinking about what it must be like having a girlfriend and being out there. Being in another country. I was talking about that and this friggin' guy texts me or writes me or whatever you did back then and says, "Charles, my dad took that picture." It was up on the

North Shore or wherever it was. "It's not a Nordic country. It's the North Shore." Maybe Peabody or wherever. He said ,"My dad took a picture of his yoga teacher and her boyfriend."

Regarding *Big Mattress*, when I took over mornings and we were doing all this crazy parody stuff of AM radio, I needed a name for the show. I didn't want The Charles Laquidara Show. We thought of it as a hippie thing with people waking up from different parts of New England. So a guy in Arlington is waking up and saying good morning to a girl in Providence. Somebody in Milford will wake up and they're on this big, big mattress. They are waking up together and saying good morning.

Today, if you're not from Boston, *Big Mattress* sounds like a porn site.

CG You were something like 25 years old doing a morning show. How did that impact your lifestyle? What time did you have to be there?

CL They kept changing drive time. At first it was 6 to 10 a.m. Then it was 5:30 to 9 a.m. I was getting up at 3:30 a.m. Sometimes I would bicycle in. During my last days in the late '80s and '90s I was living in Dover. On an almost level road it was exactly 15 miles door-to-door.

CG What time did you go to bed?

CL Maybe 9:30 or 10 p.m., except on Thursday nights when Matt Siegel and I would go to a club called Zanzibar [at Boylston Place]. We would do shooters. It was a disco place, and one night we were walking in and all these girls were going up to Matt saying, "Oh Matty, I loved that show when you talked about your wife having those breast implants." He would say, "This is Charles Laquidara," and they would say, "Oh, hi." They would totally friggin' ignore me.

I had season tickets and would take him to The Patriots. From up top there would be drunks yelling, "Hey, Chuck." I would say, "This is Matt Siegel," and they would say "Right, hey Chuck play Led Zeppelin." So I had all the guys and Matt had all the girls.

Duane Glasscock had the highest ratings in radio. Carter Alan can confirm that or Tony Berardini. His ratings were phenomenal. A really good rating in Boston was always between 2 and 4. Duane Glasscock's ratings were 13.

CG What became of him?

CL We killed him. Oedipus [program director] killed him. It was time for him to go. I was getting headaches. It was a lot of pressure and stress. After awhile I just felt like it was burning out.

[Laquidara introduced his alter ego, Duane Ingalls Glasscock, a "vile sexist" who spoke with a thick Boston accent. As an antidote to PC he initially used a vulgar catchphrase suggesting anal sexual assault. Have you ever been b____d up the ___ for being a f____g wiseguy? When told to desist it became "Have you ever been phoned in Upton, Mass. for being a lucky wise guy?" Duane opened shows with the phrase "Hello, Rangooooooon!" The Glasscock character, who hosted his "own" show on Saturday mornings, received higher ratings than Laquidara's regular weekday broadcasts.]

CG Why was there pressure and stress?

CL OMG. Saturday mornings, picture this: You walk into the Prudential building at 10 a.m. and go up to the 50th floor. All these people, the most brilliant people in the world, Eddie Gorodetsky, Billy West, Mark Gordon, at the time was one of the producers, Tom Couch, all these interns. It was like an event in the studio.

At the Prudential there was a window, and you could see people walking by. It was like theater. It was going on inside and outside. When Duane did the "bag of shit" thing people were outside waving. We were getting phenomenal ratings and 'BCN was number one.

Duane goes on the air and starts talking about "these fat cats in Beltsville, Maryland, driving around in Cadillacs and they don't know anything about ordinary people. They're in charge of radio ratings and call themselves the Arbitron Research Bureau."

(*Speaking with Duane's Boston accent.*) "They gave Tommy Hadges a lousy ratings number and Mark Parenteau only got a 4!" [Which is a phenomenal number.] "They gave me only a 13! There's four people on phones right now, and ten people outside, so I know we have at least a 14! So send them a bag of shit!"

He gave out the real address and he did that every break. I'm sure they got a lot of bags of shit. Arbitron [now Nielsen Audio] never paid attention to it. They ignored it. They didn't even write to 'BCN.

The following Monday was when Duane got fired.

CG You talk about he.

CL Before you ask that question, I'll give you an example as an answer.

So Monday Charles Laquidara, me, is doing his show, and Klee Dobra our manager pokes his head in and says, (*with a grave tone*) "Charles I want to see you after your show." He's sitting in his office with an enormous cup of black coffee which, he's so pissed off, he's stirring with a finger, sitting right across from me with the veins bulging in his neck.

"Charles Laquidara is a consummately professional disk jockey," he said. "Charles is the person who is bringing us wonderful numbers, and Charles is someone I enjoy working with. But Duane Glasscock is a fucking idiot, and Duane can never be on the radio again. He's fucking fired."

I go, "Klee you can't fire Duane. He's got great fucking ratings."

There's a long pause then he looks at me and says, "What, are you playing with a full deck? You're acting as if Duane is somebody else."

I said, "Klee you just fired him and kept me." (*Both laughing*) I had to keep the two separate, to answer your question. Duane had a Boston accent, but I didn't. Duane was not PC, and I was. It was all that and I tried to keep it separate.

CG That sounds like Andy Kaufman and Bob Zmuda. There was a long debate as to whether they were one and the same or aspects of a great prank and hoax.

What could Duane do that you couldn't do?

CL Oh shit. Duane could have girlie watch. He could send bags of shit to Arbitron. Duane could make fun of the President. He could be a Republican in a lot of ways. He talked about how PC is stupid. Even to this day, on Facebook, Duane has thousands of friends. Duane friends everybody while I only friend people I know. Most of Duane's Facebook friends are to the right of Attila the Hun.

CG Do you miss Duane?

CL No. Ask me again I didn't answer fast enough.

CG Do you miss Duane?

CL (*Emphatically*) No.

CG It sounds as though Duane provided you with some psychological balance. With Duane gone, how do you maintain yin-yang?

CL First of all, I don't have to achieve that. I've been retired for almost 20 years.

If you're talking about Charles Laquidara on the radio, how did he achieve that balance? He had to go home to his family. He also had friends who were very conservative. That's how I did it back then. As far as now goes, there's no Duane in my life.

Especially when the #metoo thing came along, there's no way I'm stepping in that shit. No way I'm getting into that one. I'm totally respectful of that movement. Trump has brought out the worst in people—and now we know who they are. Friends and neighbors have shown their dark side. That's one of the good things that Trump has done, so now I know more. I have a lot of conservative friends, but now I see a side of them I never saw before—that I didn't want to see before.

CG You appear to be financially secure, so there is seemingly little incentive to earn a living. But several months ago you did a nightclub gig in Boston at Paradise. So you appear to surface occasionally.

CL On March 14 there was a big launch party for *Daze in the Life* at the Paradise. I did that for my book. [Actually a multimedia, online site with many hours of video material and radio clips.]

Also there's a movie out, *I Am What I Play*.

[It is available for rental on Vimeo. Documentarian Roger King's look at the careers of four legendary DJs, CFNY Toronto PD/jock David Marsden, WBCN Boston's Charles Laquidara, WNEW New York's Meg Griffin, and KJR Seattle's Pat O'Day. Marsden and O'Day bring some stories from the AM Top 40 era, but the focus is on the progressive rock era of the '70s and early '80s.).

It's about me and three other DJ's who the producer says changed radio forever.

CG But now it's all gone. How do you explain that? Tea Party, *Phoenix*, 'BCN, all gone. Of things that were so vital to our life in Boston during that era, there's nothing left. What happened?

CL Things change. You can have a cigarette in your hand and light it or hold it for a hundred years. Eventually things just go away. 'BCN died a very slow, painful death. Getting out in 2000 was just in time. I just made it. I made the cut. If I stayed there much longer, it would have been horrible.

I was one of the lucky people. James Dean died in a car accident. Marilyn Monroe was still beautiful. Jane Mansfield was pretty. All those people. I didn't die, but unlike those celebrities I mentioned, my persona didn't die. In fact, the people who are still alive remember me and the great stuff we did at 'BCN. I left radio at the right time. I left 'BCN when it was still at its height. It was still a viable station. It had gone very commercial and wasn't the same as the 1960s. It had morphed into some bullshit.

As our listenership increased, because we were playing more hit songs more frequently and the music itself was changing, younger listeners wanted to hear punk and alternative rock. Also, Howard Stern had come into the radio scene and there was a lot of pressure on me to play the new music and talk about things that entertained a younger audience. For example, I remember Mark Parenteau got called on the carpet for complaining about a snowstorm when our young listeners wanted to go skiing.

It didn't take long before we all realized that most of my older listeners hated alternative rock and drifted over to WZLX. Howard Stern, meanwhile, was always complaining on his nationwide syndicated show, "When is Laquidara going to quit or die? Those suits at WBCN in Boston are running my morning show at night, which is ridiculous!" Howard and I got along really well, and I was one of the lucky ones because he would destroy competing DJ's in every other market he moved into. He was definitely kidding, tongue in cheek, saying that, but we all knew it was time for me to move out of 'BCN. So on April Fools Day 1995, Howard Stern suddenly appeared on WBCN in the morning. I appeared on WZLX in the morning, and nobody knew whether it was a joke or not for weeks. I stayed at WZLX until I retired from radio on August 5, 2000.

As you said, I'm living in Hawaii now and have some thirty-four thousand ex-listeners and a lot of new people who get turned on to my Facebook page. That's an outlet where I can vent. I can do funny things and entertain.

A lot of people use Facebook like a diary or they post pictures of dogs and kids. It's a wonderful social media thing. They try to stay out of the fray, the political fray, but I'm in it up to my ass. It's like my radio show and I control it. I open the lines up so the Trumpsters can write their bullshit. But I regulate it. If you go to my Facebook page you'll see that I have a limit of two comments per post. People can't go on and on arguing back and forth. Make a statement, a reply to their statement, then they're off. To me, Facebook is my radio show. I spend a lot of time on Facebook.

I also spend a lot of time exercising. As I get older I want to live as good a quality of life as I can. [He was born November 24, 1938] I have a trainer I work with twice a week. I exercise every day. I swim about a mile once or twice a week.

Definitely, I have a different lifestyle than in the past. I'm a bachelor now. My two kids are grown up, and I have two grandchildren with another on the way. I've moved on I guess.

I still do a lot of things I enjoy. I like getting into politics. Trump has been a wonderful cash cow for all the late night shows. God knows what all of those shows are going to do when he leaves office. Those writers are going to have to find something else to do. Right now Trump is writing all of their shows.

He's in everybody's head. He's such an asshole and whatever luck, fate, Russians, or stupid Americans put him in that job is probably the most amazing event in the history of the civilized world, or in the history of modern politics. There never will be anything like it again. There never was before. He's gotten all of these people who would never go to a protest, who basically don't give a shit, people who say I have my family and job to take care of. I don't have time for politics.

He's got all of these millions of people now politically involved. He has mothers who would never go to a march now going and hating him so much. He's brought the left together. Most of the moderate Republicans I know are almost Democrats now. Everything they think or do is liberal, because they hate Trump so much. So, he's done a fantastic service to the country and the world. He's also got to get out of office because he's making permanent decisions that are destroying the planet and democracy.

Climate change is the elephant in the room. Everybody is worried about conservative judges on the Supreme Court, paying for the kids' education, about whether gays should have rights or no, and about wars in Afghanistan. None of that shit will matter within the next few years, because the weather is not going to get better and climate change's devastating effects are going to destroy our infrastructure and our economy. So Trump has to go as quickly as possible because that dope doesn't even believe in climate change, global warming, or the effects of fossil fuel. In the meantime, the rest of us are powerless to do anything except vote for change and hunker down with our families.

All I'm saying is that I'm having a good life in Hawaii. I have Facebook and movie night once a week (*laughing*). I invite friends and neighbors and we watch movies.

CG People have perceptions of you including myself, as an oddball, free spirit. The discipline of 25 years of a morning show implies something different. Most people don't comprehend what that means; the demands of showing up, being there, and doing the gig. Having to be totally on while the listener is just getting up and having morning coffee.

It implies that given the odd hours you missed a lot. Like being on the scene and going to rock concerts.

CL Matt Siegel never went to any of the shows, because he also had to be up early in the morning. I would say that back in the day, most of my listeners, and 100% of the people I now have on Facebook, know more, and are more into the music than I am. I have a lot of favorite songs. I don't have a lot of real favorite groups. My listening is more like the average person. Not like the average music lover—the average American. I know what songs I like, but I don't go to concerts even when they come here to Maui. Once in awhile there is a concert I would love to see. I missed Amy Winehouse. I was waiting for her to come to Maui. She never came but that was a concert I wanted to see.

I'm not into the music that much. My thing on radio was that people just liked my personality. My persona. It didn't have much to do with the music I was playing. In the last half of my career 'BCN was deciding what songs I should play.

CG Who gave you the playlist?

CL Fortunately, people who really knew the music. They also knew about ratings. They talked with consultants—people like Oedipus and Tommy Hadges, Carter Alan, these people really knew their music.

CG Well Charles, even in Maui, no man is an island.

Charles Laquidara's wakeup shift was *The Big Mattress*. Photo by Charles Giuliano.

Charles turns while on the picket line during the 1979 strike. Photo by Charles Giuliano.

Laquidara talking with the media. Photo by Charles Giuliano.

Charles and Mark Parenteau. Photo by Charles Giuliano.

Striking DJs Jim Parry, Tracy Roach, and Danny Schechter. Photo by Charles Giuliano.

Jim Parry on a cold day. Photo by Charles Giuliano.

Laquidara and the media. Photo by Charles Giuliano.

Barry Savenor, smoking, with Kenny Greenblatt. Photo by Charles Giuliano.

Picket line. Photo by Charles Giuliano.

On strike. Photo by Charles Giuliano.

Laquidara. Photo by Charles Giuliano.

Tracy Roach and Oedipus update news for strikers. Photo by Charles Giuliano.

We won. Photo by Charles Giuliano.

John Hochheimer recalls on-air time with David Bowie and Elton John at WBUR

Now retired, Professor John Hochheimer of Southern Illinois University, recalls undergraduate years at Boston University's then-progressive station WBUR. He started as a high school volunteer in New York at WBAI. During freshman year at BU, in 1968, he started at WBUR. He was influenced by the free-form programming of Tom Gamache, a.k.a. Uncle T. Rock archivist David Bieber was a friend and flatmate. He once spent five hours on air with David Bowie and became friends with B.B. King and Elton John. The programming staff was fired not long after John Silber took over at BU in 1971.

Charles Giuliano Let's discuss your time at WBUR.

John Hochheimer I started in August 1968, on a work-study grant. The format was classical music during the day and news and public affairs in the evening. There was late night programming as well. When I got there, Tom Gamache, known as Uncle T, was doing his program *The Freedom Machine* from eleven until two in the morning, Monday to Friday. On Saturday there was a program called *The Jazz Grotto* that Oscar Jackson hosted. That was midnight until six, Sunday morning.

It was anything goes during Uncle T's program. There were album cuts and interviews with musicians coming through town. Because it was a non-commercial station, things could go on for as long as you wanted. Because of the format, musicians could come and hang out during both those shows. There was a piano in the studio, so we had performances. We could do whatever we wanted with no commercial breaks or interference. Tom was very popular and a lot of musicians came.

We had a program *The Drum*, which was rare programming for the African American community. The soul station was WILD, which was a day timer and shut down at sundown. *The Drum* was coordinated with the Mayor's office in Boston and something called Action for Boston Community Development. The mandate was to recruit young African American men and women and teach them how to do broadcasting, sales, marketing, news, DJ work. That was part of the alternative programming. At night we were playing music of interest to the black community.

After a year of internship, the plan was that they would be hired by commercial stations. They got a leg up into the broadcasting industry. That was in the middle, between news and public affairs. That program attracted musicians visiting town. A lot of black athletes from the Celtics and Red Sox visited the studio. Politicians came and there was discussion of education, housing, and social services.

CG In what way was Tom Gamache different from mainstream radio?

JH When I met him, he looked like the Elliot Gould character in MASH. He had the moustache, hair, and bearing. He knew a lot about the roots of rock, doo-wop, blues. He had produced a documentary called *The Evolution of the Big Beat*. For the mid-1960s, his knowledge of black music was astounding. He had eclectic taste that spanned the gamut of all kinds of music. I had heard some of that earlier at WBAI in New York, but he was able to put sets together with amazing mixes. He was a pioneer and master of that technique. He was also introducing the British Invasion and not just the Stones and Beatles. He was into Long John Baldry, John Mayall, and other blues-based players.

WBCN and WBUR were classical music stations before Tom Gamache showed up.

When I started at the station I was 18. They helped me to get a license so I could do board shifts. It was fifteen hours a week, and they started me at 6 a.m. It was just a block away from my dorm. One Saturday night I fell by to see what was happening. There were these guys hanging out and drinking wine. I came back the next week and it was jazz all night. I went to the program director and asked if part of my responsibilities might be board operator for the Saturday night show? That's how I got more and more involved.

Since BU is a Methodist school, a mandate was to record Sunday services from March Chapel. It they did the service and rebroadcasted it Sunday evening. It was pretty much up to the station manager, Will I. Lewis, to program as he saw fit. There was classical music during the day and experimental programming after 10 p.m. and on weekends. This was before NPR. I was the engineer when we did our first national program. It was into that environment that I came as a student.

In May of 1969, they organized their first fundraising drive. As a volunteer in high school I had worked on a couple of WBAI fundraising marathons. So I was put in charge, and it was a huge success. As a reward for that I was given a folk music show on Sunday nights.

CG David Bieber said that he was influenced by your programming. Can you describe working with him?

JH In addition to working at the station, my roommate and I volunteered to help incoming freshman adapt to campus life. The dorm prior to fall semester was open but largely unoccupied. This guy, David Bieber from Ohio, showed up. His sister Lorna and I had been together in classes during freshman year. He asked if he could stay with us while he looked for an apartment. Based on mutual interests in music and radio we became friends. That was August of 1968. A year later, we rented an apartment on Beacon Hill. That's when I witnessed the foundation of the Bieber archives. [Now one million objects are housed in a warehouse in Norwood, Massachusetts.]

Once a week, David and I visited record companies to get new releases. They were generous and often give them to David as well as me. Things would come to the station like posters and promotional items. When we were done with them he would take them. I asked him, "What are you going to do with this stuff?" He said, "I don't know."

When I was doing a folk music show, he was interested in meeting some of the musicians. There was a coffee house on Charles Street called Sword in the Stone. On Tuesday nights, they would have hootenannies. I spoke with Lewis and pitched the idea of a live show from the club. There were conflicts, but we fed it live to the station and recorded on reel-to-reel tapes for later broadcast. By then Gamache had moved to WBCN. His slot was available, so I went from one to two nights a week hosting the show live. For a year, artists regularly appeared on the show, which promoted them as well as the club.

Bill Staines ended up being the host at the club. During breaks I would conduct interviews. Performers included Spider John Koerner, Townes Van Zandt, and Bonnie Raitt. When she first came to town, she was the opening act for Cat Stevens at Sanders Theatre.

CG I covered that gig.

JH Bill Madison was very popular in Boston, and he was on the show. Chris Smithers became well known. A guy who came and hung out, usually with a bottle of Jack Daniels, was Don McLean pre-"American Pie."

CG What about David Bowie?

JH He wasn't on the folk music show. David Bieber was hired by assistant general manager Clark Smidt to do promotion. Another guy involved at the time was Ken Shelton [later a WBCN DJ]. I was a junior and took a course in TV production. Ken was the TA in the School of Public Communications at BU. He started hanging at the station. So there was a nucleus of people. Of the four of us, I was the one on the radio when Bieber said, "We have this guy named David Bowie coming in from Chicago." I had seen a couple of his records on Mercury but didn't think much of it.

He came around at midnight. My show was on from eleven to six in the morning, five nights a week. It was 35 hours of live programming with no commercials or restrictions on what I could play. When Bowie came, we just hung out and talked. We played music and sat in the control room for five hours. We smoked, talked, and played records all night long.

Heading back to England, his career had tanked. He was trying to revive his career. Not only was he knowledgeable of music but also the cultures from which it emerged. He had unique vision for concert performances. Until that time, musicians came on stage and sang their songs. That was it. He had this idea for lights, smoke, and people in costumes. The idea was to make the whole thing a performance event. That's where Ziggy Stardust came from. He discussed it extensively and talked about heading back to England to get support for that kind of a concert.

At that time, there was a UK folk rock band called The Incredible String Band.

They put out a double album rock opera U in Elektra. They told a whole story with lights and smoke, jugglers, acrobats with a vast array of instrumentation. When I played it for Bowie he said, "Yeah, like that."

CG Describe the Bowie persona. How did he strike you?

JH He was an interesting guy. He was young, unknown, and one of many musicians I met. He remarked on the mix of music I put together for him. He knew most of what I played, but my approach was always to try to educate. If you like this then let me turn you on to that. He was a musician I could talk to and who understood what I was trying to do.

CG What did he look like?

JH None of the makeup. He was just a regular guy with shoulder-length hair. That was hardly unusual at the time. He was wearing jeans and maybe a black turtleneck. We later knew him in many guises, but that was not the David Bowie I met.

CG David Bieber told me that after he earned a master's degree at BU in August 1968, that September he was hired as music director for WBUR. Can you describe how you interacted?

JH My former roommate was hired as music director. It was great. He was going to promote our shows and raise money for the station. He was our liaison with Steve Mindich and *The Phoenix*, as well as with the record companies. His pitch was that when they were taking artists around town, don't just visit WBCN. They may interview someone for fifteen minutes while we had a looser format and could do much longer interviews.

One night, I was doing a long Lightning Hopkins set and I got a call from B.B. King. It was quarter of four in the morning. He came by the next afternoon, and we talked for two hours. I announced he was coming on the show. About 15 minutes later, I got a call from a listener in Roxbury. She said, "I resent you bringing B.B. King on your radio station. The blues is all about pain and suffering. Black people don't want to hear that stuff anymore. We want to hear James Brown, Sly and the Family Stone."

In the middle of my interview I told him about the call and asked him to comment. He said, "Let me think about that." Some twenty minutes later he said,

"Now I want to answer that question. The blues are about pain, suffering, and loss. Everybody has had those experiences. We think nobody in the world can understand what I feel right now. When you hear the blues, you think somebody else feels my pain. It's not a black issue or a white issue. White people have sung the blues forever and they call it country music. The chords are different but the emotions are exactly the same."

He invited me to have dinner with him the next night. When he came to town, his valet called and we would get together. I saw him in Vegas and he did an Ed Sullivan thing by introducing people in the audience. The spot was on me as I stood and waved.

CG When you did the five-hour Bowie session, David commented that there was no tape to record it. The station was that poor.

JH That's correct. Also there's no photograph.

On October 25th, 1970 two guys came to the station inviting me to see Elton John at the Tea Party for three nights. "Here's the album and if you play it please tell listeners about the gig." That kind of thing happened quite frequently, particularly when David came on board.

CG I was there that night and had interviewed Elton that morning at the Midtown Motor Inn. The review ran in the *Herald Traveler* and his publicist Norm Winter later invited me to LA to hang with Elton. I always want backstage when Elton came to Boston.

JH I was backstage with him and there are six images of us in the Jeff Albertson, UMass archive. He introduced himself to me as Reg and thanked me for playing the album.

[Born Reginald Kenneth Dwight, March 25, 1947. He took the name Elton John from two musicians: saxophonist Elton Dean and vocalist Long John Baldry. His name was legally changed to Elton Hercules John on January 7, 1972.]

Ever since, I've been a huge fan and take pride in being of assistance at the beginning of his career.

CG When John Silber came to BU there were changes at WBUR.

[In January 1971, John Silber began his first year as president of Boston University. New faculty members he was authorized to recruit were brought in with minimal consultation of the departmental chairpersons. Generally, faculty regarded Silber as an autocrat. In early 1972, police broke up a demonstration opposing the restoration of armed forces recruitment. Later that year his residence was destroyed by fire, and Silber's family lost all their personal belongings. Among Silber's recruits were Saul Bellow and Elie Wiesel. During the 1970s, he accused the faculty of mediocrity and the students of fostering anarchy. Today he is credited as the architect of a distinguished university. He raised the bar for faculty and students.]

JH Just before he became president of BU in May 1970, there was a student strike. It shut down the campus and final exams were cancelled. He came with a very different vision. Until then, BU had never been prestigious compared to other colleges and universities in Boston/Cambridge. He was determined to make BU a first-rate university.

On August 24, 1971, one of his vice presidents assembled the entire WBUR staff and announced, "We're making some format changes." Will Lewis, the general manager, had been fired and Clark Smidt was gone with him.

The VP said, "Effective immediately here is the staff." He read seven names, and the rest of us we were no longer to come to the station. We were stunned. They cut not just progressive music, but the program *The Drum*, which was a central media presence for the African American community in Greater Boston. There was also a Spanish language program produced by WFCR at UMass, Amherst. It was outreach to a community of Spanish language farm workers, particularly for tobacco farms in the Connecticut River Valley. That was immediately cut as well.

The African American and Latino communities were incensed. Their only outlets for news and information were terminated by John Silber as a part of his taking control of the station. I was let go along with everyone responsible for programming.

CG Was there resistance?

JH Yeah, but what could you do? They changed the locks. We were told that if we came to the station, the campus police would be called and we would be arrested. We never heard Silber's statement, but it was implied that they didn't want any talk of resistance and revolution. He didn't want to hear loud rock and roll music. WBUR went back to a very staid program service, which it had been before Lewis.

He became general manager of KPFK, a Pacifica station in LA. I joined the station in June 1974.

When I left WBUR, I went to WBCN and became their overnight guy from September/October of 1971 to March of 1972. I left the station and went to work for ABC Dunhill Records, which had an office in Woburn.

[He moved to San Francisco, then to LA to work for KPFK. To earn more money, he became a driver for the Mary Tyler Moore production company for a year, then four more as a pool driver for movie and TV studios. He went back to school to finish a BA, then to Stanford University, earning a PhD in communications. He is now retired from Southern Illinois University.]

John Hochheimer with Elton John, backstage at the Tea Party. Photo by Jeff Albertson.

In Hollywood with (left to right) Elton John, Al Kooper, David Felton, and Charles Giuliano. Photo Giuliano archive.

Following a station visit bluesman B. B. King became a close friend. Photo by Charles Giuliano.

John Hocheimer in the studio in later years.

Roger Lifeset remembers promo guys who broke and managed rock acts in Boston

Covering jazz and rock for the daily *Boston Herald Traveler* meant constant interaction with promo guys for major record companies. New releases came in person or by mail. For major concerts at Boston Garden, The Orpheum, or Symphony Hall, they provided tickets.

There was camaraderie and tales of parking lot meets to swap product. In the fall, with a schedule of new releases, there was competition as to which company threw the best party. Now and then there was a major promo launch of a band. I helped to arrange a memorable event at Castle Hill in Ipswich.

Having just returned from hanging in LA with Norm Winter, legendary PR guy for Elton John, I was wearing my sequined Nudie's of Hollywood cowboy suit.

The promo guys were notable for variables of style and nuance. On the high end was the elegant, old school, Sal Ingemie for Columbia Records. He shared that position with mostly straight Ed Hynes. Lennie Petze promoted Epic Records. Walter Lee represented Capitol Records with its dense Beatles catalogue. Rick Alberti flacked for Elektra and A&M's Barry Korkin, and United Artists had Billy Lee Horn. Laid back Don Delacey was with RCA and presided over the one and only local Elvis date at the Boston Garden. Don favored intimate, soft-sell, hotel suite evenings. Similarly, for London Records, Brian Interland, a classy dude and collector, served up Tom Jones. At Transcontinental, which represented a number of small labels, there was John Belliveau.

The flat-out party boys were Roger Lifeset and Charlie McKenzie for Warner Brothers, and with a more subtle touch, Paul Ahern for Atlantic Records. There were a lot of memorable blowouts and harbor cruises for Boston's J. Geils band, first with Atlantic, and then with EMI/Capitol Records.

When promo guy Lifeset conned me into having an intimate, VIP party after an Alice Cooper concert, I had no clue what I was getting into. Some 300 to 400 people trashed my Harvard Square basement apartment on University Road in the legendary Murder Building.

The building was named for exotic murders including one by the Boston Strangler and another, never solved, with a Harvard anthropologist as a prime suspect. The female victim, his former student, was laid out in the ritual manner of Amazon aboriginals.

Rent was cheap and the large complex attracted musicians, artists, and hipsters. Annie Leibovitz dropped by to photograph Peter Wolf for *Rolling Stone*. Warhol associate Ed Hood held court. Nancy Michaels, a.k.a. Molly Maguire composed at her piano. Magic Dick hung out when not on the road with J. Geils. Pam Burton, who worked in record promo, was everyone's sweetheart. Tony Pink hustled. Rockers came and went. WBCN DJ Jim Parry sorted through albums while the station's ad man Kenny Greenblatt trolled the watering holes of the Square.

Kenny and I attended the Mar y Sol rock festival on Easter Weekend in Puerto Rico for the *Herald* and WBCN. We split the jungle on Easter Sunday and reported live from a bar in the Virgin Islands.

Recently, Lifeset contacted me after a lapse of decades. In the hilarious dialogue that follows we recall that Alice Cooper event and how, in Roger's words, "It went south."

Charles Giuliano Where are you?

Roger Lifeset I'm right on the line between LA and Ventura County.

I Google my own name occasionally. Your article showed up ("WBCN The Rock of Boston") and gave me a good link. That's how I got in touch with you by posting a comment to the site. The article was mind boggling to me. There were great pictures, very dated pictures of Charlie McKenzie, the "Branch" guy.

[Initially McKenzie, who became wealthy as part of the team that managed Boston, was low on the totem pole. At social gatherings Lifeset, introduced him as "This is Charlie from the Branch." Based on that I dubbed him Branch.]

I married a lady, in my third go round, that bartender Dennis Metrano introduced me to at Daisy's. [Daisy Buchanan's a watering hole on Newbury Street. At the time Metrano published a fanzine, *Sunshine*. Later he published *The Paper* in Newburyport, which I wrote for, and contributed on rock to a number of publications.]

It's where promo guys went, just as you described.

At the time he said to me and Rick Alberti, "You guys have to come down on Thursdays. That's when the stewardesses come in, and they're hot for promo guys."

I started talking to this lady, Diane. Dennis introduced me to someone I found attractive. It was happening. That little glimmer was there. We were there a couple of hours. She said, "You don't recognize me, do you?" I went, "No, not really." She said, "I'm Diane who you went out with."

I took her out when I was 16 years old. I just had my driver's license. With a friend from Quincy we drove to Nantasket Beach. If you were looking for Jewish girls that was a good spot, particularly in the summertime. I was going to college that fall, Emerson, and this was the end of summer. I took her out once and never went out with her again for a number of reasons. So this is who I'm being introduced to seven years later by Dennis. A torrid affair started.

Several years ago we were back in Boston. I went to all my old haunts: Marblehead, Swampscott. We were on the North Shore and I heard that Dennis was in Newburyport. I found him pretty quickly. We visited. He had his paper. We stayed at a hotel in the area.

CG You went to Emerson. That's where you met your wife Sherry who was best friends with my then girlfriend Nan Katsiff.

RL Sherry is still friendly with her. Now she prefers to be called Nanna. I have a picture of her in Harvard Square. In a short skirt she's walking right near Nini's Corner.

CG Before Warner Brothers did you work for Jerry Brenner?

RL I did. I worked for Jerry at Transcontinental, a national distributor, then later at Music Merchants. Sadly, Jerry passed away about two weeks ago. I hate to be the bearer of bad news. I saw a great picture of him on your website.

CG How long were you with Warner Brothers?

RL I was there the year the branch opened in 1973. We were breaking all kinds of hits. I went toe-to-toe with the national sales director, who felt that we had become less productive. I left there in 1975. I was cleaning out my desk when I got a call from ABC Records. Because of Johnny B and Charlie we used to call it ABC Downhill. At that time, for them to have three guys based in the same office was ludicrous. It was one thing for Charlie [McKenzie] and me to be at Warner Brothers. It was another thing to have three people working out of an office in Woburn right up in that general area.

For a number of reasons, ABC Records decided they didn't want us working in a branch office. They were going to rent an office of our own in an office park where they could put four desks because we had a secretary. We would work out of there as the promotion department. The distributor was in Medford. It was close to where we had the other part of the Alice Cooper saga, the Bal-a-Roue roller-skating rink. The branch was within spitting distance on Mystic Avenue.

CG You have it wrong. The skating party was for The Cars and I have photos of it.

RL Nope. I'm talking about the one for Alice Cooper. The Second Alice Cooper party was thrown in your basement apartment in Cambridge. The first Alice Cooper party was legendary—like yours. It didn't start until midnight. They were in concert that night and the party would start after the show.

Despite all the drugs and crazy shit going on, you were pretty dead-on accurate in what you wrote. Particularly, for what I could attest to, like the Alice Cooper party.

I hired the cleanup crew, as well as the guy who was going to check the guest list at the door.

CG The cleanup crew never fucking came. My apartment was totally trashed.

RL The cleanup guy came and looked in the window and went nah. (*laughs*)

CG The guy on the door was on LSD.

RL Yes, he was. I realized he was very inept at this job.

CG Gee. Thanks, Roger.

RL There's a sidelight to that you'll love.

CG Not necessarily.

RL No, this is necessary.

CG You fucking trashed my apartment.

This is how it went down.

I met you shortly after joining the *Herald Traveler* through Nan. You said, "You're my new instant best friend."

RL Yeah. I probably did. But I meant it.

CG Your exact words: "My new instant best friend."

My understanding was that it was the first Alice Cooper gig in Boston at the Orpheum Theatre.

You sent me a letter, and I wish I still had it. It said "Dear Captain." More or less, I invite you to have an exclusive VIP party for Alice Cooper after the gig. It was to be a hand-picked list of perhaps 50 of the best Boston rockers. You were going to take care of everything from booze and catered food to bartender, servers, and cleanup. I wouldn't have to lift a finger. Don't worry about a thing we'll take care of everything.

RL We sure did. (*laughs*)

CG Yeah, right, everything will be first class. It's VIP only. The best of the best. The cream of the cream. An intimate, underground, Harvard Square after party.

[My basement apartment on University Road in the legendary Murder Building.]

I told my boss, the *Herald Traveler* arts editor, Sam Hirsch, a total jerk, that I was covering Alice Cooper.

RL I remember him.

CG He said, "Who is Alice Cooper?" I said, "Well his real name is Vince [born Vincent Damon Furnier, February 4, 1948] but he calls himself Alice.

Hirsch said, "We're a respectable, family newspaper and can't write about drag queens." So I never got to cover the concert, but came running home from the gig.

That afternoon a neighbor knocked on the door and said there was a lot of stuff delivered for you to my apartment. It was all the food and booze.

I met your doorman with a couple of his pals. He showed me the list and wasn't supposed to let anyone in if he didn't have their name.

Within a few minutes there was an endless stream, and the sprawling, cave-like apartment was packed. The last straw was when a dozen drag queens floated in. I went upstairs and said to the doorman, "You can't tell me that they were on the list." His answer was, "We thought that was Alice Cooper." At that point I realized it was hopeless and said, "What the heck, come join the party."

RL That's a good version of it. Pretty close to what I know.

CG Every rocker within a hundred miles was there. We had everyone from WBCN DJ's to all kinds of bands, from J. Geils, to the Sidewinders, James Montgomery Band, Billy Squire, Modern Lovers. Loudon Wainwright was strangling his wife, Kate McGarrigle, on the kitchen floor. There was an old piano for a jam session.

Alice Cooper showed up, but was so freaked out that the band soon left.

Everyone finally left and around dawn a neighbor put a pin in my doorbell.

By about 10 a.m. I staggered into work, completely hung over. That afternoon, after work, I was totally dead and the doorbell rang. It was Maxanne from WBCN. She wanted to view the aftermath. We had tea and recapped madness from the night before.

The cleanup crew never came and it took more than a week to get things back in order. The rug was soaked with beer and cigarettes. The apartment reeked. I got you to pay for having it sent out and shampooed. Even that was pulling teeth.

RL If you can find the rug I said. (*laughing*)

CG So, Roger, you fucked me.

RL I did. (*laughing*) Now I can say it. I felt awful about it.

CG Oh, did you? How touching. You're breaking my heart.

RL The security guard was one of my trashy teenage friends from Marblehead. They were all headers. The guy who was checking names, whatever, was Wayne Ward. He didn't look right to me when I saw him that night. That's why he was perfect for the job. The people who came were all artsy fartsy deviants or whatever.

They were perfect for an Alice Cooper party.

In the middle of it, you blew a 30-amp fuse and said, "Who are all these people? How did they get in here? I thought you said there was, like, security." I went over to Wayne at that point, because I was a little concerned about it also, and I asked him, "Who are these people?" He said, "They all were invited. They all have passes and credentials."

At that point I saw one of the drag queens. He was an old drag queen, really just a deviant street person, kind of a weirdo. He was dancing around and drinking beer and eating the food. I said to Wayne, "Who's he?" He went, "Oh, that's Alice Cooper." The whole thing had gone south.

CG The band didn't stick around. It was too crazy for Alice Cooper. Years later, I would run into perfect strangers who said, "I was at your Alice Cooper party." The entire Cambridge scene showed up. Would you say we had 300 to 400 people?

RL That sounds about right. What's surprising is that the cops never showed up. How could that be?

CG It was in winter during what we call the January Thaw. It was a balmy spring-like evening and a lot of people spilled out onto the alley because it was so crowded. It ended up being a winter block party.

RL There was probably a full moon that night. That's a legitimate rock 'n' roll medal on your chest. It was a part of an overseas campaign. If you attended. You were there. You know about it. The Alice Copper party prior to that gave me the confidence to let this one rip. The one at the Bal-a-Roue, the security, I admit, was a little better. I paid a guy to make ham salad and peanut butter sandwiches. Just sandwiches and beer is what we had. For that party, Alice Cooper was going to attend. I hired a band that Charlie found called the Shittons, which was a riff on the Chiffons. They played all the '60s girl-group songs.

CG There's another part of the Alice Cooper promotion. You hired two girls from Swampscott.

RL The Dancing Beer Cans [Budweiser for Cooper, who then drank a case a day].

CG They had Budweiser beach towels formed around them. They were to greet Alice at Logan when he got off the plane.

RL Actually, they made the costumes. I was quite proud of them.

CG One of the girls, who I got to know, was upset and sent me a copy of the letter you wrote to her. In it you refused to pay them an agreed-upon fee because they had acted unprofessionally. You wrote, "I didn't pay you to shag the band."

RL That's right. Previously, I introduced them to another band and they did the same thing. They were groupies.

CG You introduced me to Captain Beefheart [Don Van Vliet, 1941–2010].

RL I don't think he's making music anymore.

CG He died a couple of years ago after a long illness with MS. I was your ace-in-the-hole for odd-shot promotions. Whenever you had something way out and off the edge, I got the call.

RL I was never wrong. You represented that fringe area—like when the Doobie Brothers came to town.

CG I hated the Doobie Brothers ["Listen to the Music" "Jesus is Allright"].

RL Of course you did. [Roger not only promoted them but was a huge fan.]

CG I thought they sucked. I think I saw them on a bill with Mott the Hoople. ["All the Young Dudes" was written for them by David Bowie.] That was a really hideous gig.

You called me about Beefheart, and we had dinner at the Half Shell. He said, "Roger I want a lobster." We watched him eat that huge lobster.

Once he met me, he wouldn't let go. He was dragging me down to New York to run around with him. I thought, this is cool driving around in a limo, but we just went to his tailor and spent the afternoon while he was fitted for stage outfits. The tailor was referred to him by Ornette Coleman.

He kept asking my opinion. He wanted to wear something dramatic to please his fans. Overall, he was very conscious of image and persona. Later, at the Berklee Performance Center, he came out in a cape holding a hatchet. The music was so far out that I don't think the costumes made much of a difference. But he was equally intense about all aspects of his career. He demanded my total critical attention and feedback, no matter what the subject. His wife, Jan, was endlessly patient and just listened.

From Ornette, he picked up free jazz clarinet. Usually, to open the gig he would just wail on it to set the mood. He got a pretty good sound, but it was entirely freestyle with none of Ornette's discipline. It amazed me that he could play so intuitively.

RL The whole Magic Band was learning how to play.

CG He asked me to go on the road with him when I mentioned that I improvised on piano. Imagine my life if I had taken him up on it?

RL That's a match made in heaven. The attraction was that Beefheart was an artist, as were you. You have maybe more in common artistically than you would have musically.

CG That's absolutely accurate. I remember that you had a favorite Beefheart song from *Trout Mask Replica*. You used to sing it to me.

RL I know the one you mean "Dachau Blues Them Poor Jews." (*singing*)

CG That's the one. Isn't it amazing that we still remember. In a lot of ways, Beefheart truly was an artist.

Then, as you mention, I wrote that two-part Sunday feature in the *Herald Traveler*. They didn't know what they had in me. It was all a fluke. I was never interested in covering mainstream, commercial rock and roll.

When Miles Davis came out with *Bitches Brew*, which totally changed fusion jazz [initiated by guitarist Larry Coryell], I wrote a five-part Sunday series on Miles. The record companies sent me all his albums and for weeks I went home each night and listened to them. From Capitol, Walter Lee sent me *Birth of the Cool*. Finally, Sal Ingemie of Columbia hooked me up with Miles at Lennie's-on-the-Turnpike. During the interview in the dressing room, he looked at me as a reflection in the mirror as he combed his hair. After that, I would hang with Miles when he came for gigs at the Jazz Workshop. Sal, who knew Miles well and talked boxing with him, was thrilled with our extended coverage.

So I guess the promo guys liked me for that. You always used to say, "You're an easy promote."

RL Don't take it the wrong way.

CG I knew what you meant. You were a con artist and hustler.

RL On my level. Would I say that to Ben Gerson [*Boston Phoenix* critic who quit covering rock to attend law school]?

CG I don't think so.

RL Because he was milquetoast. You liked the edge. You liked the lunatic fringe.

CG It was a colorful era and we were a part of it. Let's talk about Charlie McKenzie.

RL That story caught up with you. He wrapped his sports car around a tree so to speak. [March 9, 2002 at 54] It's true. A big bad-ass tree on Cape Cod when he thought he was being pursued by the police. He was being chased by the gendarmes. In those years he had done way too much blow. There were a couple of people who remained close to him. One was promoter John Sdoucous [now living in Florida]. Actually Charlie bought Cape Cod property very close to John. I think it was in Hyannis Port. There's another guy, now living here in California, Peter Wassing.

CG Wassing used to hang with Peter Wolf.

RL You would never see them separately.

CG When I first met McKenzie, he was a big goofy guy. You pulled him in to work with you for Warner Brothers

RL I didn't pull him in. He pulled himself in. I was okay with it. Charlie was the Promotion Director at the Branch. He had to work there all day. It wasn't an outside job. It was an inside job. With me, Alberti, Paul Ahern, and whatever, gone all day. In the morning, we started there but got in our cars and hit the radio stations ending up at Daisy Buchanan's. We were out and never had to come back. Once in awhile there were meetings at the branch but it was an outside job. Charlie wanted that desperately.

Warner Brothers, which was getting bigger, decided that Boston was a big kind of city. We were breaking a lot of music. They decided to beef it up. One of the ways was to bring in my current wife's former husband, Jim Saltzman, as my RPM (Regional Promotion Manager). He was there to herd me and Charlie, who were doing promotion. Then they brought in George Garrity. He was going to organize regional tours and coordinate them with radio. So we had four employees. Then they allowed us to hire, you'll remember this name, Pamela Burton. She became our secretary.

CG She was my neighbor in the Murder Building. At one point, she was dating David Bieber [promo director for WBCN]. She would make dinner and he would show up at midnight. So that didn't work.

RL Bieber was probably cataloguing yellowed copies of *The Real Paper.* (*Both laugh*)

CG When McKenzie was at the branch, he was one of the few guys who actually listened to all the demo tapes.

RL He listened to the Tom Scholz tape after Freddy Lewis left the branch to manage The Cars. When Ahern departed for the Coast, Freddy took his Atlantic job. Charlie listened to the tape and really liked it. The tape had made its way all over town. A lot of other promo guys heard it. He passed it to Ahern, who by then lived in LA. He was working for Irving Azoff, who had connections. [Personal manager, representing recording artists such as Christina Aguilera, the Eagles, Van Halen, Steely Dan, and Lindsey Buckingham of Fleetwood Mac as CEO of Azoff MSG.] Between Charlie and Ahern they really got behind the thing.

Then they got Lennie Petze who used to be the Epic guy in Boston. He had become an A&R guy for Epic. He's the guy who signed Boston to Epic.

CG Charlie and Paul got points in the deal.

RL They got points on everything. Yep. They split management.

[Tom Scholz first started writing music in 1969. While attending MIT he joined the band Freehold, where he met guitarist Barry Goudreau and drummer Jim Masdea. They later become members of Boston. Vocalist Brad Delp was added to the collective in 1970. After graduating with a master's degree, Scholz worked for Polaroid. He built a recording studio in his basement. The early demo tapes were recorded with (at various times) Brad Delp on vocals, Barry Goudreau on guitar, Jim Masdea on drums, and Scholz on guitar, bass, and keyboards. The demo tapes were sent to but rejected by record companies.

In 1973, Scholz formed the band Mother's Milk with Delp, Goudreau, and Masdea disbanding by 1974. Scholz worked with Masdea and Delp to produce six new demos, including "More Than a Feeling," "Peace of Mind," "Rock and Roll Band," "Something About You" (then entitled "Life Isn't Easy"), "Hitch a Ride" (then entitled "San Francisco Day"), and "Don't Be Afraid." Scholz played all the instruments on the demos, except for drums, which were played by Masdea, and used self-designed pedals to create the desired guitar sound.]

This demo tape was used by and McKenzie. According to Scholz, the managers insisted that Masdea had to be replaced before the band could get a recording deal. Scholz and Delp signed with Epic Records after the band did a live audition for record company executives. The duo recruited Goudreau on guitar, bassist Fran Sheehan, and drummer Sib Hashian. The band agreed to put out 10 albums over the next six years.

CG Ahern always struck me as smarter than the rest of the promo guys. He was the brains of the branch. He was always more level headed and career oriented than everyone else. McKenzie, on the other hand, just went hog wild crazy. He came into enormous wealth and morphed into The Great Gatsby.

RL Yeah. Pretty much.

CG For a time, McKenzie was flying high and believed he had the magic touch to discover and promote other bands. But nothing much came of his management ambitions.

RL Willie "Loco" Alexander and there were other things that he dabbled in.

CG Nothing panned out.

RL He was out every night at the Rat [Kenmore Square] and here and there. He liked being the guy. "Hey, that's Boston's manager." Let the good times roll.

CG By then I was in graduate school and teaching art history. Gradually, I evolved away from the rock life and got serious. But I heard about his Gatsby parties on the Cape and that he was running low on coin. Hard to believe considering the bundle he made.

You left for California.

RL I arrived here in January of 1977. I lived the whole Bicentennial thing in Marblehead where the "Spirit of '76" original painting hangs in the Town Hall. The S.S. Constitution spent the night in Marblehead harbor. Then I got a job transfer and said, "This was great, but let's get out of here."

CG Do you drive a Porsche on the Freeway?

RL Nope. I don't put my money into cars. I don't do anything, Charles.

CG Are you happy?

RL Yeah, I have a good wife and a good life. I work on my terms with the cream of the crop in my field. I wouldn't expect you to know my clients. They're smooth jazz artists. Which is something I was never into. But I was always into instrumentals. Ones you would know, I'm happy to say, are Spyro Gyra and Hiroshima.

CG What do you listen to?

RL Little. I only listen to what's related to my job. You know what I've started to do, Charles? I'm sure you can appreciate. I was into one medium. Music was it. I love that. I like movies to a certain extent. It all came at the expense of never, ever reading. I've started reading. I have a library card and I like going to the library. Unfortunately, I'm restricted to large-print books. The other ones are too hard to read. I can, but it takes the enjoyment away. I'm reading books I should have read a long time ago. I'm reading one right now that I'm sure you would appreciate. I saw a PBS special.

CG On J.D. Salinger. You're reading *Catcher in the Rye*.

RL We're simpatico here.

CG I knew you were going to say that. The Salinger documentary was amazing.

RL I read it a year and a half before it was on TV. When I saw the PBS program I said, I have to read that book again. I'm really stimulated by reading and I can't get that out of music anymore. The music of the '60s and '70s was great. Even the '50s. The music today? Forget about it. It's over.

CG The music scene we were involved with was great fun but there was absolutely no intellect. You would have conversations and people would say, "It was heavy," or "She was a nine." So this is interesting to me. I always thought you were above the fray and smart.

RL I find reading relaxing and very stimulating. I'm not saying that the music ended and I picked up a book. The music ended and I picked up nothing. I picked up a beer or a vodka soda. I particularly like having a library card. It's an adventure for me to go to the library.

Why did it all go south for Charlie? Taking his lifestyle out of the equation, it was because of the band, Boston. Tom Scholtz and his friends didn't party. Charlie was more rock 'n' roll than the band was.

I saw Charlie on the road with the band once. I was working for Warner's. It was in Pittsburgh. Boston was the headliner and the opening act was Black Sabbath. They were going nowhere, even with Ozzie. They didn't fit in. In Pittsburgh they were pretty good, but in Boston they didn't work out. I saw the band and I saw Charlie and they were on two different streams.

At the time, I remember thinking, Charlie, has to watch himself a little bit. I don't care what paper he has with them, these guys, he's way too much rock 'n' roll for them. It's not who they are. They're being good boys.

CG They were an enervating road band. Sholtz was brilliant in the studio, but that didn't equate to a stage presence. He never delivered the schedule of albums in their contract. Then there were scandals and tragedies.

RL There was a lawsuit a couple of years ago. *Boston* was the biggest debut album of all time. In the first couple of years it sold 12 million copies and a lot more since then. They couldn't make a plaque big enough for all their gold albums. It really reflects how much in sales they had. Boston was great in the studio but couldn't reproduce it on stage.

CG It was a heck of a party.

RL Life is good and we've moved on.

Warner Brothers promo man Roger Lifeset. Photo courtesy of Roger Lifeset.

Lifeset's partner in mayhem Charlie McKenzie. Photo by Charles Giuliano.

January 6, 1972

Dear Citizen,

Please understand that the midnight ALICE COOPER affair is a <u>closed</u> party.

We beg your co-operation by not inviting friends or other employees. Your invite admits only two people. This will be an intimate party.

Your man in Boston,

Roger Lifeset

Lifeset's invitation to my infamous Alice Cooper party. Bieber archives.

Promo man Paul Ahern co-managed Boston with McKenzie. Photo by Charles Giuliano.

Laid back Don Delacey promoted RCA Records. Photo by Charles Giuliano.

Charlie McKenzie, left, and WBCN DJ Mark Parenteau. Bieber archives.

J. Geils Band members (left to right) Peter Wolf, Seth Justman, and D. Klein. Photo by Charles Giuliano.

A smooth operator, Sal Ingemie promoted Columbia Records. Photo by Charles Giuliano.

Record distributor Jerry Brenner listens to Charlie McKenzie. Photo by Charles Giuliano.

The artist Paul Shapiro played with The Hallucinations at the Tea Party. Photo by Charles Giuliano.

Geils band drummer Steve Bladd. Photo by Charles Giuliano.

Magic Dick of the J. Geils Band. Photo by Charles Giuliano.

J. Geils. Photo by Charles Giuliano.

Modern Lovers at Sandy's in Beverly. Photo by Jeff Albertson.

Johnathan Richman at Sandy's. Photo by Jeff Albertson.

Roger Lifeset

At home with Cars drummer David Robinson. Photo by Charles Giuliano.

The Cars at Boston Garden. Photo by Charles Giuliano.

Ben Orr of The Cars. Photo by Charles Giuliano.

Ben Orr smoking 1979. Photo by Charles Giuliano.

David Bieber presides over a million-item archive of rock memorabilia

Archivist David Bieber discovered *Billboard Magazine* while an avid rock fan in high school. In college he became a campus correspondent for the music magazine. That continued when he matriculated to Boston University for a graduate degree in communications. For research and writing, he collected *Billboard* and other print media.

He wrote a 150-page master's thesis on the rise of alternative media. It became a calling card resulting in the position of music director for WBUR FM. While freelance writing for several publications, he later held promotion and marketing positions at WBCN and the Boston Phoenix.

David Bieber I have known you as long as anyone in Boston. You haven't missed a beat and present very realistic challenges as we discussed the other night.

Charles Giuliano When you were in graduate school at Boston University, there was no archive to do the research for your thesis. As I understand it, that's when you started to collect issues of *Billboard Magazine* and related music industry materials.

DB It started before then. I was at Miami University in Ohio as a business major. I had seen my first issue of *Billboard Magazine* in Cleveland in the spring of 1963.

I was a high school student and had to have every copy of the Top 40 list from WHK. I was completely unaware of how chart positions were established even on local playlists.

There was a notice that *Billboard* was looking for campus correspondents. They gave me a reporter's card and I was off to the races. The first two people I interviewed were Cannonball Adderley and Nancy Wilson.

In high school I had enjoyed English class but never written an article. In college I had an academic load and was taking business courses. But I was thrilled and excited to have this opportunity. On campus, they were presenting a diversified range of talent. It was all over the map regarding who I interviewed.

The *Billboard* experience went on for the next four-plus years. I interviewed everyone from Dick Gregory to Frankie Valli and the Four Seasons, Chad and Jeremy, and Johnny Carson. It became a lot more real to me than even some of the classes.

Through *Billboard* I discovered that I had an affinity for writing. I realized that I wanted to do journalism more than business. I transferred to Kent State, which offered journalism. I was writing, doing investigative reporting, and covering all kinds of concerts on campus from Ray Charles to the Temptations. Photography was a mandatory part of studying journalism. I have many pictures from that period of artists I was covering.

When I came to Boston I had one suitcase. Things were very relaxed, unlike today's real estate stampede. I was accepted at the School of Public Communications at Boston University. I found a third-floor room in a beautiful house on Bay State Road.

I took a year of classes and connected with a guy named John Hochheimer. He did an overnight show on WBUR, *The Other Side*, where anything goes. Coming from Ohio, I was totally intrigued by WBCN. I quickly discovered that Boston had never had anything like it. WBCN went on the air on March 15, 1968. I came to Boston that September.

At WBUR there was a guy known as Uncle T [Tom Gamache]. His show on WTBS was *T Time* and the one on WBUR was *The Freedom Machine*. He preceded WBCN. Boston University was unique in that they had WTBU, which you could only get in certain dorm rooms. BU also had WBUR, which was a fifth thousand-watt powerhouse station but not licensed for commercials. Uncle T started there in 1967, maybe 1968. Like Frank Zappa, he had the look of that era. He did a specialty show that was not the format of WBUR. He came out of WTBU but then had a much bigger megaphone with the FM station.

CG What was his on-air style? Where does he fit into the narrative of progressive radio?

DB It was free form and underground. The whole sense of programming was highly individual if it was Uncle T or WBCN. Later, he spent a couple of months at WBCN, but it didn't work out. With the advent of FM, there was a change as artists were focused on putting out albums rather than just singles. That came before with Beatles and Stones releases. But there was still rigidity on the AM side of the dial. They were playing even fewer songs.

There was a transition for groups that might have hit singles. They weren't just putting them on albums with other cover versions. They were creating albums with musical responsibility. The Beatles, Stones, and Dylan were doing that, but there was an expansion with the next wave of British acts and San Francisco bands. There were valid songs on albums above and beyond what the record companies deemed as singles.

It was a matter of economics as well. If you could sell an album at $3.98 for mono and $4.98 for stereo, you could make more money compared to ninety-nine cents for a single.

CG Not just Uncle T, when WBCN went from classical to rock, DJs were recruited from college radio.

DB Yes. Tommy Hadges, Joe Rogers under the name of Mississippi Harold Wilson. Later, Charles Laquidara, who had been at Pacifica, a non-profit classical station. Sam Kopper had been at a Syracuse radio station. Tommy Hadges was going to dental school. There was the seduction and lure of free albums and concerts. You were a part of the media. In addition to playing the music, there was the opportunity to meet the people who were making the music.

As the Beatles song goes "I am he as you are he as you are me and we are all together." We were all rooting for each other in a peer group sensibility.

CG Where did you come in?

DB I discovered that some of my master's degree writing corresponded to the media I was responding to. I wrote about WBCN and got to know the people there. I wrote articles that served two purposes. I was writing for *Billboard*, *Boston Magazine*, and *Fusion*, which was the East Coast counterpart to *Rolling Stone*. The publisher of *Fusion* was Barry Glovsky and the editor was Robert Somma.

I wrote about what I enjoyed, got academic credit, and I was paid. By 1970, I wrote a book-length thesis. It had ten chapters, every one of which had been published as a feature article. The theme was underground media with an emphasis on how radio and print were impacting traditional media.

By 1969 or 1970 the powerhouse of Top 40 AM radio was WABC in New York. They were playing 15 to 20 records in rotation, whereas WBUR and WBCN would be playing spoken word and underground ESP material like The Fugs. Charles knew classical music particularly well. Jim Parry was doing four train songs segueing one into the other. There was no predictability, particularly with British bands. Their first stops in America were either New York or Boston. Here they played The Tea Party or The Psychedelic Supermarket.

At the *Globe* I talked to arts editor Gregory McDonald who later created the Fletch series [a series of mystery novels]. I just said, "I want to write." He pointed to his desk and said, "You don't want to write. In that drawer, and every desk in the building, is a bottle of whiskey. People drink all the time and hate what they're doing." He gave me two albums to review and paid $10 for each. One was *The Best of the Blues Project* and the other was *The Velvet Underground*.

I reviewed them in the spring of 1969 and later went to a *Billboard* convention in New York. I ran into Steve Sesnick, who was the manager of The Velvet Underground, and Lou Reed. They remembered the byline and my two-paragraph article. We spent the day together and went to listen to the album the Velvets were working on at the time. It took *Ocean* close to 20 years to come out.

As a *Billboard* writer I got a comped subscription. I saved them, as well as other publications, which became a great resource. It was important when I was writing my thesis in 1970.

When I graduated, I had a calling card of a 150-page thesis. WBUR was expanding and becoming more aggressive about raising funds. There was more programming in diverse musical directions. I gave my thesis to Clark Smidt, who was the assistant general manager. Will Lewis was the general manager. I got my degree in August of 1970, and in September, became the music director of WBUR.

There were wonderful people coming through town. Andrew Loog Oldham, manager of The Rolling Stones, had just started a custom rock label financed and distributed by Motown. A pre-"American Pie" Don McLean talked about working with Pete Seeger.

There was an early promotional junket with David Bowie. He spent several hours at WBUR. He was still on Mercury Records. Their PR guy was Bill Coleman. Jon Landau was writing for either *The Cambridge Phoenix* or *Rolling Stone* about Bowie's first American visit. We were driving down Commonwealth Avenue when Coleman's car broke down. Landau lived over in Cambridge the other side of the bridge there at BU. He gave up the ghost and said, "I'll walk home." Coleman and Bowie walked with me to WBUR. The big regret was that we had a terrific interview, but the station was so impoverished that we didn't have any tape to capture the interview. It was conducted with myself and Hochheimer [Professor Emeritus, producer and host of *The Other Side*, WBUR, May 1969–August 1971].

When Bill Lichtenstein was open-sourcing his film *WBCN The American Revolution*, he put out a call for tapes and images. Many things have come out of the woodwork.

CG When we were teenagers, I looked forward to *Your Hit Parade* on Saturday night with Snooky Lanson and Gisele MacKenzie. There was a suspenseful countdown of the top-ten songs of the week.

[The program was heard from 1935 to 1953 on radio, and seen from 1950 to 1959 on television. It was sponsored by American Tobacco's Lucky Strike cigarettes.]

DB It was a white, middle-class take on pop music. Just as that TV show was presenting the music in a sanitized way, the record companies were doing the same thing. There was music being unleashed that could not be repressed. They had Pat Boone doing cover versions of Little Richard. You can't believe the disparity between those two performers.

CG Clearly you have a passion for the music but also an interest in the business aspect. The third component in your case is a commitment to collect the related ephemera.

DB You are right to observe the multitude of ways that this resonated with me. The discovery was the machine behind all that. There was the payola scandal that Morris Levy was the mastermind of. He was the head of Roulette Records and Strawberry Records, a retail operation in Boston. He owned Birdland and recorded everyone from Frankie Lymon and the Teenagers to Count Basie.

Levy's take on the Payola scandal was that it diverted attention from television quiz show scandals. [Charles Van Doren was fed answers to *The $64,000 Question*. The show was cancelled September 14, 1958.]

CG Wasn't Levy mobbed up?

DB Yes. *Godfather of the Music Business: Morris Levy* [2016 by Richard Carlin] is well worth reading. His life was eerily similar to that of Hesh Rabkin on *The Sopranos*. He was behind pioneering Cleveland DJ Alan Freed. He was brought down by the payola scandal.

CG In the summer we lived in a waspy community. The soundtrack of life in the 1950s includes Patti Page, Eddie Fisher, Connie Francis, Kate Smith, Johnny Mathis, Frank Sinatra, Dean Martin, Julius La Rosa, and Perry Como. It was all very safe for my generation of teenagers in America; we were straight, white, and naïve.

DB Then Elvis changed everything.

CG When the changes came with the counterculture of the mid- to late-1960s, there was a sense of danger.

DB There were prices to be paid. Whether you knew it or not, we were coming out of a very repressed period. The R&B songs from the 1950s were very coded. If you listen now, you realize that we had no idea of what they meant. But our parents did. Little Richard, Chuck Berry, and Elvis Presley got through. They had very clever messages.

I never was censored by my parents but wanted to embrace the music I was loving. There was one radio in our house on the kitchen table. It would have been logical for my parents to give me a radio which I could listen to in my room. That didn't happen. I was buying records, but we didn't have a record player.

Our first turntable was acquired in 1968, when I was learning music for my Bar Mitzvah. The rabbi, as a little side business, made a recording of what you were supposed to sing. You bought it and just played it and played it. You learned to sing along in Hebrew. I found a used turntable and plugged it into the television speaker.

The '60s begin with the assassination of President Kennedy, and ends with the resignation of Nixon. Consider all of the social and cultural changes that occurred during that time. In music, we went from the Beatles and the British Invasion to Dylan and folk rock. There was Vietnam escalation, Civil Rights, and the sexual revolution. Every couple of months something was happening. By the mid-1970s, America was exhausted.

In the months after the Kennedy assassination, as a reader of *Billboard*, they were tipping that the Beatles were coming. Beatlemania already existed in England. I was looking at the British charts and saw how dominant the Beatles were during the fall of 1963. This was leading to their appearance on the *Ed Sullivan Show*. He had an intense rivalry with Jack Paar, who had a Friday night show. Paar obtained Beatles footage and ran it even before Sullivan. It played into a frenzy that was building. There was a DJ in Washington that managed to get a copy of "I Want to Hold Your Hand." He played it even before it was available. That was destroying the Capitol Records game plan. There were already things out on Vee-Jay Records.

[Vee-Jay obtained Beatles material through British EMI. *Introducing the Beatles* was the first Beatles album released in the United States. Originally scheduled for a July 1963 release, the LP came out on January 10, 1964, ten days before Capitol's *Meet the Beatles!*]

The Beatles were on the *Ed Sullivan Show* February 9, 1964. By spring of 1964, the Beatles had eleven songs on the Hot 100, including the top five. It was unprecedented.

[When Kennedy was assassinated, the number-one record was "Dominique" by the Singing Nun. (Jeanne-Paule Marie " Jeannine " Deckers, October 71, 1933–March 29, 1985, better known as Sœur Sourire, "Sister Smile," was a Belgian singer-songwriter and a member of the Dominican Order in Belgium.]

Despite the Beatles, there were a lot of carry-overs from the 1950s. Perry Como and Dean Martin had hits into the 1970s.

CG Speaking with John and Leah Sdoucos, they described the disaster for Barry and the Remains touring with the Beatles in 1966. It was the last Beatles tour, so that's a really small window from Sullivan in 1964. They quit touring but continued making recordings.

[In January 1969, they rehearsed for their first live show in three years. Only McCartney appeared to be motivated. He said, "There's only two choices:

We're gonna do it, or we're not gonna do it, and I want a decision, because I'm not interested in spending my fucking days farting around here, while everyone makes up their mind whether they want to do it or not." There was no response and that was that.]

Some of their music was recorded in 1962 and 1963, but consider how much they produced by 1969. Some of the singles were compiled for records in the U.S., which didn't exist in the U.K. It was a time when bands were putting out two or three albums a year as well as singles.

It was the wild west as record companies were making a lot more money selling albums instead of just singles. People were getting a lot more bang for the buck. Concerts sold from $2.50 to $4.50. Not like $250 today. For Heart this summer, the top price is $350.

The inside backpages of *Billboard* give the box office gross for the top 25 concerts. For the Taylor Swift tour, for example, the single show gross is seven to eight million dollars. The top tier ticket is $499.

In January 1969, Led Zeppelin did four shows at The Tea Party. If you bought a ticket in advance it was $3.50 and at the door, $4.50. Given the capacity of the venue, the gross potential was in the range of five thousand dollars.

Absent John Bonham, they did a benefit. [The Ahmet Ertegun Tribute Concert in memory of music executive Ahmet Ertegun at the O2 Arena in London, December 10, 2007.] The first day of offer there were twenty million requests for tickets. The three surviving band members were guaranteed a hundred million each if they would tour. Robert Plant stated that he had another commitment.

The financial model changed, but I don't think that anybody involved in the business realized the potential for revenue that developed. Of course, in later years, there have been challenges. The zenith year was 1999. Along came Napster and the mantra that music was free. The artist became the lowest person on the pecking order in terms of being rewarded for the art. Like the late 1960s, "The music belongs to the people" when fans would storm the stage and rush the gates. Even $3.50 was too much to pay.

There were festivals like Woodstock and the disaster of Altamont. It's curious that as decades passed England has done really great pop festivals. In the States there were occasional festivals that Bill Graham and others would do.

Consider Fenway Park. It was the early 2000s before there was a concert there. In 1973 or 1974, I saw a charity event there. You couldn't put staging on the sacred Fenway turf. The new owners [after Tom Yawkey] allowed a show per season. You could do one Springsteen or Rolling Stones show. This summer the licensing is for twelve shows.

Why does Boston get no respect for their role in the counterculture?

DB When I came to town there was the Bosstown Sound fiasco. It was a record company creation based on the success of San Francisco bands. They were not on the same label, but there was an interconnectivity of the performers socially, musically, and communally. That was not the case in Boston. There was marketing that the Boston bands were something that consumers should buy into. The feedback and resistance to the bands was especially strong in Boston.

It wasn't until the debut album of the J. Geils Band on Atlantic that the bad air of the Bosstown Sound was blown away. Record company ads supported the underground press, *Rolling Stone*, *Creem*, *Crawdaddy*, and *Fusion*. Editorial coverage was driving that support by selling records. Hopefully, there was not too much compromise involved. I remember *Fusion* running a cover with two balloons. One was inflated with Bosstown Sound written on it. Next to it was a collapsed balloon with that inscription. It was an editorial comment that there was no Bosstown Sound.

When J. Geils emerged, there was a renewed comfort level that great music was coming out of Boston. On WBCN Maxanne Sartori was a champion of Aerosmith. That was in 1972, when Columbia Records was giving up on the band. She gave them the airplay and attention that they deserved, and she was like that with other acts. The first Bruce Springsteen radio interview is with her on WBCN. [There is a clip of that in *WBCN: The American Revolution*.]

Every four years there is turnover of the quarter million college students in Boston. Some stay on and start careers here, including in the arts and media. Unlike in other cities, the youth market is not fixed. It is in constant flux. In the mid- to late-1970s Boston was embracing the punk sound. The music was unique to New York, London, and Boston. There may have been a punk scene to a lesser extent in San Francisco or Los Angeles.

CG Are we talking about Spit and The Rat?

DB Spit was later. That was the 1980s. The Rat was '76, '77, and '78. The Paradise just celebrated its 40th anniversary. They started in September 1977. They weren't focused on punk like The Rat, Cantones, and other clubs. If you look at Paradise programming, the first night was Jon Pousette-Dart and Livingston Taylor. The fourth or fifth night was Tom Waits, and the sixth night was John Mayall. It was very diverse. There was kind of a punk underground railroad that existed between New York and Boston. The scene in New York was CBGB's and Max's Kansas City, and in Boston The Rat, and later, The Channel.

CG Where were you in all this?

DB I spent a year as music director of WBUR. Then John Silber became president of Boston University. Overnight our staff was reduced from 32 to three. He wanted to take back control of the radio station, so he let everyone go.

I knew prom guys Roger Lifeset and Charlie McKenzie. They recommended me to Danny Lipman, who had a company called Music Promotions. It was the first time I was doing creative work and ads. There was a graphic artist, Lynne Staley, who had worked at *Boston After Dark* and later *The Cambridge Phoenix/ Real Paper*. Then she was art director of the *Boston Globe* before moving to *Newsweek Magazine*.

There was no supervision and ads we were creating went back to the home offices of the major record companies. We were getting great feedback from the marketing departments of the labels. Music Promotions closed in 1973.

I continued to do freelance work for record companies in '74 and '75, as well as print supplements for radio stations. WBCN was not really paying any money. It was heartbreaking for me to work for their competitors, which I did. In '75, I worked for WCOZ. In '77, I did some work for WEEI FM. There was a very effective campaign under the umbrella term of Soft Rock. There were a lot of great catch phrases like "The Eagles without the Turkeys" and "Mac without the Yak."

These stations were eroding the WBCN audience. It was wandering in the desert. It wasn't until 1977 that T. Mitchell Hasting yielded to having a new general manager, Klee Dobra. He told Hasting that you have to invest in the station or face being totally eclipsed by competitors. Hastings gave Dobra the opportunity to hire people. One of the first people hired was Charles Laquidara. [He was with the station from 1969 to 1976.] By his own admission, Charles had taken a year off to explore other opportunities.

Charles returned rather tentatively and was unsure of his radio sea legs, so he returned as Duane Ingalls Glasscock. There was enough budget to hire me as creative services director of WBCN, where I started in March of 1978. I knew that people at WCOZ were disenchanted so I was able to convince Mark Parenteau to come onboard. Then, a year later, we hired Ken Shelton.

We had Charles doing morning, Ken midday, and Mark for afternoon drive time. That was the nucleus of the air staff well into the 1990s.

Within a month of my being hired, Hasting decided to sell the station to Mike Wiener and Gerry Carrus. They were staring to build their radio empire. This was their third station. They had an AM station in Florida and an FM station in San Jose, California. They bought WBCN for the stated price of $3.4 million. Hastings, being a crafty entrepreneur, did an end run around the minority shareholders. He made a deal as a consultant with an annual salary of $50,000 for ten years. So he got an additional half million dollars.

He abruptly ended the budget for Klee Dobra. Hastings wasn't going to invest his own money in a property he was selling. The new buyers, Wiener and Carrus, couldn't invest in a company they didn't own yet. The FCC had a much-extended evaluation period regarding the suitability of the new owners. The announcement of the sale was May 1978, but the closing did not occur until February 1979.

We were left to our own devices for that ten-month period. We were trying to do things and came up with an annual battle of the bands, *The Rock and Roll Rumble*. There was discussion of whether WBCN, The Inn-Square Men's Bar, or *Sweet Potato* magazine would pay for the pencils used by the *Rumble*'s judges. The *Rumble*, with WBCN long gone, will have its 40th anniversary in April of 2019. It's been kept going by Anngelle Wood.

CG Talk to me about your archive.

DB It was five years ago. *The Phoenix* had shut down and I was working with Stephen Mindich on his archive's transfer to Northeastern University. He said to me, as a boss, in a way that only a boss can say, although at the time he was not a boss of anything. He called to say, "A meeting is set up with Steve Samuels, and you are going to be there. Here's the address."

He was setting me up with somebody I hadn't met previously. At that time, he was the owner of the Howard Johnson's Motor Lodge Inn at 1271 Boylston Street. WBCN was formerly located at 1265.

They were creating the Verb Hotel, which occurred during the spring and summer of 2014. We struck a five-year deal, which is now entering the sixth through tenth years of a contract expansion. I installed things that I had at home.

Steve sold him, "You have to meet David who has warehouses of things," which was true. But everything was on pallets with 30 to 40 boxes on a pallet. They were shrink-wrapped and, with a forklift, put on shelves.

In Avon, I had 230 pallets. They were completely useless to me, other than the mental satisfaction that I had saved these things. My monthly rental bill was brutal to be paying for something that was largely a mirage. Nobody had ever seen or used it.

I was able to do the Verb Hotel based on the one-tenth of one percent of works that I had in my house. They were things that made the cut to stay at home rather than go in boxes.

[The boutique Verb Hotel offers a retro-chic vibe with rock 'n' roll artifacts and collectibles. There are turntables and vintage albums in the rooms.]

Over the past two years, the owner in Avon reclaimed the space, so I had to move. After extensive search, because storage is so expensive in Boston, I found a place in Norwood. It's twenty-two minutes from my house in West Roxbury.

That started the process of unpacking and brought up the points you raise, about what to do with it, and who to entrust it to? Do I have to endow it? Will somebody buy it? I want to keep it together. I would like to see these things go to people who will appreciate them. They should be used in concert with other things, so that one-plus-one equals five.

There are places where that can happen. Laurie Anderson is working with the New York Public Library. Her husband Lou Reed's papers are at Yale, which has Danny Fields' material. The University of Tulsa has Bob Dylan's papers, along with Woody Guthrie's. To varying degrees these things are a big deal. A couple of Dylan notebooks just went for twenty million dollars. A billionaire is seeing that Dylan's stuff is co-mingled with Guthrie's. There was media coverage when the Danny Fields deal was done. They had his *16 Magazine* material as well as all he had done with The Doors. He managed The Ramones. There were also x-rated homoerotic films and Polaroids, and where were they going to go? It is part of the individual landscape that goes to telling the complete story. The critical factors are space and rent. I am paying the freight and can still accommodate more content.

A hobby has turned into a business, as I do exhibitions and presentations that use the content. I'm delighted to share it for projects like the Wang Theatre and Verb Hotel. I've worked with the Antiquarian Book Fair and Spotify. [A digital music service that provides access to millions of songs] If I can pay the overhead, and keep three or four people working with me, then I'm delighted. I want to maximize the retrieval capability of the archive to get it out of boxes. We want it to be systematic so we can do the best possible exhibitions and presentations.

CG When did you connect with Stephen Mindich [publisher of *Boston After Dark/ Boston Phoenix*]?

DB I met Stephen when I was working for Danny Lipman at Music Promotions, which was in the same block as *Boston After Dark*. Music Promotions was a big advertiser with the paper.

When the *Phoenix* closed, a major question was: what would become of the archive? While I worked there, from time to time, file cabinets would get cleared out to make more space. I asked if I could have it.

They shut down the website and many writers were dismayed to find that, unless they kept hard copies, their work was no longer online.

Stephen was diagnosed with pancreatic cancer, but I was able to work with him to place the archive with Northeastern. His widow [former state Superior Court judge Maria Lopez] had a big dumpster and was throwing out things. There is no way of knowing what of value was lost.

CG What was it like working at *The Phoenix*?

DB It was adventurous. Stephen and sales director Barry Morris used all kinds of bribes like Sack Theatres movie passes to cultivate good relations with clients. It was like giving us gold.

Charlie McKenzie, before he co-managed Boston, was working for WEA [Warner Elektra Atlantic]. He controlled the budgets, and we were spending money like crazy. One year, Charlie got a leather coat in appreciation of all the advertising dollars that he funneled to *Boston After Dark*.

There were skirmishes between the advertising departments of *BAD* and *The Cambridge Phoenix*. They were a viable publication with esteemed writers. The radio stations were also looking for advertising dollars.

[Mindich later acquired *The Cambridge Phoenix* for its name and writer George Kimball. While his intent was to eliminate competition, the staff regrouped as a cooperative, *The Real Paper*, with Paul Solman as editor.]

WBCN was large at the time, but there were other alternative and underground stations like WNTN in Newton. It was an AM station, but they were also album oriented.

The names kept changing. WBCN went from being called underground, to progressive, to AOR [album-oriented rock]. Later on WBCN and WFNX [Phoenix] were competitive for the alternative category. The definitions changed, but there were certain go-to stations. What was being played and the ads had local impact but also national and international.

I would do some writing for the *Cambridge Phoenix* helping with supplements they put out a couple of times a year. They were 48 pages and called "The Earbook." They were devoted to music. I did a long profile of Scotty Brink, the program director of WRKO.

In 1972–1973, Paul Ahern was promoting Atlantic Records that had Asylum Records, which was David Geffen's label. There was a magic to what was playing on AM stations like WRKO because of the brilliance of Ahern's promotional abilities. He had new releases from Eagles, Linda Ronstadt, Joni Mitchell, as well as Tom Waits. They were getting Top-40 airplay, which was a story unto itself.

So I wrote about Brink for *The Cambridge Phoenix*. At the same time I was working with Ben Gerson of *Boston After Dark*. We went to Marblehead and did an interview with George Martin, who was producing *Marblehead Messenger* by Seatrain. We would go to New York and do an interview with Don Kirshner, who was executive producer for the ABC series *In Concert*.

Boston After Dark was also creating supplements. They were cash cows running sound equipment supplements twice a year. If you look at early issues of *Boston After Dark*, they were four to eight pages. Later there were issues with four and six sections. The arts and culture department was flush and they were spending money to make money.

CG There were hip capitalists like Mindich making a lot of money. By comparison, writers and DJs were just getting by. That was a source of resentment on the part of arts workers. There were attempts to form unions at WBCN and *The Cambridge Phoenix*. You were unusual with a position somewhere between creative and management.

DB During that era it didn't cost much to live in Boston. Particularly when you enjoyed gifts as part of the employment package. The record companies were buying concert tickets to support their acts. That's different than today regarding tour support. Labels invested in the longevity of artists who had multiple album deals. In the 1960s, it was not unusual for groups to release two or three albums a year.

There were people who understood the hip capitalist aspect of things. Rent was a hundred fifty dollars a month, an ounce of pot cost twenty-five dollars, a gallon of gas was thirty-two cents. Money went a long way. You weren't buying music, because record companies were giving it to you. I don't think we were concerned with saving while living large on other people's money.

At WBCN I was creative services director. There was a guy named Stan Cornyn, who was creative services director for Warner/Reprise. He created sampler albums and brilliant marketing strategies. Labels had an identity. Certain labels were deemed a failure, like MCA, which was known as Music Cemetery of America. On WEA [Warner Elektra Atlantic], with the autonomy of each component label, in some ways they couldn't spend it fast enough. When I was with Music Promotions, what we were spending through Charlie McKenzie was stunning.

CG You mentioned that we have known each other for a long time.

DB We met around 1971, when you were writing for the *Herald*. I recall seeing you at the Music Hall leaving at nine p.m. when the Dead played until eleven-thirty p.m.

CG It wasn't quite that bad. I never heard an encore. When the concert ended, I would grab my date and run to the car. From there, it was a rush to get to the *Herald Traveler*. You were composing a lead in your head and wrote five hundred words with a midnight deadline.

That was the first replate, when my review was dropped in. Often I went to Chinatown after filing, and papers were being dropped off as I left the restaurant. The type was so fresh that it was like reading Braille. I would read my review and go to bed. Then I was back in the office at ten a.m. Often there were several from the arts desk meeting midnight deadlines for reviews. That rarely happens anymore.

The mailbag edition was so called because it was sent to the suburbs. Delivery trucks for the *Globe* and *Herald* exchanged bundles as a courtesy. If there was breaking news, the other paper had a crack at the story.

There was a famous incident when the *Herald's* legendary society writer Rose Walsh had a scoop. She was close to the Kennedy family and learned that Jackie was engaged to Aristotle Onassis. The editors created a fake front page, which was delivered to the *Globe*. During replate they ran the scoop. It was too late for the *Globe* to catch a piece of the action. There was a big laugh about that at *The Herald*. It also highlights an era when there was real competition among newspapers. I scooped the Newport Jazz Festival riot. My colleague at *The Globe*, Ernie Santosuosso, covered the evening concert that never happened.

DB We were tastemakers and gatekeepers. We were determining what got played on radio or ran in newspapers. At that time, decisions were being made intuitively by individuals who knew the culture but had limited professional experience.

We were young and astonished by how much money Paul Ahern and Charlie McKenzie made managing Boston. Charlie was paid a fortune to walk away. There was a lot of money floating around. It did not go unnoticed. Charlie had three homes. That showed that there was money to be made in rock and roll.

CG How did it end up for him?

DB Not particularly well. He was a wonderful, affable, friendly guy who came to a bad end.

CG He was the rock Gatsby of our time.

DB What you were doing at *The Herald*, Ernie Santosuosso [and later Steve Morse at *The Globe*] was picking up on coverage of rock and pop culture in *BAD* and *The Phoenix*. The daily press wanted a share of that readership. You were writing overnight deadlines while the weekly press had a longer lead time and more column inches.

CG Ernie and I compared notes about that. We were banging it out and they had a week to polish their prose. But I always preferred instant impact and still do.

DB We were pumping out three ads in a week with a three-person operation. Michael Fremmer used to do clever radio ads.

CG In addition to reviews, we also wrote a Sunday feature for the "Show Guide" tabloid insert. That doesn't happen anymore. During one memorable streak, I was in the paper every day for a month.

DB Writers are fighting for space as newsrooms and arts sections shrink. There was respect for the voice of that writer. When you read a critic's year-end top ten list it meant something. You paid attention when someone said this is a top-ten album or movie of the summer. It meant something when that writer was quoted in an ad. Now, the bigger the words are, the smaller that attribution.

CG So much has changed. When I was freelancing I was assigned an interview/feature on the Cars. They were recording *Candy-O* [1979]. I visited them in the studio and they played the album in progress. My piece included hearing them early on when they were managed by Fred Lewis. The interview was with Ric Ocasek. The editor allowed him to see my story prior to publication. I was called in to see the text and all the lines that Ocasek crossed out.

Censorship started with *Rolling Stone* when bands and their management were allowed to preview coverage. That killed the integrity of rock journalism and I stopped reading *Rolling Stone*.

I recall walking into the greenroom at The Tea Party, grabbing a beer, talking to Duane Allman, hanging out with Jerry Garcia, or smoking a joint with Joe Cocker.

DB There were no gatekeepers because we were all in it together. They needed our coverage as much as we needed access to them. The star-making machinery took over. The marketing people are brokering access and relationships.

Dealing with publications' labels demand coverage of emerging bands as leverage for access to their top-tier talent. The marquee acts are not aware that they are being used and exploited in that fashion. There are strange and insidious deals being made. Of course, the readers have no clue what's going on.

CG A friend was assigned to shoot The Isley Brothers for *Rolling Stone*. In their hotel room he blurted out that he had read the article. They refused to be photographed until *Rolling Stone* provided access to their coverage. In hindsight, the photographer should have kept his mouth shut.

DB Much has changed and not necessarily for the better.

CG Looking back at the counterculture in Boston it was indeed a Golden Age.

Shaggy-haired David Bieber in the 1960s. Bieber archive.

David Bieber 413

Bieber at the Hard Rock Café. Photo by Charles Giuliano.

After hours with Bieber. Photo by Charles Giuliano.

The WBCN studio. Photo by David Bieber.

J.J. Jackson of WBCN. Photo by David Bieber.

WBCN studio. Photo by David Bieber.

Charles Giuliano in Provincetown 1970s. Giuliano archive.

Charles Giuliano in the back producing Moondog at Spectrum Gallery in New York. Giuliano archive.

The Bieber Archive. Photo by Charles Giuliano.

Bieber with author and hip-hop scholar Brian Coleman. Photo by Charles Giuliano.

David Bieber at his Norwood warehouse with Elvis Costello looking on. Photo by Charles Giuliano.

Bieber archive. Photo by Charles Giuliano.

Back issues of *The Real Paper*. Photo by Charles Giuliano.

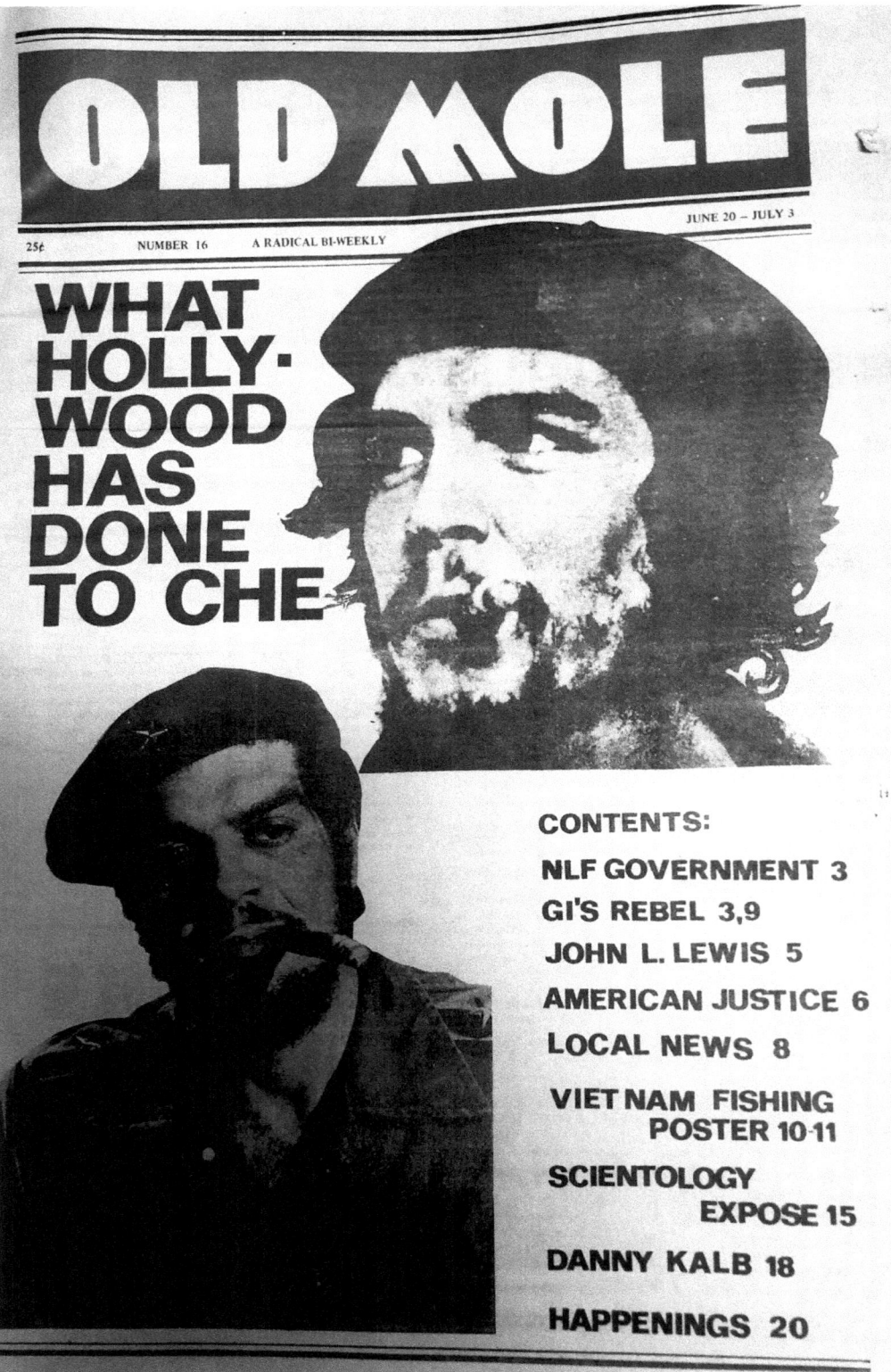

Boston's *Old Mole*. Photo by Charles Giuliano.

Steal This Book.

Bieber Archive. Photo by Charles Giuliano.

Laquidara in the WBCN library. Bieber archive.

Rock-themed lounge of Verb Hotel. Photo by Charles Giuliano.

Bibliography

Alan, Carter. *Radio Free Boston: The Rise and Fall of WBCN.* Boston: Northeastern University Press, 2013.

Blumenthal, Bob. *Jazz: An Introduction to the History and Legends Behind America's Music.* Harper Collins, 2007.

Botticelli, Jim. *Dirty Old Boston: Four Decades of a City in Transition.* Boston: Union Park Press, 2014.

Cardoso, William J. *The Maltese Sangweech and Other Heroes.* Atheneum, 1984.

Coleman, Brian. *Buy Me Boston: Local Ads & Flyers 1960s–1980s. Volume One.* Wax Facts Press, 2018.

Della Chiesa, Ron. *Radio My Way: Featuring Celebrity Profiles from Jazz, Opera, the American Songbook and More.* Pearson, 2011.

Dylan, Bob. *Chronicles: Volume One.* Simon & Schuster, 2004.

Halper, Donna L. *Images of America, Boston Radio: 1920–2010.* Arcadia Publishing, 2011.

Hentoff, Nat. *Boston Boy: Growing up with Jazz and Other Rebellious Passions.* Philadelphia: Paul Dry Books, 1986.

Kimball, George. *Four Kings: Leonard, Hagler, Hearns, Duran and the Last Great Era of Boxing.* Ithaca: McBooks Press, 2009.

Landau, Jon. *It's Too Late to Stop Now: A Rock and Roll Journal.* San Francisco: Straight Arrow Books, 1972.

Lyman, Mel. *Autobiography of a World Saviour.* Published by Jonas Mekas, 1966.

Milano, Brett. *The Sound of Our Town: A History of Boston Rock & Roll.* Beverly, Mass: Commonwealth Editions, 2007.

Milliken, Joe. *Let's Go! Benjamin Orr and the Cars.* Lanham, Maryland: Rowman & Littlefield Publishing Group, Inc., 2019.

Mungo, Ray. *Famous Long Ago: My Life and Hard Times with Liberation News Service.* University of Massachusetts Press, 1970.

Nelson, Steve. *Gettin' Home: An Odyssey Through The '60s.* Massamett Media, 2018.

Reisman, Arnie. *Clara Bow Died for Our Sins: Selected Poems and Photographs.* Summerset Press, 2015.

Reisman, Arnie. *Sodom and Costello: Selected Poems and Art.* Summerset Press, 2016.

Rooney, Jim. *In It for the Long Run: A Musical Odyssey (Music in American Life)*, University of Illinois Press, 2014.

Simon, Peter. *I and Eye: Pictures of My Generation.* Bulfinch Press, 2001.

Vacca, Richard. *The Boston Jazz Chronicles: Faces, Places, and Nightlife 1937–1962.* Troy Street Publishing, 2012.

Von Schmidt, Eric. *Baby, Let Me Follow You Down: The Illustrated Story of the Cambridge Folk Years.* University of Massachusetts Press, 1994.

Walsh, Ryan H. *Astral Weeks: A Secret History of 1968.* Penguin Press, 2018.

www.ingramcontent.com/pod-product-compliance
Lightning Source LLC
Chambersburg PA
CBHW081213170426
43198CB00017B/2605